ERRORS IN ENGLISH

AND

WAYS TO CORRECT THEM

ERRORS IN ENGLISH
AND
WAYS TO CORRECT THEM

FOURTH EDITION

HARRY SHAW

HarperPerennial
A Division of HarperCollinsPublishers

HarperCollins books may be purchased for educational, business, or sales promotional use. For information, please write: Special Markets Department, HarperCollins Publishers, Inc., 10 East 53rd Street, New York, NY 10022.

FIRST HARPERPERENNIAL EDITION

Library of Congress Cataloging-in-Publication Data
Shaw, Harry, 1905–
    Errors in English and ways to correct them / Harry Shaw.—4th
ed., 1st HarperCollins ed.
        p.   cm.
    Includes index.
    ISBN 0-06-461044-6
    1. English language—Errors of usage.   2. English language—
Grammar—1950–   I. Title.
PE1460.S516   1993
428.2—dc20   92-5313

95 96 97 PS / RRD 10 9 8 7 6 5 4 3

CONTENTS

FOREWORD

This book will help you to improve your use of language by emphasis upon those common errors, and only those, that hinder communication and impede thought. Its concern with diction, sentence structure, spelling, punctuation, grammar, and grammatical usage is not directed to the so-called niceties of usage but to those frequent errors that cause trouble, anxiety, or embarrassment. It will serve not only as a home-study guide but also as a reference book for office and home. It is detailed enough to solve most of the problems that come up in your speaking and writing.

Two basic concerns underlie and precede everything this book tries to offer about the use and abuse of words and expressions. It cannot solve either, but it can bring them to your attention.

First, little value resides in studying words and sentences unless one has something worthwhile to say and some interest and purpose is saying that something, whatever it is. Oliver Wendell Holmes once remarked, "A word is the skin of a living thought." If one's thought is nonexistent or valueless, so will be the word itself.

Reading, listening, seeing, experiencing, and, above all, *thinking* are the methods by which one insures having something to say. The book in your hand provides thousands of suggestions, none of which deals directly with this fundamental problem. But it can, and does, suggest at the outset that with rare exceptions, people tend to talk more and say less than they should. After all, speech is only the faculty or power of speaking. The ability to talk and write is one thing; thoughts and emotions are another. Spinoza once wrote that mankind would be happier if the power in men to be silent were the same as that to speak; that "men govern nothing with more difficulty than their tongues." John Ruskin wrote: "The greatest thing a human soul ever does in this world is to see something and tell what it saw in a plain way. Hundreds can talk for one who can think." It was a wise person who remarked at a meeting that it was better for him to remain silent and be thought a fool than to speak and remove all possible doubt. *Think first, talk second.*

Next, it is important to form a suitable attitude toward writing and speaking. Despite the comments that appear throughout *Errors in English*, one should not think of these processes as a long list of prohibitions, taboos, and thou-shalt-not's. The American language is a flexible medium. One should consider it the most important method he or she has for communicating clearly and interestingly with and to others.

The authors whose work you most enjoy are possibly not the greatest stylists of all time. They may repeatedly violate many of the recommendations set forth in following pages. Not by the niceties of style but by drive, imagination, and animation they compel and hold your fascinated attention. Similarly, the persons with whom you most enjoy talking may make many so-called mistakes in grammar and may frequently confuse one word with another. But they use their tongues interestingly and forcefully, however many "errors" they make while doing so.

It is true, however, that in our society few people fail to realize the importance of using good English. The late Will Rogers was never more humorous than when he remarked, "A lot of people who don't say *ain't*, ain't eatin'." (He might have noted that a lot of people who do say "ain't" are not eating very well, either.) Most of us, however, are properly concerned when others react unfavorably to mistakes we make while expressing ourselves. We understand that our use of language represents a significant form of behavior.

By learning basic good usage we can concentrate on what we wish to communicate and stop worrying about detailed methods of doing so. Freed from restraint and anxiety, we can reveal thoughts to others in the natural, easy way we should speak and write our language but all too often do not.

As you study the entries in *Errors in English*, keep these four "commandments" in mind:

Be concise. Most statements of any kind are wordy. All of us repeat an idea in identical or similar words, and then say it again. Talk should not be cryptic and mysteriously abrupt, but it should be economical. *Make it snappy!*

Be original. It's impossible to conceive of a wholly new idea or to express an old one in fresh, original diction. And yet the greatest single error in speaking and writing is the use of trite, worn-out expressions that have lost their first vigor, picturesqueness, and appeal. Avoid clichés. *Don't be a rubber stamp.*

Be specific. Much of our speech is indefinite, not clearly expressed, or uncertain in meaning. Even when we have a fairly good idea of what we wish to say, we don't seek out those exact and concrete words that would convey what we have in mind. Try to use words that have precise meaning. *Don't be vague.*

Vary the approach. The sole requirement of effective speech and writing is that they should communicate. The choice and use of words should vary from situation to situation, from person to person. At times, one's speech and writing should be racy and pungent; at other times, deliberate and formal. Communication should be appropriate. *Shift gears.*

The way you speak and write has little or nothing to do with character, intelligence, or morality. Yet each of us should always keep in mind that there are more people with power, jobs to hand out, raises to recommend, and money itself who speak and write what is known as "standard English" than those who do not. Anyone who writes and talks "unacceptably" is all too often an object of regional, racial, or national prejudice. This unfortunate truth is a harsh fact that should be squarely faced.

H.S.

PART I

WAYS TO
AVOID MAKING
ERRORS

1

UNDERSTAND WHAT
WRITING IS

Everyone who doesn't write regularly or professionally is likely to have several incorrect notions about writing and what it involves.

Such misconceptions are understandable; most people have had little experience with actual writing. Personal and business letters, a job application or two, answers on examinations, possibly a few reports at work or "research" papers for an organization constitute the slim total of isolated and fragmentary writing efforts many persons have made. It is not easy to understand a process with which we are unfamiliar.

Actually, writing is a comparatively late development in the progress of mankind from savagery to the present day. When you consider that "man" has been on the earth for several million years but has been working with an alphabet system of writing for only some five thousand years, the fact that everyone has difficulty understanding the act of writing is hardly surprising. Man discovered how to mass-produce alphabetic writing only a little over five hundred years ago. The idea that everybody should learn to read and write has been current for only two hundred years—and that idea is not universally held.

No one even knows when and where speech originated, but apparently mankind has been making understandable sounds for hundreds of thousands of years. Writing is a relatively new art form, or process, or means of communication about which little is known. Consequently, it is all the more important that the opinions we hold about writing should be accurate and helpful.

Four commonly accepted ideas about writing—all of them incorrect—should be carefully examined and discarded.

Misconception 1: WRITING IS A FORM OF SPEAKING

Although writing and speaking share a common goal of communication, they differ in several ways. A speech has been called "an essay walking on its hind legs," but effective speaking is quite different from the oral rendering of a written composition. Similarly, written composition has been prepared according to requirements and specifications not applying to speaking.

We are normally more relaxed in talking than writing, less worried about rules and errors. This is as it should be, but what many people might consider acceptable in speech they would frown upon if it appeared in writing. Some words and expressions used in writing would seem pretentious and stuffy if they appeared in speech.

Good writing is expected to be somewhat different, on occasion, from informal speech and conversation. This is a normal, justified expectation. No matter what some dictionary-makers and linguists heatedly maintain, an attitude of "anything goes" can be, and repeatedly is, costly in business and social affairs. In certain situations, using *ain't*, misspelling a word, employing an unidiomatic expression, or saying *went* when *gone* is indicated can possibly cost a job, advancement, a contract, a social opportunity, or even a potential friend. Learning to write correct English has many values, one of which is practicality.

In speaking, our sentences are shorter—or should be—than many we might construct in writing. Language is usually more direct and much simpler in speech than in writing. Conversations that sound "all right" often seem thin, shallow, and even stupid when reduced to writing. For most people, talking is habitual, natural, informal, and relaxed. Writing is none of these.

Someone reading what you have written is usually alone or in a room free from distractions. Someone listening to you is more often surrounded by others and is sometimes distracted by them. Even when you are at home, following talk over TV or radio, your mind tends to wander and you cannot recapture what you have missed by rereading something written. Most people are more eye-minded than ear-minded. Something written can be read and reread many times. A spoken message has only one hearing.

Being able to speak well is no guarantee that one can write well. Many effective talkers are poor writers; few accomplished writers are good speakers. Writing and speaking are different forms of language.

Misconception 2: WRITING SHOULD BE AS EASY AND SIMPLE AS SPEAKING

Perhaps if we had been writing as long and as much as we have been speaking, writing would be easier and simpler. But everyone learns to write several years *after* he learns to make sounds. Further, it is true that most people speak more words in a month than they write in a lifetime. A normal speaking rate is one hundred words a minute. If you talk for two hours a day—some persons talk more than this, some less—you would utter 12,000 words in a day. In a week at this rate, you would speak the length of a novel of 84,000 words. In a month, you would deliver yourself of 360,000 words; in a year more than four million. In his busy, productive lifetime, not even Shakespeare wrote nearly that much.

What is remarkable is not that our writing is bad but that it is as good as it is, considering the effort and time we spend on it.

Misconception 3: WRITING REQUIRES INSPIRATION

Regardless of training or experience, everyone finds writing so difficult that he or she often wishes some stimulus, some insight, some flash of understanding would come to provide help. Even so accomplished a writer as Voltaire, one of the world's all-time literary masters, wrote: "The necessity of writing something, the embarrassment produced by the consciousness of having nothing to say, and the desire to exhibit ability are three things sufficient to render even a great man ridiculous."

Actually, success in writing depends upon constant, unremitting, earnest application and not upon so-called "flashes of inspiration" and sudden bursts of effort. Two wise and often-quoted remarks of Thomas A. Edison are these: "There is no substitute for hard work" and "Genius is one percent inspiration and ninety-nine percent perspiration."

Robert Littell, a professional writer and editor, once wrote: "Inspiration? A question that is sure to be raised. It's not a visitation, of course, but is inside you all the time. Don't wait for it; keep on writing and writing and ever so often it will come roaring up out of your insides and take the pencil from your hands. Nobody knows how to coax it up. Don't press, as the golfers say. . . . The shy beast will come up or not, as he chooses."

The consensus of experienced writers is that the only way to woo inspiration is to apply the seat of the pants to the seat of a chair hour after hour and day after day, constantly writing and rewriting.

Misconception 4: WRITING IS A COMPLICATED SERIES OF *DO'S* AND *DON'T'S*

A major reason for the tightening up, or partial paralysis, of people starting to write is their attitude. They look upon writing as "a bunch of grammar," a long, intricate string of *thou-shalt-not's*. Actually, nearly everyone who can communicate by speaking knows quite enough "grammar" to write effectively. What is bothersome is not grammar but *usage*, a problem treated in many of the remaining pages in this book.

You do not need to know the principle of the combustion engine in order to drive an automobile. But you do need to know where to insert the ignition key, how to start the motor, how to work an automatic or manual shift, steer, follow road signs, and apply brakes. Skilled drivers are so proficient in these operations that they do them "without thinking."

Neither are skilled writers (or speakers) always consciously aware of grammar. A professional writer might be unable to define an adjective, but he would "instinctively" change the phrase "a night when the wind blew" to "windy night," if he felt the former to be too long and ineffective. You might not know what a clause and a phrase are and thus would not know how to "reduce predication." But your ear or common sense or even a little "grammar" might enable you to reduce "Diphtheria, which used to be a deadly disease, is now rare" to the shorter and more direct "Diphtheria, once a deadly disease, is now rare." Every effective writer has a working knowledge of words and their ways. And that is all that grammar is.

Try to approach writing as what it is: a flexible, resourceful medium that will help you communicate clearly and interestingly to and with others. What possible activity could be more important or more meaningful to you or to anyone?

2

PREPLAN EVERYTHING
YOU WRITE

Writing is not a single operation. It is a process consisting of three parts: preplanning, writing, and revising. Broken into its three phases, writing will both seem and actually be less complicated and difficult.

A finished piece of writing may be compared to the part of an iceberg that appears above water, one-ninth of the total mass. The remaining eight-ninths consists of preplanning (or prewriting) and revising.

You have been "speaking prose" constantly since you began to talk. You have also been engaged in a form of writing since first-grade days. Haven't you uttered many remarks to yourself before saying them aloud? Haven't you "thought through" many letters or memos before putting them on paper? Many business executives fluently dictate effective letters to a secretary or machine because they put themselves to sleep the night before planning what to say. "Thinking ahead" is not often thought of as writing, but it is an important, even essential part of that process.

If you will sit down to write *what you have thought* and not sit down to think *what you will write*, the difficulties in actual writing will diminish. They will not disappear, but they will not seem so formidable and frightening. When driving along a highway, have you ever noticed that in the distance the road seemed to rise sharply up a steep hill? As you sped along, however, the incline apparently smoothed out. The same effect will be obtained in writing if you approach it gradually through the act of planning ahead.

No matter what kind of writing you intend to do, preplanning is important. It's true, though, that if your goal is only to write better business or personal letters or other everyday types of communication, relatively little prewriting is necessary. In writing a business memo, or report, or a short book review, you are certain to do some thinking ahead but hardly an extensive or involved amount of actual planning.

But if your aim is to become a professional writer or to learn to write more effectively for pleasure and as a means of self-expression, then some genuine prethinking is essential. Prewriting is not merely a means of discovering something to write about. It involves willingness and desire to think your own thoughts. Time spent in prewriting is time spent in sorting out our own thoughts, in exploring why we have them, and in reaching some conclusions about them and why they interest us.

PREWRITING AND ORIGINALITY

We always find that we have to write from our own experience, observation, curiosity, imagination, and reflection. Naturally, we get much of our material from others in discussions or conversations, in interviews or lectures, or in reading. But we must assimilate all this material and make it our own. Otherwise, what we write will be not ours but someone else's. True originality is not so much a matter of substance as of individualized treatment. The most interesting and effective subjects for writing are those about which we either have some knowledge or genuinely want to learn something. Writing is made out of the ideas and impressions which we have obtained from various sources and made a part of ourselves.

Give some attention to items that will aid in self-analysis and provide insights into sources of originality that should come before actual writing:

Memories

Can you recall how someone, or some place, or some idea seemed to you at an earlier time in your life? What can you remember about the day you entered first grade? The first (or most memorable) Christmas you can recollect? The most cruel (or kindest) thing anyone ever did to you? Your first date?

People and Places

Who is the most entertaining (or dullest or most arrogant) person you have ever known? What one person did you most admire when you were ten years old? Whom do you most admire today? What is the most beautiful (or appealing or restful) place you have ever seen? What is, or once seemed, the most shocking sight in your town?

Incidents and Events

What was the most appalling accident you have ever witnessed? What event in your life provided the greatest excitement? Sense of achievement? Biggest disappointment? Worst embarrassment? Of all the incidents in your life, which one do you remember with the greatest pleasure? The most shame? If you could relive one day (or one hour) in your life, what would that day (or hour) be?

Imagination and Daydreaming

If you could be any person in the world for a day (or month) who would you choose to be? With what one person who has ever lived would you most like to have an imaginary conversation? If you had free choice and unlimited resources, in what city or century would you most like to spend a week or a year? What is your idea of a perfect day?

None of these topics and questions is guaranteed to produce workable ideas, but your mind probably will be triggered by a few of them. What remains to be done is to test the idea that results to see if it is usable *and* to get hold of material for its development. These necessary steps are a part of preplanning.

NEVER STOP PREWRITING

Someone has referred to preplanning as "writing on the hoof." By this is meant "writing" all the time as we go about daily activity. All authors apparently rub ideas together while walking around, eating, taking a bath, conversing, working, reading, or even sleeping. Their practice should be followed by every aspiring writer. Somerset Maugham had this to say:

> The author does not write only when he's at his desk, he writes all day long, when he is thinking, when he is reading, when he is experiencing: everything he sees and feels is significant to his purpose and, consciously or unconsciously, he is forever storing and making over his impressions.

Maugham's advice and experience were echoed by James Thurber:

> I never quite know when I'm not writing. Sometimes my wife comes up to me at a party and says "Stop writing." She usually catches me in the middle of a paragraph. Or my daughter will ask at the dinner table, "Is he sick?" "No," my wife replies, "he's writing."

Georges Simenon, the French novelist and mystery writer, is quoted as saying: "I always have two or three themes in my mind. They are things about which I worry. Before I start writing, I consciously take up one of those ideas."

Robert Penn Warren, the American novelist and poet, was once asked, "What is your period of incubation?" He replied:

> Something I read or see stays in my head for five or six years. I read a short article [about the basic story of *World Enough and Time*] in five minutes. But I was six years making the novel. Any book I write starts with a flash but takes a long time to

shape up. All of my first versions are in my head, so that when I sit down to write, I have some line developed in my head.

The acts of prewriting and writing overlap, but you are urged never to begin to write until you have incubated what you plan to say and how you plan to say that something, whatever it is. Time spent in preplanning will save time in writing. It will also help to make the finished product freer from errors and thus more effective.

3

REVISE EVERYTHING
YOU WRITE

In everything anyone writes, errors of one sort or another are inevitable. Not even a skilled professional writer can preplan, write, and proofread all at one time. Especially not skilled writers—they know from long experience that first drafts are only the beginning of the writing process.

This process has been greatly changed by the use of word processors. Word processing is the writing, editing, storing, and often printing of copy electronically. The principal value of word processing is that a user can revise his or her copy quickly and effectively. The tedious cutting and pasting connected with hand-written or typewritten copy are no longer needed. Thus the traditional distinctions between writing, revising, and editing have become blurred. But by whatever method, revision is essential for all effective writing.

In commenting on the rewriting that went into his famed novel, *The Sound and the Fury*, William Faulkner said simply: "I wrote it five separate times." Truman Capote, author of many works of fiction and nonfiction including *In Cold Blood*, said of all his work: "I write my first version in pencil. Then I do a complete revision, also in longhand. I think of myself as a stylist, and stylists can become notoriously obsessed with the placing of a comma, the weight of a semicolon. Obsessions of this sort, and the time I take over them, irritate me beyond endurance."

Want more proof? Thornton Wilder, the eminent dramatist and novelist, once said:

My wastepaper basket is filled with works that went a quarter through . . . I forget which of the great sonneteers said "One line in the fourteen comes from the ceiling, the others have to be adjusted around it." There are passages in every novel whose first writing is the last. But it's the joint and cement between those passages that take a great deal of rewriting. . . . Each sentence is a skeleton accompanied by enormous activity of rejection.

When asked about rewriting, the short story writer Frank O'Connor replied that he did so "endlessly, endlessly, endlessly." Then he added, "And I keep on rewriting after something is published."

Alberto Moravia, the Italian novelist and short story writer, commented: "Each book is worked over several times. I like to compare my method with that of painters centuries ago, proceeding from layer to layer. The first draft is quite crude, by no means finished. After that, I rewrite it many times—apply as many layers—as I feel to be necessary."

Are you still unconvinced that all writing, even that of craftsmen, requires revision? Then listen to this from James Thurber when asked "Is the act of writing easy for you?" His response:

"It's mostly a question of rewriting. It's part of a constant attempt to make the finished version smooth, to make it seem effortless. A story I've been working on was rewritten fifteen complete times. There must have been 240,000 words in all. I must have spent 2,000 hours working on it. Yet the finished version is only 20,000 words." And when asked, "Then it's rare that your work comes out right the first time?" Mr. Thurber replied, "Well, my wife took a look at a first version and said 'That's high school stuff.' I had to tell her to wait until the seventh draft."

Such comments make writing seem like hard work. Well, it is. But actually *there is no such thing as good writing. There is only good rewriting.* Those unwilling to revise and rewrite are skipping a major step toward becoming better writers. You may not wish to go to the lengths mentioned here, but some revision and rewriting are essential steps toward making any composition of whatever kind more effective and appealing.

Three kinds of alteration are possible in revision. You can (1) *substitute*, (2) *delete*, and (3) *add*.

In substituting, you can shift from one word to another that seems more accurate or meaningful (*le mot juste*). You can change the structure of a sentence. You might notice that all the sentences in a given paragraph are about the same length and, to avoid monotony, decide to combine a couple of them. If an example you have given does not seem to make your point, you can substitute another. Many other methods of substitution are possible and readily available, but these hints will give you the idea.

Similarly with deletions: Words, sentences, and entire paragraphs can be dropped when they are thought not to pull their weight, fail to make the desired point, or are just plain wordy. In fact, omission is often the most significant and telling of all exercises in revision.

In rereading something you have written, it may occur to you that something more is needed: another fact, another example, an incident or anecdote. For example, Robert Louis Stevenson, in his essay "An Apology for Idlers," wrote this sentence: "The services of no single individual are indispensable." The sentence is clear in meaning and well phrased. But isn't it possible that, when revising his essay, the author said to himself "Something is lacking"? Perhaps so, perhaps not. Anyway, Stevenson followed with this memorable sentence: "Atlas was just a gentleman with a protracted nightmare." The idea is now unmistakable and unforgettable. Just as hindsight is always superior to present sight, so "second thoughts" are often better than first ones.

Possibly the process of revising will be clearer to you if it is suggested that with everything you write you

1. Check and recheck your choice of words.
2. Consider revising the word order of certain sentences.
3. Alter some figures of speech.
4. Add a bit of dialogue, if suitable.
5. Supply an incident or anecdote to reinforce an idea.
6. Remove any section that seems stale or dull.

7. Examine, and possibly alter, the order of paragraphs.

Yet another approach to rewriting is to ask of anything you write these searching questions:

1. Does my piece of writing have a definite *central purpose* (that is, have I carefully analyzed the topic)?
2. Does my writing have *ample material*?
3. Is this material (substance) *arranged* in a clear, orderly, and logical way?
4. Is this composition *unified*?
5. Is it *clear* in all its parts?
6. Is the material presented so interestingly that it will *appeal* to its readers?
7. Is my writing *correct* in grammatical and mechanical details?

If it occurs to you that these suggestions for rewriting involve largely mechanical matters, then remember that communication is the dominant aim of all writing and that whatever blocks or slows down communication requires removal. It is for this reason that we revise and rewrite in order to remove errors that distort or bury meaning.

But something remains to be done in the rewriting process. That something is to employ whatever devices of style you can to smooth and speed your message to the minds of readers.

Scores of devices can help us communicate. The most important elements contributing to effective and pleasing style can be classified under four headings: simplicity, conversational quality, individuality, and concreteness. Other characteristics could be listed, but even these four goals involve refinements of style that can take a lifetime to perfect.

SIMPLICITY

Simplicity does not mean "writing down" to the reader and underestimating either his intelligence or his knowledge. It does mean expressing one's ideas in terms that are clear, logical, and specifi-

cally geared to the level (age, education, and so on) of the persons
for whom one is writing.

If a subject is so technical that technical terms cannot be
avoided, use them—but define them without employing a tone or
method insulting to the reader's intelligence. The level of your
reading audience will determine how many such terms should be
defined and in what detail.

If you have a choice between a long and a short word, use
whichever is clearer and more exact—usually, but not always, the
short word. Short words are more often clear and sharp, like signs
chiseled in the face of a rock; in much writing, and especially in
speaking, they are crisp and filled with zest, saying what they
"mean" and leaving as little doubt as possible in the mind of
reader or hearer. But whether we use long or short words, diction
should be as simple and clear as we can make it so that our ideas
will move smoothly.

You hear and read many words previously unknown to you.
Impressed, you may attempt what hundreds of thousands of
others have done: to employ such expressions in speaking and
writing not so much for their actual value as to show others how
"smart" you are, how "educated" you are becoming. Enlarging
one's vocabulary and using new words purposefully are both
worthwhile activities—but they lose meaning when they are
pursued for reasons of vanity, self-esteem, or "culture climbing."

No truer statement about simplicity in style exists than this: "A
book has one leg on immortality's trophy when the words are for
children but the meanings are for men." Simplicity without substance is childish; but great thoughts, like great inventions of
whatever kind, achieve much of their effectiveness and power
through simplicity. Can you think of any great work of literature,
of any great scientific discovery, that is unnecessarily and arbi-
trarily complex and involved? A good literary selection or an
important scientific discovery may be beyond our understanding,
but each probably is as simple as it can be and still be what it is.

CONVERSATIONAL QUALITY

More than most of us realize, the *conversational* quality of what we read adds an appeal that helps us to grasp the ideas being presented. Conversation is not necessarily informal and relaxed, but good conversation is never so elevated in tone that one feels condescended to. Have you noticed that some writing by eighteenth- and nineteenth-century authors, even that considered great and timeless, seems formal and pontifical? That writings of more recent vintage are often more relaxed, less didactic and "preachy"?

This difference in attitude toward both subject and reader is partly a matter of diction and sentence structure, but even more a result of later authors descending from their pedestals. Such a statement does not imply that only recent works have a conversational quality and thus are enjoyable to read. Nor does it mean that a good writer, of whatever era, will figuratively remove jacket and tie. It does imply that most effective writers have tried not to sound stuffy and ponderous, that without losing their dignity they have labored to infuse a human, friendly quality into their writing. Conversational quality means ease of expression, not sloppy thought; consideration for the reader as one "thinking with" the author and not as a person both ignorant and stupid.

Laurence Sterne wrote in *Tristram Shandy:* "Writing, when properly managed (as you may be sure I think mine is) is but another name for conversation."

INDIVIDUALITY

Related to the device of conversational tone is *individuality,* which is often a virtue and, occasionally, a vice in writing. Individuality implies "subjectivity"; when a writer is subjective, he or she is inward-centered and applies his or her own standards and judgments. A highly subjective writer tends to ignore the needs and appeals of readers and thinks exclusively of himself, his thoughts, his needs, his aspirations. Such a tendency—the direct opposite of the stylistic quality inherent in conversation—is a definite flaw.

On the other hand, the individuality growing from subjectivity can help in developing a writing style that is effectively communicative. When we read nonfiction such as essays and articles, we want and need to get the author's opinions, not merely facts, principles, and statistics. We may be dozing through a dull lecture, a flat recital of facts, but we tend to come awake when the lecturer begins to recount a personal experience, to give an eyewitness account, to express his opinions—in short, when the speaker becomes a human being and stops being an automaton or robot.

No reader wishes to be confronted with material that possesses no spark of the writer's individuality, personality, and subjective processes of thought and reasoning. Nothing is more dull and hence less communicative than writing that "goes through the motions" of setting down borrowed or plagiarized facts with no obvious stamp of the author's mind and personality. Even a research paper, one based on sources other than the writer's thought and experience, will communicate effectively only when it reveals the author's conclusions and judgments.

Prose is seldom wholly objective (unless, of course, it is merely copied from reference sources). However, an excessively subjective composition can be as ineffective as a wholly objective one. If a writer parades his opinions to the exclusion of all other considerations, if his work is studded with "I," if he is not in some respects reader-centered, he commits the error of subjectivity. If his writing is dull, lifeless, static, almost or totally devoid of emotion or personality, he commits the error of objectivity. Both errors are serious, and striking a delicate balance between them is no easy task. But it can be done.

Do such comments about individuality suggest that one must be *original* in one's writing style? The answer, both "yes" and "no," depends upon what is meant by "original." No one can reasonably be expected to produce wholly new, entirely fresh ideas and novel ways of conveying them. No one can do this often; perhaps no one now alive can do this *ever*. If he could, he would be as misunderstood as Galileo or Socrates and might lose his job or his life. But originality can and does also mean "independent thought," "individual insight," "constructive imagination." Each of these elements is attainable by nearly everyone. Goethe has wisely summed up this matter of individuality and originality:

> The most original authors of modern times are such not because they create anything new but only because they are able to say things in a manner as if they had never been said before.

If what you write, or say, reveals in some degree the imprint of your own personality, your particular individuality, then it will have never been said before in quite the same way. It will possess a genuinely important stylistic quality without which it would be dull and spiritless.

CONCRETENESS

Each of us has repeatedly read material that seemingly "made sense" but that left us with only a vague, fuzzy impression of what the author apparently intended for us to absorb. Try as we might, we could not come to grips with the author's meaning. We felt we were dealing with cotton, wool, or some soft and flabby substance that we could not grasp, handle, and move about in our own thought processes. Discouraged or annoyed, we may have decided that the selection had no meaning and no message for us and thus gone on to something else.

One major cause of such a reaction is lack of *concreteness* in writing. The author we were trying unsuccessfully to read may have been using abstract words to express ideas; he may have forgotten, if indeed he ever knew, that readers' minds respond most readily to the specific, the tangible, the concrete. For example, when we are hungry we don't think of "nutrition" or "nourishment" or even of "food." We think of steak or baked potatoes or chocolate cake.

Actually, we learned everything we know as itemized bits of experience. When we were small, a parent or some other older person pointed out a dog, said "See the dog," and ever afterward, a d-o-g had some particular and special meaning for us. Your concept of a "dog" and that of anyone else will differ, but each item of experience in our private store of meanings has a definite, concrete application. In contrast, we feel baffled by abstract words and expressions that have no direct connection with our own backgrounds.

Abstract words are useful in discussing certain ideas and are especially common in such subjects as philosophy and the social sciences, but usually they are less exact, less meaningful, and consequently less effective than concrete words. Because they refer to specific and actual objects or concepts, concrete words have meanings more or less solidly established in the minds of both writer and reader. "Something worn on the human body between shoulders and chin" is rather vague but not entirely abstract. The concept can be made less vague by referring to a *collar* and more concrete by mention of a *ruff, shawl collar, long point, spread collar,* or *button-down*. The word *neckwear* can refer to a "rather long length of soft material such as silk or wool, worn about the neck and usually under a collar." If a speaker or writer uses *necktie,* he is somewhat more specific; if he uses *four-in-hand, bow-tie,* or *necktie party,* he is being even more concrete.

Abstract words possess varying degrees of definiteness. Such words as *countryside, fear,* and *security* are not particularly specific, but they have more understandable connections with the experiences of most people than terms like *culture, duty, truth,* and *honor.* The word *carrier,* defined as a means of conveying and transporting, is somewhat abstract. It can be made less so by using such terms as *truck, car, motorcycle,* and *handcar,* or by *mule, tank, bus, half-track,* and *kayak.*

Good writers sometimes use an abstract term because nothing else will fit and then immediately make it more communicative by providing a concrete example of what is meant or by translating its meaning into terms less abstract and vague. Suppose, for example, you contend that government should intervene as little as possible in our economy and thus you employ the term *laissez-faire*. Is this expression abstract or concrete? An effective writer, Stuart Chase, unwilling to take a chance on his reader's understanding of the term, used it but immediately equated it with a city that had "no traffic system," one where every driver was on his own. Chase then explained *enforced competition* as a system in which "traffic cops protect little cars"; *governmental regulation* as similar to "traffic cops advising drivers how to drive"; *government ownership* as a procedure in which "a traffic officer throws the driver out and gets behind the wheel himself." You may agree or disagree with the writer's definitions and analogies, but at least you know what he means.

Much of what we remember from our reading of literature—especially of essays, articles, and biography—consists of incidents and anecdotes originally designed by the author to reinforce some abstract concept. The appeal of stories, plays, novels, and much poetry lies in the fact that understandable, flesh-and-blood characters are involved in understandable problems and face understandable conflicts. What happens to people, why it happens, and what the results are seem real and exciting to us because happenings are narrated and described in concrete, specific terms that we can grasp as readily as we can observe or face problems and situations in our own lives.

Nine-tenths of all good writing consists of being concrete and specific. The other tenth doesn't really matter.

Try always to make your writing as simple, conversational, individual, and concrete as you possibly can.

4

PROOFREAD EVERYTHING
YOU WRITE

When we read, we see merely the outlines, or shells, of words. Only poor readers need to see individual letters as such; most of us comprehend words and even groups of words at a glance.

But have you ever noticed how much easier it is for you to detect errors in someone else's writing than in your own? This may be because in reading someone else's writing you are *looking* for mistakes. Or it may be that you look more carefully at the writing of someone else than at your own because you are unfamiliar with it and have to focus more sharply in order to comprehend. You already "know" what you are saying.

Whatever the reason for closer scrutiny, in proofreading we narrow the range of our vision and thereby pick up mistakes hitherto unnoticed. In short, we detect careless errors not by reading but by *proofreading*.

Much of the effectiveness of proofreading depends upon the spread of your vision. The triangle on the next page will show you how wide your vision (sight spread) is. Look at the top of the triangle and then down. How far down can you go and still identify each letter in each line at a *single* glance? Your central vision is as wide as the line above the one where you cannot identify each letter *without moving your eyes at all*.

People differ in their range of vision as they do in nearly everything else. But many people have difficulty in identifying more than six letters at a single glance. Some have a span of vision embracing only three or four letters. Whatever

your span, you should not try to exceed it when you are check-
ing for errors.

If you do, you are reading—perhaps with excellent understanding—but you are not *proofreading*.

Only proofreading will enable you to eliminate errors caused
not by ignorance or stupidity but by carelessness.

Until your writing is set in type, the kind of reading that has
just been discussed is actually "manuscript" reading. When your
work appears in type it becomes "proof," a term referring to a trial
impression from a printing surface taken for inspection and correction. When you read such an impression, you are actually
proofreading. To this end, you may wish to become familiar with
what is known as "proofreaders' marks," a sample of which can be
found on page 25 (or in most dictionaries).

Word processing is making writing easier, faster, and more
error free than ever before. Writing is easier because authors
know that they can make changes easily and quickly. It is faster
because special editing features speed revisions. And word processing has made writing less tedious because writers are able to
revise and polish their work free of the tasks involved in retyping
successive drafts.

Proofreaders' Marks

ℐ	Delete	⌐	Move right
◡	Close up	⊓	Move up
ℐ	Delete and close up	⊔	Move down
tr	Transpose	=	Align horizontally
#	Insert space	‖	Align vertically
eq.#	Equalize space	⌄	Insert comma
¶	Start new paragraph	⊙	Insert period
no ¶	Run existing paragraphs together	:/	Insert colon
		;/	Insert semicolon
sp	Spell out	?	Insert question mark
STET	Let it stand	⌄	Insert apostrophe
cap	Change to capital letter(s)	⌄ ⌄	Insert single quotation marks
lc	Change to lowercase letter(s)		
ital	Change to *italic* type	⌄⌄ ⌄⌄	Insert quotation marks
rom	Change to roman type	⟨ ⟩	Insert parentheses
bf	Change to **boldface** type	⟦ ⟧	Insert brackets
⌐	Move left	=	Insert hyphen

PART II

GUIDES TO CORRECT USAGE

5

GUIDE TO GRAMMAR AND GRAMMATICAL USAGE

Grammar is that science which deals with words, forms of words, and word combinations. Broadly speaking, grammar is a descriptive statement of the way language works. What we usually call "good English" is the use of words and word forms in combinations appropriate to English as it is spoken and written by thoughtful people. Recognizing and avoiding common errors in English requires a working knowledge of English sounds, words, and the formation and arrangement of words.

Actually, grammar has nothing to do with "correctness" as such. It *describes* but does not *prescribe*. Even so, in order to speak and write without making what are generally considered minor mistakes or outright blunders, you need some knowledge of the English way of saying and writing things. Such knowledge you may have resisted for many years because you always thought that grammar is "dull," "lifeless," "not worth studying." These attitudes toward basic grammatical principles are commonly held. Nevertheless, they are both thoughtless and incorrect.

Grammar is "dull" and "dry" only when it is studied for its own sake, not when it is properly considered as a means to an end. A minimum knowledge of fundamental grammar is a powerful aid in effective writing on all levels.

Nor can grammar be thought of as "lifeless," because it is a kind of organism, filled with life and constantly developing and changing. The primary purpose of grammar is to describe change and development. Language is not based on grammar, for the latter is a controlled study and record of speech habits. Again, grammar is not a rigid set of do's and don't's; it is not something imposed by authorities. Grammar truly is a series of scientifically recorded observations about language and is subject to frequent and drastic change.

Grammatical principles may seem to you to be fixed and definite, but because both language and the grammar based upon language are progressing day by day and year by year, the language used and the grammar studied by our children and grandchildren will differ at least somewhat from practices of today.

Also, grammar is "worth studying" because, properly understood, it can help us to express our ideas clearly and effectively in both speech and writing. Weakness in writing—particularly incorrectness of sentence structure—is often due to insufficient understanding of grammar. And yet this knowledge does not have to be memorized or consciously applied. Many skilled speakers and writers are more concerned with what they have to say than with grammar, as such; they have mastered basic grammatical principles and apply them as instinctively or unconsciously as you and I might drive an automobile or run a sewing machine.

Many writers have partly or completely forgotten the grammar they learned in school, or so they think. Actually, some "unconscious" knowledge remains, because otherwise they could not make their meaning clear to other people. It is true, however, that definitions of certain grammatical terms may have been forgotten. This is unfortunate only when a lack of knowledge of the meanings of terms results in awkward or obscure phrasing.

A knowledge of terms does not guarantee acceptable or efficient writing. But surely we cannot improve our ease and surefootedness with language unless we know what is meant by

1. Parts of speech
2. Verbals
3. Phrases
4. Clauses

GRAMMAR AND USAGE

Grammar and usage overlap and are mutually dependent, but they do not mean exactly the same thing. *Grammar* is concerned with the structure of a language, the way it works. It is involved with the forms that various kinds of words take, various groups of words that are meaningful in the language, and the way language shows the varied grammatical relations it can communicate: predication, modification, and the like. Grammar remains constant, or nearly so, over long periods. Usage, however, is constantly changing. One does not have a problem in usage until a choice is involved. One can split an infinitive or not split an infinitive; one can say or write "I be" or "I am." What is involved here is less grammar than usage.

What you have had stuffed into you from early school days is *usage* rather than grammar. You have probably been expected to learn endless lists of rules and then to write sentences applying them. Over and over you have been warned by teachers and textbooks:

1. Don't say "ain't" in the classroom.
2. Don't say "I think Mary *done* it."
3. Don't use *media* as a singular noun.
4. Don't say "between him and I."
5. Don't split an infinitive.

Such cautions are matters of language etiquette, of conventional requirements, of a prescribed or accepted code of usage.

The sections that follow are intended to alert you to those items of usage, of language etiquette, that disturb or offend careful observers, teachers, and writers. They label items of divided usage and indicate what is appropriate in a given situation. They ignore some outmoded notions about usage—changes are part of the life of a language—and try to present the options, the choices, you have in writing contemporary, generally accepted English. These sections suggest that you stop worrying about rules and regulations and concentrate instead on remembering that the suitability and fitness of your language are determined by who is writing or speaking to whom about what and under what circumstances. For instance, if you wish to get someone out of your room, it might be effective and appropriate to say "Get lost," or "Beat it," or "Scram" or to use some more vigorous or even profane direction. In another situation, effective usage might suggest that you say "Please leave," or "Go away," or "Good-bye," or "*Au revoir.*" Whatever expression you select, your choice is dependent upon usage, not grammar.

Attitudes about usage have become far less rigid in recent years. Almost any expression is now considered fitting if it has the wanted and intended effect upon the person reading or hearing it. Yet everyone has faced situations in which knowledge of acceptable English is either desirable or important.

You may not wish or need to use "correct" English at all times, but it helps to know what are acceptable expressions when you are talking with, or writing to, persons you wish to impress favorably. Regardless of the idioms, accents, and other language customs of your geographic or social background, the language you write and speak will often be subjected to certain standards wherever you go. It will *have* to look or sound standard because otherwise you may find yourself being snubbed or rejected without really knowing why. Here is one of the few outright *don'ts* in this book: Don't confuse a right to complain with an excuse for ignorance.

BASIC GRAMMATICAL TERMS

Learn to Identify Each Word as a Part of Speech

A word is a letter or combination of letters, a sound or combination of sounds, forming a unit of thought capable of being used as an utterance.

Words are classified according to their use in larger units of thought—in phrases, clauses, and sentences. This functional (use) division results in eight so-called parts of speech. Every word in our language belongs to one or more parts of speech and is so labeled in every dictionary of decent quality and size. Words can also be grouped according to the purpose they serve:

Naming words: nouns and pronouns
Asserting words: verbs
Modifying words: adjectives and adverbs
Joining words: conjunctions and prepositions
Exclamatory words: interjections

Traditional and not entirely satisfactory definitions of the various parts of speech follow:

1. A *noun* is the name of a person, place, thing, or idea:

    girl   country   hat   honor

2. A *pronoun* is a substitute for a noun:

    she   it   that   somebody

3. A *verb* expresses action, a state of being, or a condition; it says, or asserts, something:

    come   be   run   remain

4. An *adjective* modifies (affects the meaning of) a noun or pronoun:

    green   some   lively   thirty

5. An *adverb* modifies (affects the meaning of) a verb, adjective, or another adverb:

    quickly   strongly   somewhat   very

6. A *conjunction* links (connects) words or groups of words:

    and   yet   where   while

7. A *preposition* shows relationship between the noun or pronoun it precedes and some other word:

    above   between   over   within

8. An *interjection* independently expresses feeling:

    ah   boo   indeed   ouch

Learn to Distinguish Between Verbs and Verbals

A verbal is a verb form incapable of acting as a predicate verb, whereas a predicate (or *finite*) verb can complete a statement about the subject of a sentence. Verbals consist of *participles, gerunds,* and *infinitives.*

A *participle* is a verbal adjective, a word having the function of both verb and adjective. As a verb form, it can take an object and be affected in meaning by an adverb. As an adjective, it can modify a noun or pronoun and can itself be modified by an adverb.

> *Present* participle: singing, speaking, asking
> *Past* participle: sung, spoken, asked
> *Perfect* participle: having sung, having been sung

> The boy noisily *eating* popcorn is rude and thoughtless.

The participle *eating* modifies *boy* and has *popcorn* for an object; it is modified by the adverb *noisily.*

A *gerund* is a verbal noun, a word having the functions of both verb and noun. As a verb form, it can take an object and be affected in meaning by an adverb. As a noun, it can be modified by an adjective and can be the subject of a verb and the object of a verb or preposition.

The present participle and the *-ing* gerund are spelled the same. Distinguish carefully between them:

> *Playing* golf vigorously can be good exercise. [*Playing,* a gerund, is the subject of the sentence in its capacity as a noun; as a verb form it takes an object, *golf,* and is modified by the adverb, *vigorously.*]
> The man *playing* golf is Warren Hibbard. [*Playing,* a participle, in its capacity as an adjective modifies *man;* as a verb, it takes an object, *golf.*]

An *infinitive* has the function of both verb and noun, as does a gerund. But an infinitive may also be used as an adjective or adverb and is often introduced by *to:*

To drive rapidly is a great thrill for her. [As a noun, the infinitive is the subject of the sentence; as a verb form, it is modified by *rapidly*.]

The best time *to fish* is early in the evening. [The infinitive acts as an adjective modifying *time*.]

The boys came *to swim*. [The infinitive is an adverbial modifier of *came*.]

Learn to Identify Phrases

A phrase, which usually serves as a part of speech, is a group of related words that does not contain a subject and predicate. Phrases may be classified as to use and form.

Use

A *noun* phrase is used in a sentence as subject or object:

Making a lot of money is his goal in life. [The italicized phrase is the subject of *is*.]

He likes *making a lot of money*. [Here the phrase is the object of *likes*.]

An *adjective* (*adjectival*) phrase is used in a sentence as a single adjective would be:

The boys *in this town* are noisy and thoughtless. [The italicized phrase modifies the noun *boys*.]

An *adverb* (*adverbial*) phrase is used in a sentence to modify a verb, adjective, or adverb:

We spent our vacation *on a farm*. [The italicized phrase modifies the verb *spent;* it answers the question "Where?"]

Form

A *prepositional* phrase is one beginning with a preposition; it may be used as adjective or adverb and, rarely, as a noun:

> The book *on the desk* is mine. [Adjective; what book?]
> He strode *into the room*. [Adverb; strode where?]
> *Without smiling* was her way of showing irritation. [Noun; subject of *was*.]

A *participial* phrase takes its name from an initial or important word:

> *Racing like mad*, we barely caught the bus.
> *Having run the last mile*, we caught the bus.

A *gerundial* phrase takes its name from the gerund it contains:

> *Playing at Candlestick Park* was his highest aim in sports.
> The crowd enjoyed *her expert twirling of a baton*.

An *infinitive* phrase takes its name from the infinitive it contains:

> *To make friends* is a worthwhile endeavor.

An *absolute* phrase is so-called because it is not directly attached to any other word in a sentence:

> John left quickly, *his objection now being a matter of record*.

Learn to Identify Clauses

A clause is a group of words having a subject and predicate. Some clauses are *independent* (main, principal); others are *dependent* (subordinate).

An *independent* clause is one that makes a complete grammatical statement and can stand alone. It may appear within a sentence or as a sentence itself:

A girl's greatest asset may be a boy's imagination.

Although only a cynic would say so, *a girl's greatest asset may be a boy's imagination.*

A *dependent* clause is one that is incapable of standing alone and for its meaning depends upon the remainder of the sentence in which it appears. Dependent (subordinate) clauses function as nouns, adjectives, and adverbs.

Noun Clause

What you said is not rude. [Subject of *is*; equivalent to "your remark."]

I do not believe *that you are my friend.* [Object of *believe.*]

Your suggestion *that you are really lazy* surprises me. [In apposition with *suggestion.*]

Adjective Clause

Girls *who have hair they consider their fortune* may have eyes which really draw interest. [The italicized clause modifies *girls.*]

The players think he is a coach *who should be taken with a grain of assault.* [Clause modifies *coach.*]

Adverbial Clause

How can I look up a word *when I don't know how to spell it?* [Clause modifies the verb *look up.*]

You can read more rapidly *than I can.* [Clause modifies the adverb *rapidly.*]

Steak is usually more expensive *than fish is.* [Clause modifies the adjective *expensive.*]

If you use a word processor, a so-called "grammar checker" (the term should be "grammatical usage" checker because there is really no such thing as "bad" or "good" grammar) it can check for and highlight misplaced sentences, awkward phrases, wordiness, and mistakes in grammatical usage. But only a human being knowledgeable about usage can decide to accept or reject the suggestions a grammar checker offers. The following pages should be helpful in this manner.

AGREEMENT OF SUBJECT AND PREDICATE

Agreement means "the state of being in accord," "conformity," "unison." As applied to grammar, the term means "correspondence in person, number, gender, or case." Thus when a subject "agrees" with its predicate, both subject and predicate verb have the same *person* (first, second, third) and *number* (singular or plural).

Few problems of agreement between subject and predicate arise, because English verbs (except *to be*) have only one form for singular and plural and for all persons except the third person singular present. But what few errors do occur are important. Usually, errors in agreement appear for two reasons: (1) the writer or speaker is confused about the *number* of the subject because of the presence of other words; (2) he or she uses a verb to agree not with the grammatical form of a subject, but with its meaning. You need to know what the *true* subject is and whether it is singular or plural.

A *predicate* (verb) normally agrees with its subject in person and number:

> The *owners* greedily *ask* too high a price. [*Owners* and *ask* are in the third person and are plural in number.]
> I *agree* to pay your asking price. [*I* and *agree* are in the first person and are singular in number.]
> *He agrees* to pay the asking price. [*He* and *agrees* are in the third person and are singular in number.]

A verb should not agree with a noun that intervenes between it and the subject:

The *cause* for all the noise and confusion *were* not obvious. [Substitute *was* for *were; cause,* the subject, is singular.]

I, together with *Eleanor* and *Sally, are* going. [Substitute *am* for *are; I* is the true subject.]

The *child,* as well as the other members of the family, *were* frightened. [Substitute *was* for *were;* the *child* is the true subject of the sentence.]

Singular pronouns require singular verbs. The following pronouns are singular: *another, anybody, anyone, anything, each, either, everybody, everyone, everything, neither, nobody, no one, one, somebody, someone.*

Each *has* his duty to perform.
No one *was* present at the time.
One of you *is* mistaken.

None (literally *no one* and also meaning "not any") may be followed by either a singular or a plural verb. It is as frequently followed by a plural verb as by one in the singular, especially when the phrase that modifies *none* contains a plural noun (*none of the men*). The standard rule, however, is that *none* requires a singular verb.

Agreement based on meaning and agreement based on grammatical form sometimes conflict. In the sentence "Each of the boys in the group *is* sixteen years old," *each* and *is* are in grammatical agreement. But in "*Each* of the boys in this group *are* sixteen years old," *are* is plural because the meaning of "each of the boys" is construed to be "all of the boys." A somewhat similar principle may be illustrated thus: "Everyone in the apartment house tuned *his* TV (or *their* TVs) to that channel." Careful speakers and writers follow grammatical agreement in such sentences; agreement based on meaning is widely employed but most appropriately in informal speech and writing.

For nouns plural in form but singular in meaning, use a singular verb.

Authorities differ about the number of many such nouns. A good rule, according to usage, is "When in doubt, use a singular verb." The following are nearly always used with singular verbs: *physics, economics, mathematics, news, politics, whereabouts, mechanics, ethics, mumps, stamina, headquarters.*

> *Physics*, they were told, *is* the study of heat, light, sound, mechanics, and electricity.
> The sad *news was* broadcast at noon.

Subjects plural in form that indicate a quantity or number require a singular verb when the subject is regarded as a unit.

> Four-fifths of the area *is* under water.
> Two from five *leaves* three.

Ordinarily, use a plural verb with two or more subjects joined by *and:*

> Both Jill and Bob *are* running for office.

When the two subjects form a single thought or have a very closely related meaning, a singular verb is frequently used:

> His kindness and generosity *is* well known.
> The sum and substance of his remarks *is* clear.

Singular subjects joined by *or* or *nor, either . . . or,* and *neither . . . nor* usually require a singular verb:

> Either Mimi or Dick *is* at fault.
> Neither the boy nor his father *was* found guilty.

If the subjects differ in number or person, the verb agrees with the nearer subject:

> Neither Phil nor the other boys *know.*
> Either they or I *am* liable for damages.

Relative pronouns referring to plural antecedents generally require plural verbs.

> Each of *those* who *are* there should listen carefully.
> He is one of the most able *students* who *have* ever attended that school.

If *only* or some similar qualifying word precedes *one*, the verb in the subordinate clause is singular:

He is the *only one* of those in this room who *listens* carefully.

A verb does not agree with a predicate noun:

The best part of a children's party *is* the ice cream and cake.
Ice cream and cake *are* the best part of a children's party.

After the expletive *there*, the verb is singular or plural according to the number of the subject that follows. Always use a singular verb after the expletive *it*.

There *are* [not *is*] strong sentiments in his favor.
There *were* [not *was*] baseball, tennis, and swimming.
In the field there *stands* [not *stand*] a towering tree.
It *is* [not *are*] men who must wash the dishes.

A collective noun takes a singular verb when the group is regarded as a unit, a plural verb when the individuals of the group are regarded separately.

The crew *has asked* him to help with coaching.
The crew *are coming* on board in a few hours.
The family *was named* Gregson.
The family *were seated* at the dinner table.

AGREEMENT OF PRONOUN AND ANTECEDENT

A pronoun does not always agree with its antecedent in case, but it should agree in *gender, number,* and *person*:

The *girl* picked up *her* books. [Feminine, singular, third]
The *women* took off *their* coats. [Feminine, plural, third]
The *man* removed *his* hat. [Masculine, singular, third]
The *boys* raised *their* voices. [Masculine, plural, third]

Singular pronouns refer to singular antecedents:

Has anyone here forgotten *his* promise?
Each passenger will have a berth to *himself*.
Everybody is expected to do *his* share.

In the last sentence above, *everybody* may refer to men and women. Only in colloquial English could you say, "Everybody is expected to contribute *their* share." You may write "Everybody is expected to contribute his or her share," although this construction sounds somewhat artificial. In grammar—and in few other situations and places—men are considered more important than women.

A pronoun agrees with the nearer of two antecedents:

He hated everything and everybody *who* caused his defeat.
He hated everybody and everything *that* caused his defeat.
Either Jack or his sisters will lose *their* chance to go.
Either Jack's sisters or he will lose *his* chance to go.

A collective noun used as an antecedent takes either a singular or plural pronoun, depending upon the sense of the sentence.

The group of girls was shouting *its* praises. [The group acted as a unit.]
The group of girls raised *their* umbrellas. [The group acted as individuals.]
The group *was* divided in *its* [not *their*] opinion of the speaker.
Members of the group *were* divided in *their* [not *its*] opinion of the speaker.

CASE

Case is one of the forms a noun or pronoun takes to indicate its relationship to other words in the sentence. There are only three important cases in English: nominative (subjective); genitive (possessive); and objective (accusative).

A noun or pronoun is in the *nominative* case (subject of a sentence) when it indicates the person or thing acting; in the genitive (*possessive*) case when it denotes the person or thing owning or possessing; in the *objective* case when it indicates the person or thing acted upon.

There is no change in the *form* of a noun to denote the nominative and objective cases. Word order in the sentence provides the only clue:

The child rode his tricycle. [*Child* is in the nominative case, *tricycle* in the objective.]

The tricycle was ridden by the child. [*Tricycle* is in the nominative case, *child* in the objective.]

The possessive case does involve a change in the form of a noun, but the case of nouns usually causes little trouble.

Grammatical problems often arise because many *pronouns*, unlike *nouns*, have distinct forms for the nominative and objective cases. Such problems appear most frequently with *personal* pronouns (*I, you, he, me, him*) and with *relative* and *interrogative* pronouns (*who, whom, whose*).

Nominative Case

The subject of a sentence or a clause is in the nominative case.

If the subject is a noun, rest easy; it would be uncommon for one to get its grammatical form wrong. If the subject is a pronoun, you still should have little trouble:

He and *I* [not *me*] volunteered to go.
Who [not *whom*] is speaking, please?

A predicate complement is in the nominative case.

A *predicate complement* is a noun (no difficulty with case), a pronoun (nominative case, essentially), or a predicate adjective (no case involved) used after a linking verb.

After a linking (copulative, coupling) verb, use only the nominative case of a pronoun:

That was *she* [not *her*] calling on the telephone.
It was *they* [not *them*] who invited us to the dance.

In colloquial speech one often hears (and perhaps says) "It's me" or "This is me," or "That's him." Such expressions are growing more acceptable, but careful speakers and writers continue to use the nominative case in such constructions.

Objective Case

The object of a verb or preposition is in the objective case.

All nouns and the pronouns *it* and *you* cause no difficulty in this construction. But carefully choose between *who* and *whom*, *I* and *me*, *she* and *her*, *he* and *him*, *they* and *them*, *we* and *us*:

> *Whom* did the police blame for the accident?
> The superintendent accused *me*.
> That is a blow to *her*.
> A group of *us* is going to the lecture.
> Did you invite both *him* and *her* to our party?
> To *whom* did you mention our party?

The indirect object of a verb is in the objective case.

An *indirect object* is a noun or pronoun before which *to* or *for* is expressed or understood:

> Give *me* a fuller explanation, please.
> If you do *him* a favor, he will not be grateful.
> Tell *whom* my bad luck? Didi? I certainly shall not.

The subject, object, or objective complement of an infinitive is in the objective case:

> *Whom* did you take him to be? [That is, you did take *him* to be *whom?*]
> His father made *him* say that. [*Him* is the subject of *to say*.]
> My eagerness to kiss *her* was great. [*Her* is the object of *to kiss*.]
> Did Jack think him to be *me?* [*Me* is the objective complement of *to be*.]

Nominative or Objective Case

So far, so good; now we come to the real trouble spots. If you do not fully understand the function of pronouns, particularly *who*, *whoever*, *whom*, and *whomever*, now is the time to learn them once and for all time.

Who and *whoever* are used as subjects of verbs or as predicate pronouns. *Whom* and *whomever* are used as objects of verbs and of prepositions.

The following sentences illustrate correct use of *who* and *whoever:*

The question of *who* is eligible is unimportant. [*Who* is the subject of *is;* the entire clause *who is eligible* is the object of the preposition *of.*]

This article offers good advice to *whoever* will accept it. [*Whoever* is the subject of *will accept;* the clause *whoever will accept it* is the object of *to.*]

A stranger here, he does not know *who* is *who.* [The first *who* is the subject of *is;* the second *who* is a predicate pronoun.]

These sentences illustrate proper use of *whom* and *whomever:*

That is the boy *whom* I saw at the beach last summer. [*Whom* is the direct object of *saw:* "I saw whom."]

Jack always tells his problems to *whomever* he meets. [*Whomever* is the direct object of *meets:* "He meets whomever."]

Give the present to *whomever* you wish. [*Whomever* is the object of the preposition *to.*]

The case of a pronoun must not be affected by words that come between the pronoun and its antecedent. The case of a word always depends upon its *use* in a sentence:

Jill asked Gray *who* he thought would be elected. [Check by omitting *he thought.*]

Who do you think is responsible for that decision? [Check by omitting *do you think.*]

I winked at the girl *whom* no one thought we had invited. [Check by omitting *no one thought.*]

An appositive should be in the same case as the noun or pronoun it identifies or explains:

We, *you* and *I*, are silly to take this chance.

The judge gave both of us, *Fred* and *me*, a stern lecture.

A few of us, those *whom* you asked, are delighted to accept.

An elliptical clause of comparison, preceded by *than* or *as*, requires the case called for by the expanded construction:

You are as strong as *I* (am). [Nominative]
This story interested you more than (it interested) *me*. [Objective]
I do not love her as much as *he* (loves her). [Nominative]

Genitive (Possessive) Case

/ A noun or pronoun linked immediately with a gerund should preferably be in the possessive case:

She dislikes *your* being more attractive than she is.
The coach praised John for *his* taking extra practice sessions.

When the use of a possessive with a gerund causes awkwardness, rephrase the sentence:

Awkward: No rules exist against *anyone's* in this section speaking his mind.
Improved: No rules exist against any section *member's* speaking his mind.

Avoid using the possessive case of an inanimate object:

Awkward: The *tree's* leaves were turning brown.
This machine will quickly wax and polish the *dance hall's* floor.
Improved: The *leaves of the tree* were turning brown.
This machine will quickly wax and polish the floor *of the dance hall* (or *the dance hall floor*).

Use the possessive case in accordance with established idiom.
Despite the suggestions given above, such expressions as the following are idiomatic and thus desirable: a day's work, a moment's notice, a dime's worth, a stone's throw, a summer's work, at his wits' end, three years' experience, tomorrow's weather report, the law's delay, two semesters' study.

PRINCIPAL PARTS OF VERBS

An English verb has three principal parts: *present tense* (present infinitive), *past tense, past participle* (go, went, gone). A good way to recall these parts is to substitute those of any verb for the following:

I play today.
I played yesterday.
I have played every day this week.
I swim today.
I swam yesterday.
I have swum every day this week.

Do not misuse the past tense and past participle. The past tense and past participle of most English verbs are formed by adding *-d, -ed,* or *-t* to the present infinitive: *ask, asked, asked; deal, dealt, dealt.* Such verbs are called *regular,* or *weak,* verbs. Verbs which form the past tense and past participle by a vowel change as well as by the occasional addition of an ending are called *irregular,* or *strong,* verbs: *do, did, done; ride, rode, ridden.*

Wrong: The dog *has bit* the child seriously. [*Has bitten*]
Joe *drunk* a pint of cold milk. [*Drank*]
Snow *has fell* for 22 hours. [*Has fallen*]

When in doubt about the correct forms of the past tense or past participle, consult your dictionary. If no additional forms follow the main entry, the verb is regular (formed with the endings *-d, -ed,* or *-t*).

Do not carelessly omit the ending of a regular verb:

We are *supposed* [not *suppose*] to arrive on time.
Yesterday I *asked* [not *ask*] for another examination.

Learn the principal parts of frequently used regular and irregular verbs. Here is a list of 50 troublesome verbs. Study them; put them into the three expressions suggested earlier.

bear	bore	borne (born, *given birth to*)
begin	began	begun
bid	bid	bid (*as in an auction*)
bid	bade	bidden (*as in a command*)
bite	bit	bitten (bit)
blow	blew	blown
break	broke	broken
burst	burst	burst
catch	caught	caught
choose	chose	chosen
come	came	come
dig	dug	dug
dive	dived	dived
do	did	done
drag	dragged	dragged
draw	drew	drawn
drink	drank	drunk
drown	drowned	drowned
eat	ate	eaten
fall	fell	fallen
fly	flew	flown
forget	forgot	forgotten (forgot)
freeze	froze	frozen
get	got	got (gotten)
go	went	gone
hang	hung	hung (*object*)
hang	hanged	hanged (*person*)
know	knew	known
lay	laid	laid
lead	led	led
lend	lent	lent
lie	lay	lain (*recline*)
lie	lied	lied (*falsehood*)
lose	lost	lost

pay	paid	paid
raise	raised	raised
ride	rode	ridden
rise	rose	risen
run	ran	run
set	set	set
sing	sang	sung
sit	sat	sat
speak	spoke	spoken
swim	swam	swum
take	took	taken
tear	tore	torn
wake	waked (woke)	waked (woke)
wear	wore	worn
wring	wrung	wrung
write	wrote	written

LINKING AND AUXILIARY VERBS

Most verbs assert (indicate) action, but some express a static condition or state of being, not of action. Nearly all such "inactive" verbs are *linking* verbs (also called *copulative* or *joining* verbs). A linking verb can "couple" two nouns or pronouns or a noun and an adjective: "This *is* my brother"; "The dog *looks* sick."

Another variety of verb which can cause trouble is the *auxiliary* verb—one that "helps out" another verb in forming tenses, voice, mood, and certain precise ideas. Usually an auxiliary verb has little meaning of its own, but it does change the meaning of the main verb it accompanies:

The man of the soil *has been* pushed more and more out of the American economy.

A careful analysis of the oxygen content *should have been* made at the time.

The following are suggestions for handling linking and auxiliary verbs.

1. Distinguish between a linking verb and one that expresses action.

The most common linking verb is *to be*. Other linking verbs are *appear, become, feel, grow, look, prove, remain, seem, smell, sound, stand, taste, turn*. Still other verbs occur in only a limited number of linking contexts: "*slam* shut," "*ring* true." Distinguish carefully between meanings of the same verb when it asserts action and when it does not:

The sky *looks* overcast today. [Linking]
Jane *looks* closely at every page she reads. [Action]
We *felt* downcast over our defeat. [Linking]
Marian *felt* her way through the dark room. [Action]

2. Use the correct auxiliary verb.

The most common auxiliary verbs are *to be, to have*, and *to do*. Other auxiliaries are *can, could, dare, let, may, might, must, need, ought, shall, should, used, will, would*.

Meanings for these frequently used auxiliary verbs are given in your dictionary. Be sure you know the right word. Do not, for example, use *should* if *would* is needed or *ought* if *must* is indicated. Also, do not confuse *of* with *have*.

Inaccurate: You *should of* told me about that.
               The child *might of* been seriously injured.
               Can I borrow your slide rule, please?
               I *had ought to* leave by now.
               Leave me think for a few minutes alone.
Accurate: You should *have* told me about that.
               The child might *have* been seriously injured.
               May I borrow your slide rule, please?
               I *ought to have* (should have) left by now.
               Let me think for a few minutes alone.

TENSE AND TONE

Tense indicates the time of the action or time of the static condition (state of being) expressed by a verb. The three divisions of time—past, present, future—are shown in English by six tenses.

The three primary, or simple, tenses are the *present* tense, the *past* tense, and the *future* tense. The three secondary, or compound, tenses are the *present perfect*, the *past perfect*, and the *future perfect*.

Within some tenses verbs also have certain *tones* that express precisely what the writer wishes to say: *simple tone* (I study); *progressive tone* (I am studying); and *emphatic tone* (I do study).

Use the correct tense to express precise time. Unlike a highly inflected language, such as German, English has few tense forms; English verbs reveal change in tense only by inflection or by the use of auxiliary words.

Difficulty with tense usage arises from not knowing the functions of the six tenses or from not thinking carefully about the exact time element involved. The following brief table and comments on each tense should help you to use the precise tenses needed to convey your ideas:

ACTIVE VOICE

Present	I see (am seeing)
Past	I saw (was seeing)
Future	I shall see (shall be seeing)
Present perfect	I have seen (have been seeing)
Past perfect	I had seen (had been seeing)
Future perfect	I shall have seen (shall have been seeing)

PASSIVE VOICE

Present	I am seen (am being seen)
Past	I was seen (was being seen)
Future	I shall be seen
Present perfect	I have been seen
Past perfect	I had been seen
Future perfect	I shall have been seen

VERBALS
(NONFINITE VERB FORMS)

Present infinitive	to see (to be seeing)
Perfect infinitive	to have seen (to have been seeing)
Present participle	seeing [none]
Past participle	seen [none]
Perfect participle	having seen (having been seeing)
Present gerund	seeing [none]
Perfect gerund	having seen (having been seeing)

Present tense indicates that the action or condition is going on or exists now:

He *walks* to his office every day.
The truth *is* known.

Past tense indicates that an action or condition took place or existed at some definite time in the past.

She *mailed* the package yesterday.
The summer of 1989 *was* hot.

The *future tense* indicates that an action will take place, or that a certain condition will exist, in the future:

We *shall leave* at noon tomorrow.
Our glee club *will be singing* there next month.

The future may be stated by the present tense accompanied by an adverb (or adverbial phrase) of time. Such constructions as the following are common:

I am going to San Diego soon.
This Thursday the boat leaves for Honolulu.

Present perfect tense indicates that an action or condition was begun in the past and has just been completed or is still going on. The time is past, but it is connected with the present. The present perfect tense *presupposes* some relationship with the present:

You *have been* a nuisance all your life.

The weather *has been* too cold for hiking in the woods.

I *have* long *been* an Alfred Hitchcock addict.

Past perfect tense indicates that an action or condition was completed at a time now past. It indicates action "two steps back." That is, the past perfect tense presupposes some relationship with an action or condition in the past tense:

The roads were impassable because ice sheets *had formed* during the night.

He lived in Berkeley. He *had been* there for several months.

Future perfect tense indicates that an action or condition will be completed at a future time:

I *shall have died* by that time.

The weather *will have moderated* before you leave.

The three secondary, or compound, tenses always indicate completed action, whether it be in the present (present perfect tense), in the past (past perfect tense), or in the future (future perfect tense).

Use the correct tone to express precise meaning. The *simple* tone is a concise statement of a "snapshot" or instantaneous action of a verb: I *talk* (present tense), I *talked* (past tense), I *shall talk* (future tense), I *have talked* (present perfect tense), I *had talked* (past perfect tense), I *shall have talked* (future perfect tense).

The *progressive* tone forms in each of the six tenses are built by using proper tense forms of the verb *to be* followed by the present participle of the main verb: I *am talking, was talking, shall be talking, have been talking, had been talking, shall have been talking.*

The *emphatic* tone forms are formed by the verb *to do* and the present infinitive of the main verb. The emphatic tone is used in only present and past tenses: I *do talk*, I *did talk*.

Watch carefully the sequence of tenses. When only one verb is used in a sentence, it should express the precise time involved. When two or more verbs appear in a sentence, they should be consistent in tense. Most important, remember that the tense of a verb in a subordinate clause depends on the tense of the verb in the main clause.

The present tense is used in a dependent clause to express a general truth:

Some people did not believe that the earth *is* a planet.

The present tense is used alone to express a "timeless" truth:

Thought *makes* the whole dignity of man.

Do not allow the tense of a verb to be attracted into the past when it should be present: "Last summer, I visited a small village in France; the houses *were* old and picturesque." (It is conceivable that the village has been destroyed, but is that what is meant?)

Passages in some short stories and novels are written in the present tense although the action occurred in time which is past. This use is called the *historical present*.

Use a present infinitive except when the infinitive represents action completed before the time of the governing verb:

I intended to *see* [not *to have seen*] you about it.
Everyone is pleased *to have had* you as a visitor.

A present participle indicates action at the time expressed by the verb; a past participle indicates action before that of the verb:

Traveling all over the world, he *sees* many remarkable people.
Having been a good worker, he *was* able to get many letters of
    recommendation.

When narration in the past tense is interrupted for reference to a preceding event, use the past perfect tense.

In April they *pruned* the trees which *had been damaged* by
    sleet.
He *told* me that he *had been* ill for a month.

VOICE

Verbs are classified as to *voice*, active or passive. A verb is in the *active* voice when the subject is the performer of the action or is in the condition or state named. In the *passive* voice, the subject does nothing, is inactive or passive, and has something done to it.

The engineers *threw* a bridge across the river.
A bridge *was thrown* across the river by the engineers.
The lookout *sighted* the ship on the horizon.
The ship on the horizon *was sighted* by the lookout.
Tom *laid* the book on the table.
The book *was laid* on the table by Tom.
We *rested* on the beach.

In the first three examples above, the point of view and the emphasis are quite different. The verbs which are *active* stress the doers of the action—engineers, lookout, and Tom; the verbs which are *passive* stress the recipients of the action—bridge, ship, and book.

Choice of active or passive voice depends upon context, upon relative importance of the doer and the recipient of the action. Since intransitive verbs rarely fulfill the conditions that make verbs active or passive, only transitive verbs can have a passive voice.

In the last example above, *rested* is in the active voice because the subject, *we*, is in the state or condition named.

Never use an intransitive verb in a passive voice construction:

Incorrect: Your books have been lain on the table.
Correct: Your books have been laid on the table.

Avoid frequent use of the passive voice. Doers and agents are usually more appealing than those who sit still and do nothing. Use of the active voice normally provides greater force, strength, and life than does the passive. Use the active voice whenever you wish to imply action, mental or physical; use the passive voice in impersonal writing ("These results *were noticed*") and as little elsewhere as possible. Your reader will prefer "Fred *kissed* Joy passionately" to "Joy *was kissed* passionately by Fred." Fred and Joy probably do not care what voice you use, and may be sorry you mentioned them, but it is likely that Joy was as "active" as Fred.

ADJECTIVES AND ADVERBS

Ordinarily, it is not difficult to determine when an adjective *or* adverb should be used. *Adjectives* "go with" nouns and pronouns; *adverbs* "go with" verbs, adjectives, and other adverbs. And yet misuse of adjectives and adverbs is common for three main reasons: (1) After linking verbs, an adjective is used if reference is to the subject, an adverb if reference is to the verb itself; (2) idiomatic usage often violates the distinction between adjectives and adverbs; (3) some adjectives and adverbs have identical or similar forms. Keep in mind the following fundamental distinctions.

Adjectives

An *adjective* modifies a noun or pronoun by describing, limiting, or in some other way making meaning more nearly exact. An adjective may indicate quality or quantity, may identify or set limits. Consequently, adjectives are of three general types: descriptive (a *red* hat, a *hard* lesson, a *damaged* thumb); limiting (the *fourth* period, her *former* home, *many* times); proper (an *American* play, a *Colorado* melon).

Some adjectives—indeed, most—have endings that mark them as adjectives. The more important of these include:

-*y:* rocky, funny, dreamy, fussy, muddy
-*ful:* harmful, faithful, hurtful, sinful
-*less:* stainless, timeless, lawless, guiltless
-*en:* golden, wooden, given, hidden, rotten
-*able* (-*ible*): favorable, desirable, credible
-*ive:* obtrusive, submissive, impulsive
-*ous:* amorous, ridiculous, generous, marvelous
-*ish:* mannish, selfish, Danish, fortyish
-*al:* cordial, optional, experimental, judicial
-*ic:* metric, philosophic, authentic, artistic

-ary: primary, visionary, contrary, secondary
-some: meddlesome, tiresome, handsome, troublesome

An adjective may modify a noun directly ("this *yellow* light thrown upon the color of his ambitions") or indirectly ("the survivors, *weary* and *emaciated*, moved feebly toward the ship"). In sentences such as "The water felt *cold*" and "The corn is *ripe*," each adjective is related to the subject, the word it modifies, by a linking verb. (A linking verb has little meaning of its own; it functions primarily as a connection between subject and predicate noun or predicate adjective.) In the sentences above, *cold* and *ripe* are called *predicate adjectives* or *complements*.

Adverbs

An *adverb* modifies a verb, adjective, or other adverb by describing or limiting to make meaning more exact. Adverbs usually tell *how, when, where, why, how often,* and *how much.* In "A low cry came *faintly* to our ears," the adverb modifies the verb *came* and tells *how.* In "We were *nearly* ready to leave," the adverb modifies the adjective *ready.* In "Close the door *very* softly," the adverb modifies the adverb *softly.*

Adverbs have the following characteristics:

1. Adverbs are commonly, but not always, distinguished from corresponding adjectives by the suffix *-ly: bad, badly; sure, surely; cold, coldly.*
2. Certain adverbs are distinguished from corresponding nouns by the suffixes *-wise* and *-ways: endways, sideways, lengthwise.*
3. Certain adverbs are distinguished from corresponding prepositions in not being connected to a following noun:

   Adverb: He ran *up.*
   Preposition: He ran *up* the street.
4. Like adjectives, but unlike nouns and verbs, adverbs may be preceded by words of the *very* group (intensifiers):

The *most exotically* dressed girl. . . .
He went *right* by.

Some Guidelines

1. *Do not use an adjective to modify a verb.*

The form of a word does not always reveal whether it is an adjective or adverb. Most words ending in *-ly* are adverbs, but *holy, sickly, fatherly,* and *manly* are adjectives. Also, some adjectives and adverbs have the same form: *quick, little, early, fast, kindly.* Finally, a few adverbs have two forms quite different in meaning: *late, lately; sharp, sharply.*

Wrong: He drives his car too *rapid.* [*Rapidly*, an adverb, should modify the verb *drives*; *rapid* is an adjective.]
He dresses *neat* when she is going to a party. [Use *neatly.*]
Shakespeare's Portia acted *womanly.* [Use *in a womanly way.*]
The preacher spoke *abrupt* to me. [Use *abruptly.*]

2. *Do not use an adjective to modify another adjective.*

Wrong: Judy is a *real* keen chess player. [Use *really*, an adverb.]
That is a *sturdy* tailored overcoat. [Use *sturdily.*]
Dick drove his convertible *plenty* fast. [Use *very*, or *quite*, or *exceedingly.*]

3. *After such verbs as* appear, be, become, feel, look, seem, smell, taste, *the modifier should be an adjective if it refers to the subject, an adverb if it describes or defines the verb.*

Correct: This coffee tastes *good.* [Adjective]
The dance hall looked *beautiful.* [Adjective]
Jim appeared *sick* when he left the room. [Adjective]
She looked at him *lovingly.* [Adverb]
Karen feels *intensely* that she was slighted. [Adverb]
Joe tasted *carefully* before he swallowed. [Adverb]

4. *Be accurate in using words that may be either adjectives or adverbs.*

Correct: Sue was a *little* girl. [Adjective]
Please come a *little* nearer. [Adverb]
Bob was a *kindly* man. [Adjective]
Bob spoke *kindly* to everyone. [Adverb]
Get here quickly; be an *early* bird. [Adjective]
I hope you will come *early.* [Adverb]

5. *Be accurate in the use of comparatives and superlatives.*
Grammatically, *comparison* is the change in form of an adjective or adverb to indicate greater or smaller degrees of quantity, quality, or manner. The change is commonly indicated by the endings *-er* and *-est* or by the use of adverbial modifiers: *more, most, less, least.* The three degrees of comparison are *positive, comparative,* and *superlative:*

large	larger	largest
slow	slower	slowest
slowly	less slowly	least slowly
wise	wiser	wisest
wisely	more wisely	most wisely

Some comparisons are irregular: *good, better, best; little, less, least.*

Some adjectives are logically incapable of comparison because their meaning is absolute: *perpendicular, unique, round.* Only in informal speech and writing can something be *more impossible* or *more final* or *more fatal.*

Comparative degree is used to show relationship between two persons, objects, or ideas:

Fred is *taller* than I.
This box contains *less* than the other one.

Superlative degree is used to show relationship among three or more:

Alan is the *smartest* child in his class.
This desk is the *most attractive* of the four on display.

CONJUNCTIONS

A *conjunction* is a linking word used to connect words or groups of words in a sentence. Conjunctions are of two main kinds: *coordinating*, which join words or groups of words of equal rank, such as *and, but, for, or, nor, either, neither, yet*; and *subordinating*, which join dependent clauses to main clauses, such as *if, since, because, as, while, so that, although, unless*.

Certain coordinating conjunctions used in pairs are called *correlative* conjunctions. Most frequently used of these are *both . . . and, either . . . or, neither . . . nor, so . . . as, whether . . . or, not only . . . but also*.

Another kind of conjunction is the *conjunctive adverb*, a type of adverb that can also be used as a conjunction joining two independent clauses. Some examples are *accordingly, also, anyhow, besides, consequently, furthermore, hence, however, indeed, likewise, moreover, nevertheless, still, then, therefore, thus*.

1. *Distinguish among the meanings of conjunctions and conjunctive adverbs.*

Conjunctions, particularly those which are to join clauses, must be chosen with care, for they always show logical relationships of ideas. Often a careless writer will use *and* where the relationship of clauses needs to be more accurately expressed, probably by use of subordination. Compare emphasis and meaning in these sentences:

> The search for the chemical formula has been rewarding *and* further investigation will make the rewards even greater.
> *Although* the search for the chemical formula has been rewarding, further investigation will make the rewards even greater.

Depending upon your expressed purpose, you may coordinate or subordinate ideas in one of several ways. But unless you know the purpose (meaning) of conjunctions and conjunctive adverbs, you are likely to have trouble.

1. Purpose—*along the same line or in the same direction of thought:* and, both . . . and, not only . . . but also, also, besides, furthermore, in addition, indeed, likewise, moreover, similarly, whereby, whereupon

2. Purpose—*contrast:* although, but, however, instead, nevertheless, not only . . . but also, notwithstanding, still, whereas, yet

3. Purpose—*affirmative alternation:* anyhow, either . . . or, else, moreover, or, still, whereas, whether

4. Purpose—*negative alternation:* except that, however, instead, neither, neither . . . nor, nevertheless, nor, only, whereas

5. Purpose—*reason, result, purpose, cause:* accordingly, as, as a result, because, consequently, for, hence, inasmuch as, in order that, since, so, so that, that, thereby, therefore, thus, whereas, why

6. Purpose—*example:* for example, indeed, in fact, namely

7. Purpose—*comparison:* indeed, in fact, moreover, so . . . as, than

8. Purpose—*time:* after, as long as, as soon as, before, henceforth, meanwhile, once, since, then, till, until, when, whenever, while

9. Purpose—*place:* whence, where, wherever, whither

10. Purpose—*condition:* although, as if, as though, if, lest, once, provided, providing, though, unless

11. Purpose—*concession:* although, insofar as, notwithstanding the fact that, though, unless, while

2. *Use correlative conjunctions to correlate only two ideas.*

Dubious: *Both* the wind, tides, heavy rain, *and* darkness conspired against us. [Delete *both* or two of the four subjects.]
Neither poverty, ill health, *nor* the indifference of others could keep John from entering college. [Delete one of the three subjects or otherwise rephrase the sentence.]

3. *Avoid using a conjunctive adverb to join words or phrases or dependent clauses.*

> *Dubious:*   Ned's favorite foods are steak, broccoli, *also* ice cream. [. . . broccoli, *and* ice cream]
> At last report he was losing the decathlon; *still* was trying hard. [. . . *but* he was still trying hard]

4. *Be careful in using* like *as a subordinating conjunction.*

In recent years the use of *like* in clauses of comparison has greatly increased ("It looks *like* he might succeed"). A popular cigarette tastes good "like a cigarette should"; we no longer avoid *like* "like we used to."

In standard English, however, *like* is used as a preposition with no verb following: "He looks like an athlete." For clauses of comparison, use *as* or *as if* in strictly formal English:

> My wet shoes felt *as if* [not *like*] they weighed a ton.
> I am named for my father *as* [not *like*] my father was named for his.
> You must do *as* [not *like*] I tell you.

GLOSSARY OF GRAMMATICAL TERMS

The following list briefly defines those elements of grammar that are most often and most importantly involved in the writing of English sentences. Several of the items have been treated in greater detail at appropriate places earlier within the text.

absolute expression   An absolute expression (also called nominative absolute) is one that has a thought relationship but no direct grammatical relationship with the remainder of the sentence in which it occurs. An absolute expression is usually composed of a noun or pronoun and a participle: *"The game being lost,* we left the stadium." *"The purpose of our field trip having been explained,* we set out with enthusiasm."

active voice   The form of an action-expressing verb which tells that the subject does or performs the action.

agreement Correspondence, or sameness, in number, gender, and person. When a subject agrees with its verb, they are alike in having the same *person* (first, second, or third) and *number* (singular or plural). Pronouns agree not only in person and number, but also in gender.

Martha is my cousin.
Martha and *Sue are* my cousins.
A *woman* hopes to retain *her* youthful appearance.
Many *women* retain *their* youthful appearance.
Gary is one of those *boys* who *are* always well-mannered.

antecedent The substantive (noun or pronoun) to which a pronoun refers is its antecedent:

The *girl* has lost *her* chance. [*Girl* is the antecedent of *her.*]
Remember that *pronouns* agree with *their* antecedents in gender, number, and person. [*Pronouns* is the antecedent of *their.*]

appositive A substantive added to another substantive to identify or explain it. It is said to be "in apposition":

One important product, *rubber,* is in short supply in that country. [*Rubber* is in apposition with *product.*]
More hardy than wheat are these grains—*rye, oats,* and *barley.* [*Rye, oats,* and *barley* are in apposition with *grains.*]

An appositive agrees with its substantive in number and case. It is set off by commas if its relationship is loose (nonrestrictive) and is used without punctuation if the relationship is close (restrictive).

article The articles (*a, an, the*) may be classed as adjectives because they possess limiting or specifying functions. *A* and *an* are indefinite articles; *the* is the definite article: a phonograph, an error, the surgeon.

auxiliary A verb used to "help" another verb in the formation of tenses, voice, mood, and certain precise ideas. *Be* (*am, is, are, was, were, been*), *have* (*has, had*), *do* (*does*), *can, could, may, might, shall, should, will, would, must, ought, let, used* are examples.

He *has* left town for the weekend.
We *should have been* working with the stevedores on the dock.
Will you please turn off the light?

comparison   The change in form of an adjective or adverb to indicate greater or smaller degrees of quantity, quality, or manner.

complement   A word or expression used to complete the idea indicated or implied by a verb. A *predicate* complement (sometimes called *subjective* complement) may be a noun, a pronoun, or an adjective that follows a linking verb and describes or identifies the subject of that verb. An object (objective) complement may be a noun or adjective that follows the direct object of a verb and completes the meaning.

Mr. Black is a *lawyer.*
Jane is *mournful.*
The club members are *youthful.*
They called the dog *Willie.*
We dyed the grass *green.*

complex sentence   A sentence containing one independent clause and one or more dependent clauses.

compound sentence   A sentence containing two or more clauses that could stand alone.

compound-complex sentence   A sentence containing two or more independent clauses and one or more dependent clauses:

You may send candy, or you may send flowers, but you must certainly send something to Mother because she expects a gift.

conjugation   The changes in the form of a verb to show tense, mood, voice, number, and person.

conjunctive adverb   An adverb that can also be used as a conjunction coordinating two independent clauses: *also, furthermore, nevertheless, besides, however, therefore, thus, so, consequently, hence, likewise, still, then, moreover.* For example:

"The library is open on Saturday; *therefore* you can take the books back then."

context   The parts of a piece of writing or of speech that precede or follow a given word or passage with which they are directly connected. If we say that such and such a passage in a novel is obscene but that in its *context* it is significant and not shocking, we mean that what comes before or follows provides meaning which is important, even essential, to understanding and judgment.

declension   The inflectional changes in the form or use of a noun or pronoun to indicate case, number, and person. "To decline" means to give these grammatical changes.

CASE	SINGULAR	PLURAL
Nominative	*man, I, who*	*men, we, who*
Possessive	*man's; my, mine; whose*	*men's; our, ours; whose*
Objective	*man, me, whom*	*men, us, whom*

determiner   A determiner may be an article (*a, an, the*), a possessive (*my, your, its, their, hers, his*), a demonstrative (*this, that, those*). In general, a determiner is any member of a subclass of adjectival words that limits the noun it modifies and that usually is placed before descriptive adjectives.

direct address   In this construction, also called the *vocative*, the noun or pronoun shows to whom speech is addressed: "*Jimmy*, where are you?" "What did you say, *Mother*?" "After you mow the grass, *Fred*, please take out the garbage."

direct quotation   A quotation that reproduces the exact words written or spoken by someone: "Please use your dictionary more often," the office manager said. "These letters will all need to be retyped."

ellipsis (elliptical clause)   The omission of a word or words that are not needed because they are understood from other words or from context. In the following examples, the words shown in brackets are often omitted in speaking and writing:

Some drove to Miami, others [drove] to Palm Beach.
While [we were] swimming, we agreed to go to a movie later.

expletive   A word or phrase added to fill out a sentence or to provide emphasis. The latter function is performed by exclamatory or profane expressions. The more frequently employed function of the expletive is complementary, however; in this sense, *surely, indeed, why,* and *yes* may be considered expletives. *It* and *there* are commonly used as expletives:

It was Alice sitting there.
It is a truism that men love freedom.
There are 2,400 people present.

Some grammarians further classify *it*. For example, the late Professor Paul Roberts discussed "impersonal *it*," "situation *it*," and "expletive *it*," illustrating each as follows:

Impersonal:	It is raining.
	It is Wednesday.
	It snowed last night.
Situation:	It was Ben who started the trouble.
	It's Lois and the children.
	Was it the cat?
Expletive:	It is hard to believe that Dave is sixteen.
	It is true that we were once great friends.

finite verb   A verb form or verb phrase that serves as a predicate; it has number and person. The nonfinite verb form cannot serve as a predicate. Nonfinite forms are participles, gerunds, and infinitives.

gender   The gender of nouns and pronouns is determined by sex. A noun or pronoun denoting the male sex is called *masculine: man, boy, lord, executor, he.* A noun or pronoun indicating the female sex is called *feminine: woman, girl, lady, executrix, she.* Nouns that denote no sex are referred to as *neuter: house, book, tree, desk, lamp, courage.* Some nouns and pronouns may be either masculine or feminine and are said to have *common* gender: *child, teacher, friend, doctor, visitor, it, they.*

idiom   The usual forms of expression of a language; the characteristic way in which it is put together. In speaking of French idiom, for example, we refer to such a distinct usage as putting the adjective after its noun or the fact that an adjective in French has forms for singular and plural and for masculine and feminine gender. *Idiom* also refers to expressions that are accepted but that differ from usual constructions, such as *a hot cup of tea, how do you do*, and *jump the gun*.

impersonal construction   A method of phrasing in which neither a personal pronoun nor a person as noun is stated as the actor. The passive voice is used, or words like *it* or *there* (see *Expletive*).

I have four reasons for my decision. [Personal]
There are four reasons for this decision. [Impersonal]
We must consider two suggestions. [Personal]
It is necessary to consider two suggestions. [Impersonal]

indirect object   A noun or pronoun that precedes the direct object of a verb and before which the word *to* or *for* is understood. When an indirect object follows the direct object, a preposition (*to, for*) is actually used: "Yesterday I bought *him* a soda." "Yesterday I bought a soda for *him*."

indirect question   Restatement by one person of a direct question asked by another: "When will you pay me?" [Direct] "Joe asked when I would pay him." [Indirect]

indirect quotation   Restatement by one person in his or her own words of the words written or spoken by someone else: Eileen said, "I'll be there on Sunday." [Direct] Eileen said that she will be here on Sunday. [Indirect]

infinitive   A word that functions as both verb and noun and that also may be employed as an adjectival or adverbial modifier. The infinitive is usually introduced by the sign *to: to* speak, *to* sing. Like a gerund, an infinitive can take an object and be modified by an adverb; in its function as a noun, it can be the subject or object of a verb and the object of a preposition.

Will you please *return* by the next plane. [Please *to return;* infinitive as verb and part of predicate]
The person *to see* is the manager. [Infinitive as adjective]
She is waiting *to tell* us of her recent trip. [Infinitive as adverb]

inflection   (1) A change in the form of a word to show a change in use or meaning. *Comparison* is the inflection of adjectives and adverbs; *declension* is the inflection of nouns and pronouns; *conjugation* is the inflection of verbs. (2) A change in the pitch or tone of voice.

intensifier   A word or element used to strengthen, increase, or enforce meaning. *Certainly* and *extremely* are examples of intensifiers.

interjection   The interjection (1) has no grammatical connection with the remainder of the sentence, and (2) expresses emotion—surprise, dismay, disapproval, anger, fear. Grammarians distinguish two kinds of interjections. First are those forms used only as interjections, never occurring otherwise in speech: *oh, ouch, tsk-tsk, whew, alas.* Some of these contain sounds not used otherwise in English and consequently difficult to represent in writing; *tsk-tsk,* for example, is an inadequate representation of the clucking sound made to indicate disapproval. Second are the forms that occur sometimes as interjections and sometimes as other parts of speech: *goodness, well, my.* The two groups are hard to separate, since many words now used only as interjections originate from other parts of speech: *Alas,* for example, has its root in a word meaning "wretched."

intransitive verb   See *transitive verb.*

irregular verb   Sometimes called strong verbs, irregular verbs do not follow a regular pattern in forming their principal parts. Instead, these are usually formed by a change in the vowel: *see, saw, seen; choose, chose, chosen.* Your dictionary is your guide.

juncture   This word has several meanings, all of which involve the act or state of "joining" or "connecting." In linguistics, *juncture* indicates that words as we speak them are not usually separated to the extent that they are in writing. Our words tend to flow together without the pauses that in writing are shown by spaces. For example, if we speak the sentence quoted elsewhere, "The person who can do this well deserves praise," we would need briefly to interrupt our flow of sound after either *this* or *well* in order to be fully understood. Such interruptions vary in length and are frequently combined with variations in *pitch*.

linking verb   This verb is also called a *joining* verb, a *copula*, a *copulative* verb, or a *coupling* verb. It does not express action, but only a state of being. It serves to link the subject with another noun (predicate noun), pronoun (predicate pronoun), or adjective (predicate adjective). These words following the linking verb are called predicate complements or subjective complements. Common linking verbs are the forms of *to be*, *look, seem, smell, sound, appear, feel, become, grow, prove, turn, remain, stand.*

modify   To limit or describe or qualify a meaning in some other specific and closely related way, adjectives are used with nouns and pronouns and adverbs are used with verbs, adjectives, and other adverbs. Limiting: *five* acres, the *only* meal. Descriptive: *blue* skies, *large* houses, speak *rapidly.*

mood   The mood (or mode) of a verb indicates the manner in which a statement is made. Thus, if we wish merely to express a fact or ask a question of fact, we use the *indicative* mood: "The building *is* tall." [Statement] "*Is* the building tall?" [Question] If we wish to express a desire or a condition contrary to fact, we use the *subjunctive* mood: "Oh, how I wish I *were* in Austria!" [Desire] "If I *were* rich, I should give you your wish." [Contrary to fact] If we wish to give a command, we use the *imperative* mood: "*Shut* the gate, please."

The indicative and imperative moods are not troublesome, and the use of the subjunctive has largely disappeared. However, careful speakers and writers employ the subjunctive to express the precise manner in which they make their statements. *Were* and *be* are the only distinct subjunctive forms now in general use, although our speech still retains numerous subjunctive forms in sayings handed down from times when this mood was more widely used: Heaven *forbid*, if need *be*, *suffice* it to say, *come* what may.

As indicated above, use the subjunctive mood, not the indicative, to express a condition contrary to fact. Also use the subjunctive in expressions of *supposition* and to indicate that a condition is *highly improbable* even though not completely contrary to fact: "He worked as if he *were* never going to have another opportunity." "Suppose he *were* to ask you to go with him!"

Use the subjunctive in clauses introduced by *as though* or *as if* to express doubt and uncertainty: "He talks as if he *were* the only clever person in the house."

Use the subjunctive in *that* clauses expressing necessity or a parliamentary motion: "It is essential that he *appear* at the meeting of the group." "I move that the contractors *be authorized* to proceed with the work."

As indicated above, use the subjunctive mood to express a desire (wish, volition). In parallel constructions, do not shift the mood of verbs: "If I *were* in your position and *was* not prevented, I should certainly speak up." [Change *was* to *were*.]

Differences between the indicative and subjunctive may be illustrated thus:

INDICATIVE	SUBJUNCTIVE
I take (am taken)	(if) I take, (be taken)
you take (are taken)	(if) you take (be taken)
he, she, it takes (is taken)	(if) he, she, it take (be taken)
we take (are taken)	(if) we take (be taken)
I took (was taken)	(if) I took (were taken)
I am, we are	(if) I be (we be)
you are, you are	(if) you be, you be
he is, they are	(if) he be, they be
I was, we were	(if) I were, we were

nonfinite verb   A verb form that cannot serve as predicate, since it shows neither person nor grammatical number. Nonfinite verb forms—the verbals—are gerunds, participles, and infinitives.

object   The noun, pronoun, noun phrase, or noun clause following a transitive verb or a preposition.

Your book is on the *floor.* [Object of preposition]
She struck *him* with a newspaper. [Object of verb]
I see *what you think.* [Object of verb]

A *simple* object is a substantive alone; a *complete* object is a simple object together with its modifiers; a *compound* object consists of two or more substantives.

The Popes built the *house.* [Simple]
The Popes built *the large yellow house on the slope.* [Complete]
The Popes built *the house and the barn.* [Compound]

object complement   A word, usually a noun or adjective, used after the direct object of certain verbs and intended to complete the meaning of a sentence: "We have chosen Margie *leader.*" "Let me make this story *simple.*"

participle   A verb form having the function either of a verb used as part of the predicate or of an adjective. The three forms are *present, past,* and *perfect* participle.

The player *swinging* the bat is Henry.
I have *finished* my essay.
Having finished my essay, I turned it in.

passive voice   The form of an action-expressing verb which tells that the subject does not act but is acted upon. Literally and actually, the subject is *passive.*

person   The change in the form of a pronoun or verb—sometimes merely a change in use, as with verbs—to indicate whether the "person" used is the person speaking (*first* person), the person spoken to (*second* person), or the person or thing spoken about (*third* person): *I* read, *you* read, *he* reads, *we* read, *you* read, *they* read, *it* plays.

possessive The case form of nouns and pronouns indicating ownership or some form of idiomatic usage: the *man's* hat, a *week's* vacation, *my* job.

predicate The verb or verb phrase in a sentence that makes a statement—an assertion, an action, a condition, a state of being—about the subject. A *simple* predicate is a verb or verb phrase alone, without an object or modifiers; a *complete* predicate consists of a verb with its object and all its modifiers; a *compound* predicate consists of two or more verbs or verb phrases.

The next player drove the ball 200 yards down the fairway. [*Drove* is the simple predicate; *drove the ball 200 yards down the fairway* is the complete predicate.]
  I *wrote* the article last night and *submitted* it this morning. [Compound predicate]

regular verb Also called weak verbs, these are the most common verbs in English. They usually form their past tense and past participle by adding -*d*, -*ed*, or -*t* to the present infinitive form: *move, moved, moved; walk, walked, walked; mean, meant, meant.*

sentence A *sentence* is a group of words containing a complete, independent thought or a group of closely related thoughts. It may also be defined as a group of words (or even one word) conveying to reader or listener a sense of complete meaning. A sentence must contain a *subject* and a *predicate*, expressed or understood. The subject is the name of the person or thing about which the verb makes a statement. The predicate is what is said of the subject; it must contain a verb which can make a complete, independent statement.
  Sentences may be classified according to grammatical structure as *simple, compound, complex,* or *compound-complex.*
  A *simple sentence* contains only one subject and one predicate and expresses only one thought.

The sun is shining.
The boy and the girl talked and danced.

A *compound sentence* contains two or more independent clauses. The clauses of a compound sentence are grammatically capable of standing alone, but they are closely related parts of one main idea.

The hours are good but the pay is poor.
She read and I wrote letters.

A *complex sentence* contains one independent clause and one or more dependent (subordinate) clauses.

The woman said that she had walked for over an hour.
He is an athlete whose muscles are unusually supple.

A *compound-complex sentence* contains two or more independent clauses and one or more dependent clauses.

Since the day was unpleasant, we stayed indoors; Ned studied, and I worked on my stamp collection.

strong verb   See *irregular verb.*

subject   The person or thing (noun, pronoun, noun phrase, noun clause) about which a statement or assertion is made in a sentence or clause. A *simple* subject is the noun or pronoun alone; a *complete* subject is a simple subject together with its modifiers; a *compound* subject consists of two or more nouns, pronouns, noun phrases, noun clauses.

substantive   An inclusive term for noun, pronoun, verbal noun (gerund, infinitive), or a phrase or a clause used like a noun. The following are examples of substantives:

My *hat* is three years old. [Noun]
They will leave tomorrow; in fact, *everyone* is leaving tomorrow. [Pronouns]
Your *playing* is admired. [Gerund]
To better myself is my *purpose*. [Infinitive, noun]
From Chicago to Los Angeles is a long distance. [Noun phrase]

What you think is *no problem of mine.* [Noun clause, noun
   phrase]
Do *you* know *that he is a thief?* [Pronoun, noun clause]

syllable   In phonetics, a segment of speech uttered with one
impulse of air pressure from the lungs; in writing, a character
or set of characters (letters of the alphabet) representing one
sound. That is, a syllable is the smallest amount or unit of
speech or writing.

syntax   The arrangement of words in a sentence to show their
relationship. It is a rather vague and general term, but one for
which our language has no adequate substitute. Syntax is a
branch of grammar.

transitive verb   Verbs are classified as either transitive or intransitive. A *transitive* verb is regularly accompanied by a direct
object that completes the meaning of the verb: "They *refused*
his resignation." An *intransitive* verb requires no direct object:
"He *will obey.*" Whether a verb is transitive or intransitive
depends upon meaning, upon the idea the writer wishes to
show: *will obey* in "He *will obey* our orders" is transitive.

verb phrase   A verb together with an auxiliary or auxiliaries, or
with its object or its modifiers: *is going, was finished, shall have
taken, will have been taken, studied the assignments, flows
slowly, whispers nonsense to himself.* Distinguish between a
verb phrase and a *verbal* (participle, infinitive, gerund).

vowel   In phonetics, a speech sound articulated so that there is a
clear channel for the voice through the middle of the mouth. In
spelling and grammar, a letter representing such a sound: *a, e,
i, o, u,* and sometimes *y.*

weak verb   See *regular verb.*

word order   An English sentence consists not of a string of
words in free relationship to one another, but of groups of
words arranged in patterns. Words in an English sentence have
meaning because of their position. That is, they have one mean-

ing in one position, another meaning in another position, and no meaning in still another position.

EXERCISES IN GRAMMAR

Parts of Speech, Grammatical Functions (I)

Use a capital letter to indicate that the word, phrase, or clause italicized in each sentence below has the grammatical function of A—a noun (*naming* word); B—a finite verb (*asserting* word); C—an adjective (*modifying* word); D—an adverb (*modifying* word); E—a preposition or a conjunction.

1. I *am* ready to help you at any time.
2. He was charged with driving too *fast* for road conditions.
3. I had still another *reason* for calling you.
4. It is of primary importance in swimming to *learn* to breathe properly.
5. You read faster *than* I do.
6. I don't want the people *sitting* over there to hear this.
7. You can *at least* try.
8. Who is *in charge* around here?
9. The best seat will go to *whoever comes first*.
10. *Insofar as* information is available, we will keep you posted.

Parts of Speech, Grammatical Functions (II)

Follow the directions given above.

1. Someone *has to have been monkeying* with this set, the way it works now.
2. *Doing* what other people expect you to do is his idea of morality.
3. *To whatever extent* I can help you, you can count on me.
4. The aphorism that truth lies *at the bottom of the cup* is often misleading.
5. *Whomever you want to invite* will be all right with me.

6. Courage *at two o'clock in the morning*, according to Napoleon, is the kind that counts.
7. To get up and *try* again, no matter how often you fail, is the mark of a hero.
8. I will repeat my last remark for the benefit of those *who came in late*.
9. These supplies, *however you came by them*, are going to prove useful.
10. We usually admire the people who like us; we do not always admire those *we like*.

Recognition of Verbals

Each of the following sentences contains two verbals. Pick out each verbal and classify it by an identifying letter: *G*—gerund; *P*—participle; *I*—infinitive.

1. Dressed in his football uniform, Martin seemed to be unusually muscular.
2. Thinking that her mother was not at home, the little girl went to the cupboard to get a handful of her favorite cookies.
3. Am I to understand that cleaning out an attic is a simple procedure?
4. Running full before the wind in a stiff breeze, the sailor was determined not to jibe.
5. Training a puppy to go out at regular intervals takes patience and vigilance.
6. Jay earned money to put himself through college by composing rock tunes.
7. His throat parched, John tried to unstick his tongue from the roof of his mouth.
8. Having calculated the risk, the gambler decided to put all his chips on one throw of the dice.
9. To appear as tall as the soprano, the tenor had to wear elevator shoes.
10. Refreshed after a night's sleep, the astronauts found the going easier.

Recognition and Classification of Phrases

Underline the phrases in the following sentences. Indicate the form of each phrase: *Prep*—prepositional; *Ger*—gerund; *Inf*—infinitive. Then indicate the function of each phrase: *N*—noun; *Adj*—adjective; *Adv*—adverb. Each sentence contains two such phrases.

1. At last a gentle rain fell upon the dry fields.
2. Students usually have to study at night.
3. Martin played most of the game with a broken finger.
4. The son of the circus strong man wanted to feed the elephants.
5. Putting both hands into the box, Jane pulled out all the candy she could grasp.
6. Rowing a boat is a good way to develop shoulder muscles.
7. Billy stepped importantly from the plane into a waiting car.
8. To breed a champion hog is the dream of many 4-H Club members.
9. Having packed his bags, Errol phoned for a bellboy.
10. The thing I like most about clothes is buying them.

Recognition and Classification of Dependent Clauses

Underline the dependent clauses in the following sentences. Classify each such clause: *N*—noun clause; *Adj*—adjective clause; *Adv*—adverb clause. Each sentence contains two dependent clauses.

1. When Jim telephoned, I was in the basement with the men who were cleaning up the mess.
2. What we wanted most was to find the cherry tree we had seen the day before.
3. Although the seal dived into the pool after her, Gladys, who was a strong swimmer, still had hope of getting the fish.
4. If you have finished your tirade, Dick, I suggest that we join the party.

5. I can't see why anyone would want it, since it isn't really oblong.
6. After the party was over, Stanley looked around for the girl who had come with him.
7. When he threw me out of the house, I realized that he just didn't want to buy a television set.
8. It was clear that Ken was a little uncouth, but we needed a man who could manage the turnstiles.
9. It doesn't matter why he got in; we have to decide how we're going to get him out.
10. Until we know otherwise, we must assume that Sellers is not on our side.

Kinds of Sentences

Indicate the kind of sentence formed by each of the following groups of words, using these symbols: S—single; Cp—compound; Cx—complex; CC—compound-complex.

1. After we had been driving for miles on the rolling, twisting road, a wave of nausea suddenly swept over me.
2. My brother hurries through dinner, changes into old clothes, and works in the lab for two hours.
3. Since Jack could scarcely distinguish a yellow-bellied sapsucker from a double-breasted blue serge, he was asked to resign from the Birdwatchers' Club.
4. Smiling nonchalantly, the little man tossed the bundle over his left shoulder.
5. No one could understand how the chickens escaped, but Polly knew.
6. Some readers do not know how to use the card catalog, and they waste time looking for books in the library.
7. The symbol of Martin's club is a corn cob pipe.
8. When the group reached the ski hut, some people built a fire, and others prepared dinner.
9. The forecast was for fair and warmer weather, but the day dawned dark and cool.

10. We don't know, but we suspect that the dean's wife has rebellious thoughts.

EXERCISES IN USAGE

Agreement and Case

In this exercise apply the standards of edited English rather than those of informal speech. Consider word contractions acceptable if they are in standard form. Write a capital letter to indicate that the sentence shows an error connected with: *A*—agreement of the subject and predicate; *B*—agreement of pronoun and antecedent; *C*—case indicating subject or object; *D*—case (genitive) indicating possession or attribution; *E*—none of these: The sentence is acceptable as it stands.

1. He is the only one of the people on this block who do not take the morning paper.
2. Aunt Tilda was really eloquent on the subject of Bert coming in late for dinner.
3. Either the operators or the foreman are to blame for the accident.
4. The spring series of lectures on Elizabethan dramatists was well attended.
5. We suspected the perpetrator of this joke to be either his sister or he.
6. You should keep the drainpipe's slant to about one-quarter inch to the foot.
7. Eight slices of pie divided by four make two apiece.
8. Everybody working on Sunday or a holiday will have their pay doubled.
9. I asked Sally if that was her brother or she who came in.
10. He said that whomever he stayed with would have to get used to him getting up early.
11. Father told Hy and me that we would be well rewarded for the weeks work.
12. The worst of my worries and difficulties was that nobody would believe me.

13. I finally collared the dog, after a week's watching, who had been digging up the garden.
14. It became clear to Mack and I that none of the fish in that pond was going to take a hook.
15. Either chemistry or physics is required in the third year.
16. Give these old skates to whomever you think can use them.
17. What I have written down here are the things you are to bring back from town.
18. Neither Parsons nor I am eligible for the scholarship.
19. Either you or Dolly swims better than her.
20. He is one of those people who have to be told everything twice.

Verbs, Adjectives, Adverbs, Conjunctions

In this exercise, following current standard usage, *shall* and *will* or *should* and *would* are regarded as interchangeable forms in the first person; you will not be asked to distinguish them. In the second and third persons, *shall* still implies determination and *should*, obligation. Use a capital letter to indicate that the sentence contains an error involving: A—the form of a verb (confusion of principal parts, wrong mood, or use of a substandard form); B—tense or sequence of tenses; C—use of adjective for adverb or vice versa, or the wrong form of either; D—misuse of conjunctions (preposition or coordinating conjunction used for subordination, and so on); E—none of these: The sentence is acceptable as it stands.

1. He looked as if he were about to explode, but with an apparent superhuman effort he controlled himself.
2. If I knew then what I know now, we would never have drifted apart.
3. I have never learned to play a piece of music, like you can, at first sight.
4. He has lived for several years in the Arctic before he settled down here, and has many fascinating stories to tell about his life there.

5. If I had had her experiences, I would write a book—maybe several books.

6. Before the party started, I made the irritating discovery that someone had got into the refrigerator and drank most of the cokes.

7. He's a very retiring neighbor and never comes over without I ask him to call on us.

8. We would have liked to have had Jed on our team, but he's too prejudice to join us.

9. If we keep very quiet and talk soft enough, we may get close enough to take a picture.

10. Only in recent years was it discovered that the more distant galaxies seemed to be receding from us at enormous speeds.

11. If I would have known you were coming to town, I'd have got tickets for a play.

12. I had never swum in the ocean before, and I was surprised at how bitterly it tasted.

13. I can remember having the same experience; however, you'll get use to it.

14. I'm sorry the Petersons have already left; I should have liked to have seen them.

15. It's surprising how swiftly the time has passed, and I can hardly realize that at the end of the month I'll be here a whole year.

16. In the part of the country where I was born, every boy wanted to have a rifle, a pony, moreover a couple of good dogs.

17. If the fishing here turns out to be as good as I have heard of its being last year, I shall not have wasted my time in coming so far.

18. She was the wittiest and intelligentest speaker whom up to that time I had ever listened to.

19. After a long discussion that grew fairly warm at times, it was voted that the club president was directed to invite two speakers, on opposite sides of the question.

20. I wouldn't have tried to ride your bicycle, had I known the chain was broke.

Exact Connectives

In each sentence below, a blank indicates the omission of a connective word or phrase. Write a capital letter to indicate the expression that fits the context and most precisely shows the relation between the two parts of the sentence. Do not overlook correct punctuation.

1. Several teams on the Coast appear to be almost exactly balanced this year; _____ I wouldn't be surprised if the season ended in a three-way tie for the title. [A—of course; B—moreover; C—in fact; D—for example; E—anyway]
2. A translation of a Latin passage into English is usually much longer than the original, _____ English uses separate words to express relations that in Latin are shown by inflections. [A—primarily because; B—chiefly for the reason that; C—although; D—consequently; E—in any case]
3. The difference is that the writer of ordinary fiction is permitted to introduce genuine surprises now and then just as life does, _____ the writer of detective stories is required to play strictly fair with the reader and present only solutions that have been clued beforehand. [A—but; B—however; C—in contrast; D—whereas; E—on the contrary]
4. It is a good rule of style to choose short, homely words instead of showy ones; _____ one should avoid an obviously affected, Hemingwayesque simplicity. [A—in any case; B—at the same time; C—whenever possible; D—in contrast; E—notwithstanding]
5. Nobody knows how the public will react to the proposal of a guaranteed annual income; _____ I'm not sure how I feel about it myself. [A—however that may be; B—in any event; C—consequently; D—for that matter; E—at the same time]

Review

Each sentence below, continued through five lettered segments, contains an error in grammar. (You are to apply the standard of *edited* English rather than that of informal speech, but contractions are acceptable if they are in standard form.) Use a capital letter to indicate the segment with the error.

1. (A) Had I known that you were taking (B) the same route to school as we, (C) I'd have suggested you riding (D) in the same car with (E) John and me.

2. (A) He lay looking like something (B) the cat had dragged in, (C) having swum too far and (D) drank enough salt water (E) to make anybody feel bad.

3. (A) The latest of his exploits is (B) to have caught four touchdown passes (C) in one game, though he has been (D) looking so good lately that I (E) was not much surprise to hear of it.

4. (A) He was an effective storyteller (B) who we knew had traveled a great deal, (C) and his account of adventures (D) among savage tribesmen were (E) thrilling to both Joey and me.

5. (A) He failed in algebra because he is (B) one of those people who begin to study (C) too late, but if he had started earlier (D) and worked harder, (E) he may have passed the course with ease.

6. (A) Once in possession of the house, I (B) planned to make great changes, and (C) would have completed them (D) if I didn't run out of money (E) before I had well begun.

7. (A) We were held spellbound by the glass blower, (B) marveling at how he could work so fast and careful (C) in turning out little colored animals; (D) there is not many an artist who combines (E) so much speed and expertness.

8. (A) They're now freshmen in college, and (B) their chief worry is whether four years (C) from now they're going to be as many jobs (D) available to graduates as there are at present, (E) but I think there're going to be plenty of jobs.

9. (A) The intellectual level of foreign movies, (B) according to many critics, (C) are usually superior to (D) that of those produced in America, (E) especially in the category of satire.

10. (A) The members of the early class (B) and we in ours

learned too late that (C) if we had listened to the assignments (D) and wrote up all the reports listed in them (E) we might not have landed in the mess we're in now.

ANSWERS TO EXERCISES IN GRAMMAR

Parts of Speech, Grammatical Functions (I)

1. *B*	3. *A*	5. *E*	7. *D*	9. *A*
2. *D*	4. *A*	6. *C*	8. *C*	10. *E*

Parts of Speech, Grammatical Functions (II)

1. *B*	3. *E*	5. *A*	7. *A*	9. *D*
2. *A*	4. *D*	6. *C*	8. *C*	10. *C*

Recognition of Verbals

1. Dressed—*P*; to be—*I*
2. Thinking—*P*; to get—*I*
3. to understand—*I*; cleaning out—*G*
4. Running—*P*; to jibe—*I*
5. Training—*G*; to go out—*I*
6. to put—*I*; composing—*G*
7. parched—*P*; to unstick—*I*
8. Having calculated—*P*; to put—*I*
9. To appear—*I*; to wear—*I*
10. refreshed—*P*; going—*G*

Recognition and Classification of Phrases

1. At last—*Prep, Adv;* upon the dry fields—*Prep, Adv*
2. to study—*Inf, N;* at night—*Prep, Adv*
3. of the game—*Prep, Adj;* with a broken finger—*Prep, Adv*
4. of the circus strong man—*Prep, Adj;* to feed the elephants—*Inf, N*
5. putting both hands—*Par, Adj;* into the box—*Prep, Adv*
6. Rowing a boat—*Ger, N;* to develop—*Inf, Adj*

7. from the plane—*Prep, Adv;* into a waiting car—*Prep, Adv*
8. To breed—*Inf, N;* of many 4-H Club members—*Prep, Adj*
9. Having packed his bags—*Par, Adj;* for a bellboy— *Prep, N*
10. about clothes—*Prep, Adj;* buying them—*Ger, N*

Recognition and Classification of Dependent Clauses

1. When Jim telephoned, *Adv;* who were cleaning up the mess, *Adj*
2. What we wanted most, *N;* we had seen the day before, *Adj*
3. Although the seal dived into the pool after her, *Adv;* who was a strong swimmer, *Adj*
4. If you have finished your tirade, *Adv;* that we join the party, *N*
5. Why anyone would want it, *N;* since it isn't really oblong, *Adv*
6. After the party was over, *Adv;* who had come with him, *Adj*
7. When he threw me out of the house, *Adv;* that he just didn't want to buy a television set, *N*
8. That Ken was a little uncouth, *N;* who could manage the turnstiles, *Adj*
9. Why he got in, *N;* how we're going to get him out, *N*
10. Until we know otherwise, *Adv;* that Sellers is not on our side, *N*

Kinds of Sentences

1. *Cx*	3. *Cx*	5. *CC*	7. *S*	9. *Cp*
2. *S*	4. *S*	6. *Cp*	8. *CC*	10. *CC*

ANSWERS TO EXERCISES IN USAGE

Agreement and Case

1. A	5. C	9. E	13. B	17. E
2. D	6. D	10. D	14. C	18. E
3. A	7. A	11. D	15. E	19. C
4. E	8. B	12. E	16. C	20. E

Verbs, Adjectives, Adverbs, Conjunctions

1. C	5. E	9. C	13. A	17. E
2. B	6. A	10. B	14. B	18. C
3. D	7. D	11. A	15. B	19. A
4. B	8. A	12. C	16. D	20. A

Exact Connectives

1. C	2. A	3. D	4. B	5. D

Review

1. C	3. E	5. E	7. B	9. C
2. D	4. D	6. D	8. C	10. D

6

GUIDE TO CORRECT
WORD USAGE

Skillful writers leave little to chance. Just as their tones and sentence structures are chosen to be effective for their subjects and appropriate for their audiences, so do they select suitable words to achieve their purposes.

Think how the wording of a single sentence might vary depending on whether it was addressed to close friends, your parents, teachers, a prospective employer, a church or town official, a judge, and so on. Think how it might vary with the age of the listener—a younger brother or sister, perhaps, as opposed to an aged aunt or uncle. The use of words is not a matter of choosing absolutely "good" words and avoiding absolutely "bad" ones but of selecting those that will help achieve the effect you want.

Diction refers to the choice of a word or words for the expression of ideas. Defined in this way, diction applies to *both* writing and speaking, although the sections here deal with writing. The following sections will help make your writing more effective.

Because there are many words to choose from, because many ideas require expression in different shades of meaning and emphasis, and because outright errors in usage should be avoided, diction is troublesome for all writers and speakers. Just as a reputable builder carefully selects materials for the construction of a house, so must writers use care in choosing the words they use. Effective communication, the primary aim of writing and speaking, is impossible without effective choice and use of words.

Diction, like sentences, should be *correct*, *clear*, and *effective*, but no standards can be absolute. Our language is constantly changing. Also, diction, like fashions in dress and food, is influenced by changes in taste. Again, what is acceptable in daily speech and conversation may not be suitable in formal writing. The use of this or that word cannot be justified by saying that it is often heard or seen in print. Advertisements, newspapers, magazines, and even some "good" books exhibit faulty diction, or at least diction that is not acceptable in formal writing.

As you study the following sections, keep your dictionary constantly at hand. You may disagree with some of the statements made, but it is sensible to be guided—at least at first—by the work of authors whose skill in communicating commands respect.

SUMMARY OF COMMON PROBLEMS IN DICTION

In choosing and using words, remember that

1. words should be in *current and national use*
2. words should be in *reputable use*
3. words should be *exact* and *emphatic*

Keep in mind two primary recommendations about diction:

1. *Be specific.* Much of what we write and speak is indefinite, not clearly expressed, of uncertain meaning. Even when we have a fairly good idea of what we wish to say, we don't search hard enough for those exact, specific, and concrete words that would get across what we have in mind. *Be definite. Don't be vague.*
2. *Be concise.* Most statements of any kind are wordy. All of us, in both speech and writing, tend to repeat ideas in identical or similar words—and then write or say the same things once again. Neither speech nor writing should be abrupt or cryptic, but both should be economical. *Make it snappy!*

Current and National Use

In writing, it helps to remember that words mean what your readers think they mean, not necessarily what you think they do. The first method of insuring clear communication is to use words that are in *current* and *national* use.

Current Use

Words should be understandable to readers and listeners of the present time. Words do go out of style and out of use. (You must have struggled with the meanings of words and expressions used by Shakespeare and other earlier writers.) Except for somewhat doubtful purposes of humor, avoid using antiquated expressions.

1. Obsolete Words An *obsolete* word is one that has passed completely out of use. An *obsolescent* word is one that is in the process of becoming obsolete. One dictionary, however, may label a given word "obsolete"; another may label the same word "obsolescent"; still another, "archaic." Your dictionary may include *infortune* for *misfortune*, *yestreen* for *last evening*, *garb* for *personal bearing*, *prevent* for *precede*, *eftsoon* for *soon afterward*, *twifallow* for *plow again*, *anon* for *coming*.

2. Archaic Words An *archaic* word is an old-fashioned word, one that has passed from everyday use but may still appear in Biblical expressions, proverbs, and legal language. Effective, up-to-date general writing will not include terms such as *enow* for *enough*, *methinks* for *it seems to me*, *lief* for *willing*, *wot* for *know*, *glister* for *glisten*, *whilom* for *formerly*, *pease* for *pea*, *oft* or *ofttimes* for *often*, *marry* as an expression of surprise or astonishment, *bedight* for *array*, *cote* for *pass by*, *presents* for *this document*, and *beget* for *procreate*.

3. Poetic Words Words that have been (and are still occasionally) used in poetry rather than prose are known somewhat loosely as *poetic diction*. Poetic words, sometimes so labeled in dictionaries, are usually archaic words found in poetry composed in (or intended to create the aura of) a remote past. Examples are the use of the endings *-st, est, -th,* and *-eth* on present tense verbs: *doest, couldst, wouldst, leadeth, doth.* Other examples are contractions such as *'tis* and *'twas.* Usually considered "poetic" are words like *glebe, ope, orb, 'neath, eye of night, acold, thee, thine, thou, ye,* and *fain.*

4. Neologisms A *neologism* is a newly coined word or phrase or an established term employed in a new sense. Not all neologisms are contrived and artificial, but many are and consequently have short lives. Columnists, broadcasters, sports commentators, and advertising copywriters repeatedly concoct neologisms. Some of their coinages are colorful, attention-getting, and picturesque, and presumably will prove permanently valuable. If they do not fill a real need, they will quietly disappear from the language.

Words are coined in various ways:

1. As needed words in the fields of science, technology, and business, to describe new inventions, discoveries, applications, and occupations: *astronautics, astrogate, automation, H-bomb, cyclotron, computerize, realtor, beautician.*

2. By adaptation of common words—often by analogy, for example, by adding *-ize* to nouns to form verbs or adding a suffix like *-wise* to form adverbs: *vacationize, signaturize, bookwise, city-wise, taxwise.* Most "-ize" and "-wise" coinages are rarely suitable in formal writing.

3. Through the combination of two or more common words. Those are the so-called portmanteau words: *brunch* (*break*fast and *lunch*); *cheeseburger* (*cheese* and ham*burger*); *chortle* (*ch*uckle and sn*ort*); *motel* (*mo*tor and ho*tel*); *smog* (*sm*oke and f*og*); *transistor* (*trans*fer and *resistor*); *cinemaddict* (*cinema* and *addict*); *stagflation* (*stagnation* and *inflation*).

4. By using the initial letters or syllables of common

words: *loran* (*long range navigation*); *radar* (*radio detecting* and *ranging*). Such a word is an *acronym*.
5. As virtually or completely new information: *gobbledygook; blurb; jeep; bazooka.*
6. As registered trade names or trademarks and their derivatives: *Kodak, kleenex, Dacron, simonize, technicolor, Caterpillar* (tractor).

Depending on the dictionary you own, newly coined words that appear may have no label or be labeled "informal" or "colloquial" or "slang," with perhaps a brief history of their origin or originator. If you use neologisms, be sure they are appropriate to both content and reader, that is, easily understood by the people you are addressing.

These lines from the English poet Alexander Pope are sound advice:

> *In words, as fashions, the same rule will hold,*
> *Alike fantastic if too new or old:*
> *Be not the first by whom the new are tried,*
> *Nor yet the last to lay the old aside.*

National Use

Television, radio, the telephone, films, and easy transportation have helped to make American English *national.* That is, writers or speakers can assume they will be understood by American readers or listeners if they use words and phrases common to all parts of the country. Words should be in *national use.*

Applying this principle suggests that the writer should be aware of other limitations of diction besides geographic regions. The comments that follow deal with the subdivisions in vocabulary that can prevent or hinder a reader's understanding.

1. Americanisms and Briticisms Broadly defined, an English *nationalism* is a word or phrase common in or limited to the English used by a particular one of the English-speaking nations.

Americanism and *Briticism* refer to words or word meanings that are common, respectively, in the United States and the British Isles. Dictionaries label many such expressions "U.S.," "Chiefly U.S.," "British," "Scottish," or the like, not to guide us in our writing—except when we write to someone in a non-American country—but to help us understand them when we come across them in the writings of anyone writing in English anywhere in the world. For example, here are different terms associated with cars and motoring in the United States and Great Britain:

American Usage	*British Usage*
battery	accumulator
gasoline	petrol
paved road	metalled road
hood (of a car)	bonnet
trunk (of a car)	boot
fender	wing

2. Localisms A *localism* is a word or phrase used and understood primarily in a particular section or region. Along with certain grammatical constructions and characteristic pronunciations, localisms identify a speaker's *regional dialect*.

Various areas of the United States have localisms that add flavor to speech but may not be immediately intelligible in other areas. For residents of one of these areas, such expressions seem quite clear since they themselves have known and used them from childhood. Dictionaries label or define many words according to the geographic area where they are common. Here are some examples:

Northern (most of New England, parts of northern New Jersey and northern Pennsylvania):
  pail: "bucket" (Midland and Southern)
  swill: "slop" (Midland and Southern)
  brook: "small stream"
  down-easter: "native of New England, especially Maine"

choose: "wish"
selectman: "town official"

Midland (the rest of New Jersey and Pennsylvania; northern Delaware, Maryland, and Virginia west of the Appalachians; West Virginia, Kentucky, Tennessee, and westward):
blinds: "window shades"
skillet: "frying pan"
green beans: "string beans"

Southern (part of Virginia; North Carolina, South Carolina, and Georgia west to the mountains):
chitlins: "chitterlings"
harp, mouth harp: "harmonica"
snap beans: "string beans"
butternuts: "brown overalls"
corn pone: "corn bread"
chuck: "throw"
tote: "carry"
poke: "sack"

Southwestern:
mesa: "flat-topped rocky hill"
mustang: "half-wild horse"
mesquite: "spiny tree or shrub"
maverick: "unbranded animal"
longhorn: "breed of cattle"

Western:
grubstake: "supplies or funds"
coulee: "narrow valley"
rustler: "cattle thief"
potluck: "food available without special preparation"
dogie, dogy: "motherless calf"

Should localisms be used? If a particular localism is in general use on all levels in your home region, then it is widely enough understood to be acceptable, although it will mark your writing as stemming from that region. If you have any doubt about whether the word or phrase will be understood, choose a substitute that is in more general use.

3. Shoptalk The specialized or technical vocabulary and idioms of people in the same work or the same way of life are known as *shoptalk*, the language people use in discussing their particular field of activity. *To talk shop* is the verb form of this expression.

For your writing to be in national use, avoid introducing words and expressions peculiar to, or understood only by, members of a particular trade, profession, science, industry, or art. Legal shoptalk, medical jargon, and sports talk, for example, have special meanings for those in these fields and occupations. So do more than forty other classifications of words that have special labels in your dictionary: astronomy, entomology, psychology—all the way from aeronautics to zoology.

In the last generation alone, many new words and meanings have come from fields like chemistry, electronics, nuclear physics, automation, and other sciences, arts, and recreations.

When technical words are widely used or have extended meanings, their subject labels may be dropped. Some examples (made popular by special fields) are *broadcast* (from radio), *telescope* (from astronomy), *weld* (from engineering), *diagnose* (from medicine), *daub* (from painting), and *mold* (from sculpture).

A specialist writing for or speaking to other specialists uses numerous technical terms. In that circumstance, shoptalk is appropriate. But it is another matter for nonspecialists. Few of us could understand a technical article in *Electronics* magazine. More of us could understand its treatment in *Scientific American*. All of us might understand it if it were adapted for a general-circulation magazine.

Use common sense in dealing with shoptalk. Consider the "average" educated reader and find terms that require no special or technical knowledge unless they are indispensable to what you want to say and unless you carefully define them when you use them.

4. Foreign Words and Phrases For most Americans, a foreign word or phrase is one that comes from a non-English language. Tens of thousands of foreign words have come into our language from Greek, Latin, and French, and thousands more have come from other languages. Depending on your dictionary, you will find from 40 to 150 foreign-language abbreviations used for word origins and meanings.

Two things happen to these foreign words and phrases: (1) If they have been widely used or used over a long period, or both, they are Anglicized and become part of our everyday language, to be recorded in dictionaries like any common word. (2) If the conditions of (1) have not been met, the word or phrase remains foreign; as such, it is indicated in dictionaries as foreign, partly as a guide for writers to use italics if they use the word or phrase. Anglicized examples include *a priori*, *à la mode*, *blitz*, *chef*, *habitué*, and *smorgasbord*. Non-Anglicized examples include *Anno Domini*, *fait accompli*, *cause célèbre*, *ex libris*, *mañana*, and *Weltschmerz*.

If the word or phrase has been Anglicized or if no good English equivalent exists, use it. But why *merci beaucoup* for "thank you" or *Auf Wiedersehen* for "good-bye"? Even *a* or *an* serves better than *per*: $5 *an* hour.

Reputable Use

The choice and use of words in today's writing is more relaxed, freer from rules, and closer to the way we actually speak than ever before. This freedom of choice, however, does not mean that "anything goes" and that no standards of diction exist. In all careful writing, one should try to use words and expressions that are standard and reputable, considered to be in good and acceptable usage.

Many reputable words and expressions, however, are neither exact nor effective. This section contains suggestions for using words that (1) call things by their names; (2) are as concrete and specific as meaning allows; and (3) are direct, economical, and idiomatically sound.

1. Exact Diction Any of several words may be available to convey a general meaning, but often a particular word or phrase will express your meaning more precisely than any other. It is your task and opportunity to find this word or phrase. In this search, a thesaurus is an excellent reference book. Frequently, too, your choice is from several words with nearly identical meanings, and a study of the synonyms for an expression listed in a dictionary or thesaurus will help you choose a more precise term. For example, before allowing a word like *happy* to stand in one of your papers, find out whether one of the following adjectives will communicate your meaning more precisely: *blithe, cheerful, gay, sportive, jocular, jolly, jovial, joyful, joyous, merry.*

For another example, consider the overworked word *pretty.* We speak and write of a pretty day, a pretty flower, and so on. The word *pretty* is entirely reputable and carries a general meaning that cannot be called misleading or incorrect. Perhaps it would be more exact and accurate to write that a certain person is *attractive* or *charming* or *personable* or *winsome* or *exquisite* or *fair* or *comely* or *sensuous* or *engaging.* These words are not synonyms for *pretty,* but one of them may more exactly convey the impression you want to give.

But do not let the use of synonyms lead you into error: two words may be synonymous in one meaning but not in another. *Steal* and *pilfer* share a meaning—"to take without permission"— but *steal* can also mean "to move so slowly as to be unnoticeable." We can write "The shadows were *stealing* across the yard," but not "The shadows were *pilfering* across the yard."

Exactness and precision in diction require clear and careful thinking. Effective diction is achieved when the reader understands as nearly as possible what the writer intended to communicate.

2. Specific Diction A *general* word names a broad concept: class names of nouns (*animal, clothing, devices, land, street*); conventional verbs with many meanings (*go, move, say*); and broad adjectives and adverbs (*good, bad, gladly, fast*). Especially colorless diction results from overuse of the forms of *to be* (*am, is, are, was, were*).

A *specific* word names a more limited concept (*collie, leotard, flashlight, pasture, boulevard*). As a verb, a specific word will have a more particular meaning and a more limited use (*totter, amble, saunter, drawl, shout*). A specific word is a vivid, hence a *clear* word; an active, hence a *lively* word; and a fresh, hence an *interesting* word.

Some general words are so vague that they only approximate an idea. With the aid of a thesaurus or dictionary, you can find specific words for any of the following general words and phrases:

aspect	field	manner	quality
case	fine	matter	question
character	great	nature	situation
condition	instance	nice	state
cute	involved	personality	style
degree	item	persuasion	thing
element	job	phase	type
factor	lot	point	vital
feature	lovely	problem	way

General: a *fine* day
a *great* game
the *first* thing

Specific: a *memorable* day
a *record-setting* game
the first *argument* (*question, principle, problem, etc.*)

3. Concrete Diction An *abstract* word gives no clear picture; it is a mental construct like *beauty, culture, efficiency,* or *wealth.* A *concrete* word expresses something that can be perceived by the senses: *lilacs, crimson, drumbeats, jogging, lemony, jagged.* "He *closed* the door" pictures movement; "He *slammed* the door" gives both picture and sound. *Weep* suggests sight and feeling; *sob* adds hearing and movement.

Specific and concrete nouns, colorful and dynamic adjectives and adverbs, verbs that tell of action or relate to the senses, specific and concrete phrases—all help make writing more direct, forceful, and effective.

Ordinarily, and within the bounds of common sense, choose the concrete, specific word over the general, abstract one. This sentence uses reputable words and is clear in meaning:

If you have committed a crime, escape to the woods with ammunition and clothing. People there will give you food and you need worry about nothing.

Notice the greater effectiveness of these sentences from Merimée's short story, "Mateo Falcone":

If you have killed a man, go into the *maquis* of Porto-Vecchio with a good gun and powder and shot. You will live there quite safely, but don't forget to bring along a brown cloak and hood for your blanket and mattress. The shepherds will give you milk, cheese, and chestnuts, and you need not trouble your head about the law or the dead man's relatives, except when you are compelled to go down into the town to renew your ammunition.

4. Colloquialisms A *colloquialism* is a conversational word or phrase that is permissible in, and often indispensable to, an easy style of speaking and writing. A colloquialism is not substandard or illiterate; it is an expression that is more often used in speech than in writing and more appropriate in informal than in highly formal speech and writing. The origin of the word is the Latin *colloquium*, for "conversation." Our word *colloquy* means "speaking together"; the word *loquacious* means "given to talking, fond of talking."

Colloquialisms are thoroughly reputable and can be used in all writing that is not painstakingly precise, learned, or stilted. If the tone of some paper that you are writing is formal, you should employ only a few colloquialisms and only those that do not alter the mood and intent of your work. But do not avoid colloquialisms entirely, because if you do your writing may sound affected and artificial. A good rule is to use colloquialisms thoughtfully and carefully and not to rely on them as a substitute for more exact and appropriate expressions.

Dictionary words and phrases are marked as colloquial ("Colloq.") when the editors judge them to be more common in speech than in writing or more suitable in informal than in formal discourse. In some dictionaries the label used is "Informal." A large number of words and phrases are so labeled. The term applies to many expressions because informal English has a wide range and because editors differ in the way they interpret their findings. Certain contractions, such as *don't, shouldn't,* and *won't,* are considered "acceptable" colloquialisms; other expressions, however, such as *brass tacks, jinx, enthuse, flop,* and *ad,* should be avoided. No objective rule or test will tell you when to use a colloquialism and when not to. In general, use a colloquialism when your writing would otherwise seem stiff, artificial, and labored.

The following are examples of colloquialisms (as in dictionaries and linguistic studies, no attempt is made to indicate their comparative rank or acceptability): *angel* (financial backer), *brass* (impudence), *freeze* (stand motionless), *phone, gumption, cute, hasn't got any, show up, try and, take a try at, flabbergast, fizzle, flop, root for, make out, fill the bill.*

You might use any or all of these colloquialisms if you are reporting the conversation of a person who would characteristically use them in speech. You might use several in writing in which the tone is light or humorous or breezy. But whenever you use colloquialisms, be certain that they are in keeping with the purpose and tone of your writing.

5. Idiomatic English *English idiom* or *idiomatic English* concerns words used in combinations with others. Of Greek origin, the word *idiom* meant "a private citizen, something belonging to a private citizen, personal," and, by extension, something individual and peculiar. An idiomatic expression may violate grammar or logic or both and still be acceptable because the phrase is familiar, deep-rooted, widely used, and easily understandable—for the native born. "How do you do?" is, for example, an accepted idiom, although an exact answer would be absurd.

A few generalized statements may be made about the many idiomatic expressions in our language. One is that several words, when combined, may lose their literal meaning and express something that is only remotely suggested by any one word: *birds of a feather, blacklist, lay up, toe the line, bed of roses, dark horse, heavy hand, open house, read between the lines, no ax to grind, hard row to hoe.*

A second statement about idioms is that parts of the human body have suggested many of them: *burn one's fingers, all thumbs, fly in the face of, stand on one's own feet, keep body and soul together, keep one's eyes open, step on someone's toes, rub elbows with, get one's back up, keep one's chin up.*

A third generalization is that hundreds of idiomatic phrases contain adverbs or prepositions with other parts of speech. Here are some examples: *walk off, walk over, walk-up; run down, run in, run off, run out; get nowhere, get through, get off.*

agree	*to* a proposal
	on a plan
	with a person
contend	*for* a principle
	with a person
	against an obstacle
differ	*with* a person
	from something else
	about or *over* a question
impatient	*for* something desired
	with someone else
	of restraint
	at someone's conduct
rewarded	*for* something done
	with a gift
	by a person
wait	*at* a place
	for a person
	on a customer

Usage should conform to idiomatic word combinations that are reputable and, therefore, generally acceptable. Remember, however, that many acceptable idioms are also trite. A good dictionary contains explanations of idiomatic usage following key words that need such explanation. It is important to consult your dictionary when using certain words such as *prepositions* with nouns, adjectives, or verbs. The following are examples of idiomatic and unidiomatic expressions containing troublesome prepositions.

Idiomatic	*Unidiomatic*
accord with	accord to
according to	according with
acquaint with	acquaint to
adverse to	adverse against
aim to prove	aim at proving
among themselves	among one another
angry with (a person)	angry at (a person)
as regards	as regards to
authority on	authority about
blame me for it	blame it on me
cannot help talking	cannot help but talk
comply with	comply to
conform to, with	conform in
correspond to (a thing)	correspond with (a thing)
desirous of	desirous to
graduated from (high school)	graduated (high school)
identical with	identical to
in accordance with	in accordance to
in search of	in search for
prefer (one) to (another)	prefer (one) over (another)
prior to	prior than
responsible for (to)	responsible on
superior to	superior than
treat of (a subject)	treat on (a subject)
unequal to	unequal for

It should be pointed out that many educated users of the language do not always follow accepted idiomatic usage. In everyday conversation, such a speaker is as likely to say "blame it on me" as "blame me for it" and "angry at" a person as "angry with." But in careful, formal writing the distinctions just listed should be followed.

Collecting idioms can be fun. For instance, what can you make of these idioms?

make a date; *make* as if; *make* believe; *make* a fool of; *make* heavy weather of; *make* good; *make* off; *make* ready; *make* up; *make* a meal of; *make* a fuss; *make* a mess; *make* trouble; *make* a pass

Or these?

break one's *heart;* have one's *heart* in the right place; wear one's *heart* on one's sleeve; change of *heart;* after one's own *heart; heart* and soul; set one's *heart* on; eat one's *heart* out; take to *heart*; cold hands, warm *heart*; one's head rules one's *heart*; sick at *heart*

6. Figurative Language Many words have an exact meaning (*denotation*) and a suggested or implied meaning (*connotation*).

The exact, literal meaning of a word is referred to as its *denotation*, its dictionary definition. It is thus different from an associated meaning, or *connotation,* that the word might have for an individual (or group) because of personal experience.

Assume that you see a small four-footed animal on the street and refer to it as a *dog.* If your purpose in using the word is to refer to the animal in exact terminology, you have succeeded in applying a denotative term that is plain, straightforward, and objective. But suppose that one grandparent of the dog was a fox terrier, another a bulldog, the third an Irish terrier, and the fourth a collie. You can denotatively express these facts by referring to the animal you see as a *dog of mixed breed.* Here you have continued to use objective phrasing. But if your purpose is to speak exactly and objectively, it would be unwise to call the dog a *mongrel.* True, this term means the same as a *dog of mixed breed,* but it is likely to arouse mingled feelings of approval or disapproval toward that dog.

Nearly all words mean more than they seem to mean. They have associated meanings, a surrounding fringe of suggestive, or connotative, values. For example, a dictionary definition of the word *gold* is "a precious yellow metal, highly malleable and ductile, and free from liability to rust." But with gold have long been associated riches, power, happiness, evil, and unhappiness. Around the core of meaning that the dictionary definition gives are associations, suggestions, and implications. These connotations are not always present, but you should be aware of this suggestive power of words.

A writer's obligation is to convey sensible comments clearly. But good writers search for words that suggest more than they say, that stimulate the reader's associated meanings: *baby sister*, not *girl; enigma*, not *problem; home,* not *house; mother*, not *woman*. By exact, or denotative, definition, a horse is "a large solid-hoofed, herbivorous mammal," but to anyone who has ever owned, loved, and cared for a horse the word suggests many associated meanings. New Orleans is "an industrial trade center," but its name suggests such images as Crescent City, Old French Quarter, Mardi Gras, Sugar Bowl, Superdome, and Dixieland jazz.

A *figure of speech* is one method of using words out of their literal, or ordinary, sense in order to suggest a picture or image. "He is a saint" and "sleeping like a baby" are illustrations of, respectively, the two most common figures of speech: metaphor and simile.

A *metaphor* is a term applied to something to which it is not literally applicable. That is, a metaphor is a figure of speech in which a term is transferred from the object it ordinarily designates to an object that it may designate only by comparison or analogy, as in the phrases "evening of life" (later years, old age) and "A mighty fortress is our God" (strength, power).

A *simile* expresses the resemblance of one thing to another, but it does so by using the words *like, as*, or *as if.* "She is *like* a cool breeze," "heart *as* cold *as* an iceberg." Figurative language, which is often vivid and imaginative, can add color and clarity to writing.

Found occasionally in prose are the following figures of speech, which, like parts of speech, appear in both writing and speaking. In addition to metaphor and simile, these include:

1. *Synecdoche:* A figure of association. Use of a part (or an individual) for the whole class or group, or the reverse.
   Part for Whole: We have fifty *head* of cattle on our farm.
   Whole for Part: Central defeated Stratfield in the homecoming game.

The two schools did not play, but their football teams did.

2. *Metonymy:* A figure of association somewhat like synecdoche. Use of the name of one thing for that of another suggested by it, as in "the bottle" for "strong drink":
   We all agree that the tailor *sews a fine seam.*

3. *Personification:* Giving nonhuman objects the characteristics of a human being.
   The waves *murmured,* and the moon *wept* silver tears.

4. *Hyperbole:* Exaggeration, or a statement exaggerated imaginatively, for effect; not to be taken literally. Some similes and metaphors express hyperbole:
   The young student, *innocent as a newborn babe,* eagerly accepted the bet.
   The sweet music *rose and touched the farthest star.*

Because figurative language is colorful and imaginative, it adds vigor and effectiveness to writing. But do not think of figurative language as a mere ornament of style; do not use it frequently; do not shift abruptly from figurative to literal language; and bear in mind that a direct, simple statement is often preferable to a series of figures and always preferable when the figures are artificial, trite, or overly elaborate. Many worn-out similes are trite phrases: *happy as a lark, cool as a cucumber, busy as a bee, mad as a hornet, quick as a wink, smooth as silk, right as rain, quiet as a mouse, hot as blazes, like a chicken with its head cut off.*

Mixed figures are those in which the images suggested by the words and phrases are unrelated. Similes or metaphors are especially likely to become mixed; they seem to describe an event or process that cannot happen or exist. Here are some examples of mixed and inappropriate figures:

After football season many a football player who was a tidal wave on the football field has to put his nose to the grindstone and study.

Three of us were the kingpins on the roost in our high school.

At any party there is always a rotten apple that throws a monkey wrench in our food and drink.

I hope to get to be a wheel here, but I don't expect to do much trotting around when I get out.

When I graduate, I hope to become a well-oiled cog in the beehive of industry.

Inexact and Ineffective Diction

You are cautioned about flaws that will lessen whatever effectiveness you may have otherwise achieved. Regard the comments that follow not as a series of *don'ts* but as a list of weaknesses in diction that are always—or nearly always—to be avoided.

1. **Illiteracies** *Illiteracies* are nonstandard words and phrases not normally accepted in either informal or standard usage. Also called *barbarisms* and *vulgarisms*, illiteracies are characteristic of uneducated speech; they should be avoided in writing unless put into the mouths of people being characterized as uneducated. Illiteracies are not necessarily coarse, and are frequently colorful, but they should not be used without a specific purpose.

Dictionary editors apply different restrictive labels to "illiterate" or "vulgar" English; what may be marked *illiterate* in one dictionary may be termed *dialect* or *nonstandard* in another. And because most dictionaries record primarily "standard" usage, many illiteracies are not listed at all.

The following words and phrases are examples of illiteracies: *acrossed* and *acrost, ain't, anywheres, as how, being as, being as how, borned, brung, to burgle, concertize, couldn't of, disremember, drownded, drug* (past tense of *drag*), *et* (past tense of *eat*), *fellers, hisself,* I *been* or I *done, irregardless, mistakened, nohow, nowheres, ourn, them's* (for *those are*), *them there, this here, youse.*

2. **Improprieties** One class of improprieties includes words that are acceptable as one part of speech but are nonstandard as another; they may be nouns improperly substituted for verbs, verbs for nouns, adjectives for nouns, adjectives for adverbs, adverbs for adjectives, prepositions for conjunctions. Another class includes misuses of principal parts of verbs.

A word that is identified as more than one part of speech may be so used without question, but do not remove a word from one part of speech and place it in another until standard usage has sanctioned this new function. The following are examples of grammatical improprieties:

Nouns used as verbs:	*grassing* a lawn, *suppering,* to *author, ambitioned, passengered*
Verbs used as nouns:	a *sell, advise*
Adjectives used as adverbs:	dances *good, awful* short
Verb forms:	*come* for *came, don't* for *doesn't, says* for *said, done* for *did, hadn't ought, set* for *sit, of* for *have*
Other combinations:	*them kind; being that, being as* or *being as how* for *because* or *since; except as* for *unless*

For guidance consult your dictionary, which labels every word according to the part (or parts) of speech that it is. Note also the usage label—colloquial, dialect, slang, and so forth—since the same word may be acceptable as one part of speech but not as another.

Another class of improprieties includes words that are similar or vaguely similar to other words and are used inaccurately in their place. Such words include homonyms and homographs.

Homonyms are two words that have the same or almost the same pronunciation but are different in meaning, in origin, and frequently in spelling; for example: *real* and *reel; made* and *maid; hour, our,* and *are; accept, except; stationary, stationery.*

Words that are near-homonyms may also cause confusion: *farther* for *further, father* for *farther, genial* for *general, morass* for *morose, loose* for *lose, imminent* for *eminent.*

A person of such distinction is certainly one to *immolate.* (Should be *emulate.*)

The tennis player *lopped* the ball to the back of the court. (Should be *lobbed.*)

To be an engineer one has to be able to use a *slight* rule. (Should be *slide* rule.)

All of us took too much for *granite*. (Should be *granted*.)

When I slipped and fell I was *humidified*. (Should be *humiliated*.)

Such confusion may result from hearing words inexactly rather than seeing them in print and relating their meaning to their appearance as well as their sound.

Homographs are two or more words that have the same spelling but are different in meaning, origin, and perhaps pronunciation. Examples include *slaver* (a dealer in slaves) and *slaver* (drool or drivel); *arms* (parts of the body) and *arms* (weapons); *bat* (club, cudgel) and *bat* (flying mammal).

3. Exaggeration To *exaggerate* is to misrepresent by overstatement: "I thought I'd die of embarrassment"; "That outfit is older than Noah"; "That is a horrible (or *ghastly* or *frightful*) tie you are wearing"; "I was scared to death."

Occasionally, exaggeration can be used to good effect, but it is *never* exact and not intended to be taken literally. It is more often misleading and ludicrous than appropriate and picturesque. Be cautious when using such words as *gigantic, tremendous, wonderful, phenomenal, staggering, thrilling, terrible, gorgeous, horrible, marvelous,* and *overwhelming.*

4. Affectation *Affectation* is artificial behavior intended to impress others, a mannerism or way of talking, acting, or writing that involves show or pretense. In language, it becomes apparent when a writer uses words that are not customary or appropriate to the person using them. Deliberately trying to be different or learned or impressive often results in misinterpretation, confusion, and annoyance for the reader. Pretense is an even greater sin against effective English than "bad grammar."

For example, compare these two sentences:

Affected Diction:	After liquidating her indebtedness she was still in possession of sufficient resources to establish a small commercial enterprise.
Effective Diction:	After paying her debts, she still had enough money to set up a small business.

For example, a recent magazine contained this paragraph:

The opportunity for options in life distinguishes the rich from the poor. Perhaps through better motivation, the upper levels of the poor could be tempted into the option track. It is important to motivate such people close to the breakthrough level in income because they are closest to getting a foot on the option ladder.

What this writer probably meant was, "The more money you have, the more choices you have." He or she fell into the error of affectation.

5. Euphemisms One form of affectation is the use of *euphemisms.* A euphemism is a softened, bland, inoffensive expression used instead of one that may suggest something unpleasant. In effective writing it's a good idea to call things by their names. In avoiding such nonreputable expressions as *croak, turn up one's toes to the daisies, kick the bucket,* and *take the last count,* you may be tempted to write *pass away* or *depart this life* rather than the short, direct word *die.* Other examples of euphemisms that should usually be avoided are *perspire* for *sweat, prevaricate* for *lie, expectorate* for *spit, mortician* for *undertaker, separate from school* for *expel, intoxicated* for *drunk, abdomen* for *stomach, obsequies* for *funeral,* and *love child* for *illegitimate.*

Here are a few euphemisms recently noted in magazines and newspapers:

preowned car (secondhand car)	problem skin (acne)
senior citizens (old people)	custodial engineer (janitor)
experienced tires (retreads)	motion discomfort (nausea)
mortical surgeon (undertaker)	food preparation center (kitchen)

sanitary engineer (garbage
   collector)

extrapolation (educated guess)

comfort station (public toilet)

creative conflict (political
   demonstration)

6. Jargon and Gobbledygook *Jargon* has two basic meanings: (1) the language of a particular trade, profession, or group, such as legal jargon or medical jargon; (2) unintelligible or meaningless talk. The first of these meanings is discussed under the headings of technical words (shoptalk) and slang. In its second sense, jargon involves the use of vague terms, "big" words, and indirect, round-about ways of expressing ideas.

In an attempt to make writing "fine," the users of jargon will write "The answer is in the negative" rather than "No." For them, "bad weather" is "unfavorable climatic conditions." Jargoneers also employ what has been called "the trick of elegant variation." They may call a spade a spade the first time but will then refer to "an agricultural implement."

Gobbledygook is a special kind of ineffective writing. The term was coined by a former congressman, grown weary of involved government reports, who possibly had in mind the throaty sounds uttered by a male turkey.

The term *gobbledygook* is often applied to governmental and bureaucratic announcements that have been described as "masterpieces of complexity." For example, in a pronouncement from a Washington bureau "the chance of war" was referred to, in gobbledygook, as "in the regrettable eventuality of a failure of the deterrence policy."

Another example is the plumber who wrote to inform an agency of the U.S. government that he had found hydrochloric acid good for cleaning out pipes. Some bureaucrat responded with this gobbledygook: "The efficiency of hydrochloric acid is indisputable, but the corrosive residue is incompatible with metallic permanence." The plumber responded that he was glad the agency agreed. After several more gobbledygookish letters, an official finally wrote what should have been written originally: "Don't use hydrochloric acid. It eats the hell out of pipes."

Realizing how absurd gobbledygook is may ensure your never

using it. Who, for instance, would prefer "An excessive number of culinary assistants may negatively impact the flavor of the consommé" to "Too many cooks spoil the broth"?

7. Slang *Slang* is the nonstandard vocabulary of a given culture or subculture. It consists of coinages and figures of speech that are often characterized by raciness and spontaneity. Slang may also be defined as language peculiar to a particular group, language by which members of the group recognize and relate to other members of the group. The groups may be based on age—much slang begins with high school or college students—but it may come from any segment of the population: musicians, sports figures, lawyers, doctors, engineers, and even ministers and priests. Most slang terms eventually pass into the obscurity of dictionaries of obsolete slang, but some endure in wider and more general use.

Slang expressions may take one of several forms:

1. *Neologisms* (newly coined words) that remain slang, although not all neologisms are slang. A newly coined word for a new thing, such as virtual reality, will probably enter the language as a standard word; on the other hand, a newly coined word for something that already exists and has a name, such as *upper* (amphetamine), will probably be labeled as slang.
2. Words that are formed from others by abbreviating them: *legit, simp, psych out* or *psych up, snafu, mod.*
3. Words in general use that are given extended meanings: *bird* (which has been a slang term for "girl" for centuries), *creep, off the wall, grass, pot, pits, jerk, guts, grease, pad.*
4. Phrases that are made up of one or more newly coined words or one or more general ones: *blow your top, go into orbit, freak out, pork barrel, shoot the bull, conk out, cool it, bum steer, ripped off.*

Slang has no place in formal writing and only a limited place in informal writing. Why? First, many slang words and expressions last for a brief time and then pass out of use. If they are used, they violate the principle of national use. Second, using slang expressions prevents searching for the exact words needed to express your meaning. Calling someone a "creep" hardly conveys an exact and full impression. Third, most slang does not serve the primary aim of writing, which is to convey a clear and exact message from writer to reader. Finally, slang is not suitable in most formal or careful informal writing because it is not in keeping with the context. Words should be appropriate to the audience, the occasion, and the subject.

There are, however, some arguments in favor of slang in certain situations. It does express feeling. It also makes for effective shortcuts in expression and often prevents artificiality in writing. Furthermore, when used in recording dialog, it can convey the actual flavor of speech.

8. Triteness The term *trite* applies to words and expressions that are worn out from overuse. A trite expression is sometimes called *hackneyed language* or a *cliché*. The origins of the words *triteness, hackneyed*, and *cliché* are revealing: the first comes from the Latin word *tritus*, which means "to rub, to wear out"; *hackneyed* is derived from the idea of a horse or carriage let out for hire, devoted to common use, and thus worn out in service; *cliché* comes from the French word *clicher*, which means "to stereotype."

Thus trite language resembles slang in that both are rubber stamps, "stereotyped plates" of thought and expression.

Clichés may be tags from common speech, overworked quotations, or outworn phrases from newspapers. They save writers the task of stating exactly what they mean, but their use results in writing that is stale and ineffective. Such words and phrases may seem humorous; they are, indeed, often used for humor or irony. Used seriously, they suggest that the speaker or writer is naive or lazy.

Because trite words and expressions are familiar, they are likely to occur to us more readily than others that are more effective. Look suspiciously at each word or phrase that leaps to mind until you can be certain the expression is exact and unhackneyed. Hundreds of examples could be cited, but here are some colorful expressions that are now ineffective because of overuse:

brave as a lion   gentle as a lamb   pure as new fallen
    snow

brown as a berry   green as grass   sadder but wiser

cold as ice   like a blundering   strong as an ox
    idiot

fight like a tiger   like a fish out of   trees like sentinels
    water

free as the air   like a newborn   wild as a March
    babe   hare

Here are some more trite words and phrases:

a must, all in all, along this (that) line, and things like that, any manner or means, aroused our curiosity, as a matter of fact

battle of life, beating around the bush, believe me, bigger and better things, bitter end, bright and early, brings to mind, butterflies in my stomach, by leaps and bounds

center of attraction, chills (shivers) up and down my spine, come into the picture, conspicuous by its absence

dear old (high school, college, alma mater), depths of despair, doomed to disappointment, dull thud

each and every, every walk of life

fair land of ours, few and far between, fill the shoes of, first and foremost, fond memories, force of circumstances

get our (their) wires crossed, give it a try, give out (up), goes without saying, grand and glorious, great (guy, job, thrill, etc.), green with envy

hang one on, honest to goodness

in dire straits, in glowing terms, in the best of health, in the long run, in this day and age, interesting (surprising) to note, intestinal fortitude, irony of fate

last but not least, last straw, leaves little to be desired, live it up mad dash for, make the world a better place, more than pleased, Mother Nature

necessary evil, never a dull moment, nick of time, no fooling, no thinking person, none the worse for wear, needs no introduction

out of this world

proud possessor, psychological moment

raining cats and dogs, real thrill

sad to relate, safe to say, sigh of relief, sight to behold

take a back seat, the time of my life, thing of the past, tired but happy

wee small hours, wide open spaces, words fail to express, wunderbar, without further ado

9. Wordiness To be really effective, diction must be economical. Writing should be neither clipped nor sketchy, but using more words than are needed weakens the force and appeal of all writing and most speech.

Conciseness alone does not guarantee good writing, but it is impossible to write forcefully if you use three or four words where one would serve adequately. (The Golden Rule contains only eleven words. The Ten Commandments are expressed in seventy-five words. Lincoln's Gettysburg Address contains only 267 words.) The moral of "few words for many" is in the following: To the question of whether rules should be observed, an administrator wrote, "The implementation of sanctions will inevitably eventuate in subsequent repercussions." What he meant, and should have written, was "Yes."

Here are examples of some wordy expressions and their concise counterparts:

I would appreciate it if	please
in the month of June	in June
it has come to our attention that	(begin with the word following that)

it is interesting to note that	(begin with the word following that)
in the event that	if
at the present time	now
on condition that	if
in regard to	about
inasmuch as	since
are of the opinion	believe
in accordance with	by
before long	soon
at this point in time	now

When meaning is expressed or implied in a particular word or phrase, repeating the idea by additional words is useless. One word of two or three expresses the idea, and the others add nothing. Common examples are using *again* with many verbs beginning with *re-;* using *more* or *most* with absolute-meaning adjectives; and using *more* or *most* with adjectives and adverbs that already end in *-er, -est.* The following are examples of such expressions:

repeat again	recur again
more better	necessary need
long length	first beginnings
endorse on the back	each and every one
completely unanimous	cooperate together
rise up	fellow classmates
most perpendicular	more perfect
more paramount	resume again
loquacious talker	meet up with
audible to the ear	consensus of opinion
more older	many in number
most unkindest	visible to the eye
descend down	final end
individual person	revert back
join together	reduce down
complete monopoly	cover over
this afternoon at 3 P.M.	back up
most unique	personal friend .

Wordiness takes many forms. *Affectation, euphemisms, jargon* and *gobbledygook,* and *trite expressions* are frequently wordy. Once again, use all the words you need to express your ideas fully and clearly, but try hard to eliminate the deadwood.

EXERCISES IN WORD USAGE

Areas of Usage

In this exercise, assume that the standard of word choice is that of careful but not overformal or affectedly "fine" American speech or writing. By this standard, each of the sentences below contains one or more questionable expressions. Write a capital letter to indicate that in order to make the sentence acceptable, you would have to substitute (in one or more places): A—the correct form of a word or phrase (for an impropriety or illiteracy); B—a current American expression (for a regional, British, or old-fashioned one); C—a more formal expression (for slang, argot, or jocular usage); D—a fresher or simpler expression (for hackneyed language or occupational jargon); E—a more straightforward or frank expression (for a euphemism, a would-be elegance, or affectedly fine writing). If the sentence fits more than one category, choose the first one it fits.

1. In this crowning victory, the veteran left-hander gave everything he had.
2. I resent your calling me a dropout, being that actually I was thrown out.
3. In the little town where I grew up, a courthouse idler could achieve lasting distinction by unusual distance and accuracy of expectoration.
4. We made two stops to take on petrol during the race.
5. The gathering at Harold's was supposed to be a cram session, but I'm afraid we spent most of the time just goofing off.
6. Having finally reached the top of the divide, we all got out and left the car cool off.

7. Everybody wanted to ride with Claude, because he really drives a hot car.
8. Mr. Powers is out of the office today, but I reckon you can see him tomorrow.
9. I have observed that fanatics or radicals in any political cause tend to prevaricate when it suits their purposes.
10. In response to your inquiry regarding our ability to supply earth-moving equipment immediately, I wish to state that the answer is in the affirmative.

Improprieties and Mistaken Identities

Each sentence in the pairs below may contain careless or faulty diction. Write a capital letter to indicate that of the two sentences: A—the first only is acceptable; B—the second only is acceptable; C—both are acceptable; D—neither is acceptable.

1. I found the book rather *dissatisfying*. I don't like the *hustling and bristling* to and from work in rush-hour crowds.
2. I have nothing to gain by the deal, and my curiosity is entirely *disinterested*. There are usually many causes of an *economical* depression.
3. Football had a *derogative* influence on his study habits. Whether you go or stay is *immaterial* to me.
4. Thanksgiving makes me conscious of *materialistic* things that I usually take for granted. He easily passed the *entry* requirements of the college.
5. The movies supply *vicarious* pleasures. I was interested in the close *contrast* exhibited by many details of their two lives.
6. I was embarrassed by that *phase* of the incident. While in England he *frequented* the British Museum.
7. The two events are entirely *disassociated*. Although you can't see it move, a glacier is in *continual* motion; it never stops.
8. A really accurate *translation* of a poem is impossible.

The conductor started the second movement with a *flourish* of his baton.

9. Information *achieved* from libraries is sooner forgotten than that from life. It was truly a *pathetic* case.

10. He *obtained* his goal of getting a job in the circus. He was *too reticent* to take part in sports.

Idiomatic Usage

Each sentence in the numbered pairs below may contain an example of nonstandard idiomatic usage. Write a capital letter to indicate that: A—the first sentence only is acceptable; B—the second sentence only is acceptable; C—both are acceptable; D—neither sentence is acceptable.

1. I could not agree to his proposal that we nominate Sellers for vice-president. He thought Sellers was the best candidate, but I could not agree with him.

2. I am often impatient with being delayed in expressway jams. My father is often impatient with me.

3. Prior to the final test, we were given several review exercises to study. Of approximately three subjects, he passed only English.

4. When John forgets a date with me, I get angry at him. He is annoyed with me when I am late.

5. I prefer cooked breakfast food over the dry cereals. I don't like this hat, and wish I hadn't bought it during a spur of the moment.

6. Obedience to the traffic laws saves a driver from tickets and fines. Less and less original dramatic programs are broadcast on television.

7. Mother often tells me I am prone toward sloppiness in doing my chores. She always adds that I seem oblivious to her criticism.

8. Statistics show that fewer licenses for horse-drawn vehicles are issued each year. A well-trained horse is always obedient of commands given it.

9. Many people who are expert at swimming are not able

to dive well. He was angry that she was unmindful of his wishes.

10. Everybody was surprised to find him capable to play the piano so well. She was astonished that he thought her careless about his feelings.

Figures of Speech

Each sentence below contains figurative language (metaphor or simile) that may and may not be effective. Write a capital letter to indicate your judgment of the figurative language. (If the sentence fits more than one category, choose the first one it fits.) A—bad because mixed (combines two or more incompatible images); B—bad because incongruous or absurd (produces an effect not intended by the writer); C—bad because trite (weakened by overuse); D—reasonably fresh and effective (or at least not obviously faulty).

1. Collins took the pass over his shoulder and, running like a deer, covered the 50 yards to the goal line unmolested.
2. Many people are prevented by poverty from pursuing the higher fields of education.
3. While we talked, the kittens continued their intricate game, skittering back and forth over the floor like blown leaves.
4. Her smile disclosed a perfect row of teeth that shone like diamonds.
5. The social bridge between them was now so far apart that neither felt like keeping up the correspondence.
6. The poor schoolmaster was destined to be unlucky in love, and after a year his headlong pursuit of Miss Darby ended in flat disappointment.
7. Mrs. Peebles ruled her husband with an iron hand, and during her lectures the unfortunate man couldn't get a word in edgewise.
8. It was one of those stinging cold Arizona nights, with a

sky full of the enormous desert stars shuddering and, I imagined, blowing on their hands.

9. From my experience as a player and a coach, I would say that poor footwork is the greatest stumbling block in learning to play tennis.

10. The romantic intentions of the summer night were embarrassingly obvious—not a ripple on the dreaming lake, and a little mood music coming from the leaves overhead.

The Exact Word

In each of the following sentences you are to supply the missing word from the list given below it. Write a capital letter to indicate the word that most *exactly* fits the meaning and idiom of the context.

1. I have decided to ignore his criticism entirely, and nothing he can say will _____ me to make a reply. (*A*—aggravate; *B*—irritate; *C*—provoke; *D*—exasperate; *E*—nettle)

2. His failure to show up at the eight o'clock class was a rather frequent _____ . (*A*—event; *B*—incident; *C*—accident; *D*—episode; *E*—occurrence)

3. Carrying the surveying equipment proved to be an awkward and exhausting task; before we had gone far I began to wish that I had chosen a less _____ load. (*A*—heavy; *B*—weighty; *C*—ponderous; *D*—massive; *E*—cumbersome)

4. It takes more courage to be patient and persevering under long-continuing _____ than to face a momentary danger boldly. (*A*—calamity; *B*—misfortune; *C*—disaster; *D*—mischance; *E*—catastrophe)

5. Something was preventing the water from entering our part of the irrigation system, and it took us several hours to locate and remove the _____ . (*A*—obstacle; *B*—impediment; *C*—obstruction; *D*—hindrance; *E*—barrier)

6. It was some comfort to him that nobody else would ever know, but for a long time his conscience continued to ＿＿ him with having betrayed his better nature by a selfish act. (*A*—blame; *B*—censure; *C*—condemn; *D*—reprove; *E*—reproach)

7. Having been left alone and with nothing in particular to do, he decided to spend the afternoon in an aimless ＿＿ through the surrounding fields and woods. (*A*—excursion; *B*—ramble; *C*—tour; *D*—trip; *E*—jaunt)

8. It is impossible to call a person or family ＿＿ without implying that there is something at least faintly absurd or pretentious about them. (*A*—polite; *B*—urbane; *C*—cosmopolitan; *D*—genteel; *E*—well-bred)

9. These shameless elderly gossips were never known to spare an ounce of charity for anybody outside their own circle, but they spent endless time on one another's aches, pains, and operations in loud expressions of ＿＿ . (*A*—commiseration; *B*—sympathy; *C*—compassion; *D*—condolence; *E*—pity)

10. This silly piece of criticism has neither seriousness of argument nor decency of manner, and the writer's comments are to be dismissed as merely ＿＿ . (*A*—trifling; *B*—playful; *C*—petty; *D*—frivolous; *E*—insignificant)

ANSWERS TO EXERCISES

Areas of Usage

1. D	3. E	5. C	7. C	9. E
2. A	4. B	6. A	8. B	10. D

Improprieties and Mistaken Identities

1. D	3. B	5. A	7. D	9. B
2. A	4. D	6. B	8. C	10. D

Idiomatic Usage

1. *C*	3. *A*	5. *D*	7. *B*	9. *C*
2. *B*	4. *B*	6. *A*	8. *A*	10. *D*

Figures of Speech

1. *C*	3. *D*	5. *A*	7. *C*	9. *B*
2. *A*	4. *B*	6. *B*	8. *D*	10. *D*

The Exact Word

1. *C*	3. *E*	5. *C*	7. *B*	9. *A*
2. *E*	4. *B*	6. *E*	8. *D*	10. *D*

GLOSSARY OF DICTION

The following list, alphabetically arranged for easy reference, contains words and expressions often misused or confused. The list, not all-inclusive, is a capsule presentation of some common violations of good usage. If the material given below does not apply to your problem, if you want more detailed information, or if you do not find listed the word or phrase you are seeking, consult your dictionary.

A few of these expressions are always to be avoided, but many are unacceptable only in formal English. Remember especially that no stigma attaches to the label "colloquial"; it indicates that a given expression is more appropriate in conversation and in informal discourse than it is in formal writing.

Usage is so constantly changing that expressions now restricted in some way may later be considered standard. Furthermore, because no dictionary or textbook (including this one) is a final authority, some usages are disputed. Probably no two linguists would agree on all the comments that follow. But this illustrative list should be serviceable as a starter.

This glossary is not intended to hamper or restrict your speech. It should serve to acquaint you with what is considered the usage of educated people when they are writing formally. It should also serve as a guide on those few occasions when you need to be on your best behavior and to speak as correctly as you can. Several of the proscribed words and expressions in this glossary will be considered acceptable in the daily speech of almost everyone but not in carefully prepared writing.

Standard English, so-called, has nothing to do with character, intelligence, morality, or even aesthetics. Yet all of us should remember that there are more people with power, money, jobs to hand out, and grades to assign who speak and write standard English than those who do not. Anyone speaking "unacceptably" is all too often the object of regional, racial, or national prejudice. This harsh fact and unfortunate truth should be squarely faced.

a, an The choice between *a* and *an* depends upon the initial sound of the word that follows. *An* should be used before a vowel sound, *a* before a word beginning with a consonant sound: *an* adult, *a* picture; *an* honor, *a* historian.

ability, capacity *Ability* means the power to do something, physical or mental (*ability* to speak in public). *Capacity* is the ability to hold, contain, or absorb (a room filled to *capacity*).

absolutely This word means "completely," "perfectly," "wholly." In addition to being greatly overused as an intensifier, it is both faulty and wordy in an expression such as "absolutely complete." Never use *absolutely* or any other such modifier with words like *complete, perfect, unique* (see *unique*).

accept, except *Accept* means "to receive" or "to agree with"; *except* means "to omit" or "to exempt." (I will not *accept* your offer. The men were punished but Ned was *excepted*.) As a preposition, *except* means "other than." (Everyone *except* me was on time.)

ad A colloquial abbreviation, much used, for *advertisement*. In strictly formal writing, avoid such abbreviations as *ad, auto* for *automobile, phone* for *telephone, exam* for *examination*.

advise This word, meaning "to counsel," "to give advice to," is overused in business letters and other forms of communication for "tell," "inform." (I am pleased to *inform* [not *advise*] you that the check has been received.)

affect, effect As a verb, *affect* means "to influence" or "to assume." (This book has *affected* my thinking.) *Effect* as a verb means "to cause" and as a noun means "result." (Your good work will *effect* an improvement in your mark for the term. This play will have a good *effect* on youth.)

ain't This contraction is considered illiterate, dialectal, or colloquial and is cautioned against in standard English, both written and spoken. The word, which stands for *am not,* is often informally used even by educated people, but it has not been accepted in the sense that *isn't* (for *is not*), *aren't* (for *are not*), and *weren't* (for *were not*) have been.

alibi Used colloquially to mean "an excuse or any kind of defense," the word precisely and correctly should be used to mean "a plea or fact of having been elsewhere when an offense was committed." *Alibi* is often used in the loose sense mentioned above and is now a trite and jaded expression.

all right, alright The former expression is correct but has been overworked to mean "satisfactory" or "very well." *Alright* is analogous to *altogether* and *already* (both standard words) but is not yet an acceptable word in standard usage.

almost See *Most, almost.*

already, all ready The former means "earlier," "previously." (When she arrived, her friend had *already* left.) *All ready* means "all are ready." (They will leave when they are *all ready.*)

altogether, all together *Altogether* means "wholly," "completely." (He was not *altogether* pleased with his purchase.) *All together* means "all in company" or "everybody in one place." (The family was *all together* for the holidays.)

alumnus, alumna   An *alumnus* is a man graduate; an *alumna* is a woman graduate. The respective plurals are *alumni* and *alumnae*. To refer to graduates of a school as *alum* or *alums* is colloquial or slangy.

among, between   The former shows the relationship of more than two objects; *between* refers to only two or more than two when each object is considered in its relationship to others. (We distributed the candy *among* the six children. We divided the candy *between* Jill and Gray. Understanding *between* nations is essential.)

amount, number   The former is used of things involving a unified mass—bulk, weight, or sums. (What is the *amount* of the bill?) *Number* is used of things that can be counted in individual units. (I have a *number* of hats and coats.)

and etc.   A redundant expression. *Etc.* is an abbreviation for the Latin phrase *et cetera*, meaning "and so forth." Omit the *and* in *and etc.*

and/or   Primarily a business and legal expression, *and/or* is objected to by purists and other especially fastidious users of English. It is somewhat vague and also has business connotations objectionable to some people. Although it is a useful time-saver, in formal English you should avoid using it.

and which, that, who; but which, that, who   Correct sentence structure provides that these phrases should appear in clauses only if preceded by clauses that also contain *which, that,* or *who.* ("This is the first book *that* I bought *and that* I treasure," not "This is the first book I bought *and that* I treasure.")

anyway, anyways   *Anyway* means "in any case," "anyhow." (She was planning to go *anyway.*) *Anyways* has the same meaning as *anyway,* but it is considered either dialectal or colloquial when used to mean "in any case."

apt, liable, likely   *Apt* suggests fitness or tendency. (She is *apt* in arithmetic.) *Liable* implies exposure to something burdensome or disadvantageous. (You are *liable* for damages.) *Likely* means "expected," "probable." (We are *likely* to have snow next month.) *Likely* is the most commonly used of the three terms. Distinction in meaning has broken down somewhat, but *apt* and *liable* used in the sense of "probable" are sometimes considered colloquial or dialectal.

as   One of the most overworked words in the English language. It is a perfectly good word, but *since, because,* and *when* are more exact and effective conjunctions. (*Since* [not *As*] it was snowing, we decided to stay indoors.) *As* is often misused in place of *that* or *whether.* (I doubt *that* [not *as*] I can go.) In negative comparisons some writers prefer *so . . . as* to *as . . . as.* (He is not *so* heavy *as* his brother.) In general, use *as* sparingly; nearly always a more exact and effective word can be found.

as good as, if not better than   A correctly phrased but awkward and mixed comparison. A statement will be more effective when *if not better* is put at the end. (*Awkward:* My work is *as good as, if not better than,* your work. *Improved:* My work is *as good as yours, if not better.*)

awful, awfully, abominably   These and such other expressions as *terrible, ghastly,* and *horrible* are loose, overworked intensifiers. If you really need an intensifier, use *very* (which see).

bad, badly, ill   *Bad* is an adjective meaning "not good," "not as it should be." *Badly* is an adverb meaning "harmfully," "wickedly," "unpleasantly," "inefficiently." *Ill* is both an adjective and an adverb and means "sick," "tending to cause harm or evil," or "in a malevolent manner," "wrongly." (She was very *ill.*) *Bad* and *badly* are often incorrectly used with the verb *feel.* ("I feel *bad* today"—not *badly,* unless you mean that your sense of touch is impaired.)

badly   A colloquial expression for "very much." Avoid its use in this sense in formal writing and speaking.

balance, remainder   The latter term means "what is left over." *Balance* has many meanings, but its use as "remainder" is considered colloquial. (He ate the *remainder* [not *balance*] of the meal.)

be sure and   This expression is considered both colloquial and unidiomatic. (When you get there, *be sure to* [not *sure and*] write to me.)

beside, besides   *Beside* is normally a preposition meaning "by the side of." *Besides* is an adverb meaning "moreover," and, infrequently, is a preposition meaning "except." (The old man sat *beside* the stove. I can't go because I have no money, and *besides* I don't feel well.)

between   See *Among, between.*

bunch   A colloquialism for "a group of people," "crowd," or "set." (Our *set*—or *group* or *crowd* or *gang*—was closely knit at that time.)

but which   See *And which.*

calculate, reckon, guess   These words are localisms for "think," "suppose," and "expect." Each of the words has standard and acceptable meanings, but in the senses indicated here they should always be avoided except in informal conversation.

can, may, might   *Can* suggests "ability," physical and mental. (He *can* make good progress if he tries hard enough.) *May* implies permission or sanction. (The office manager says that you *may* leave.) The distinction between *can* and *may* (ability vs. permission) is illustrated in this sentence: "Lee thinks that you *can*, and you *may* try if you wish." *May* also expresses possibility and wish (desire): "It *may* snow today" (possibility). "*May* you have a pleasant time" (wish, desire). *Might* is used after a governing verb in the past tense, *may* after a governing verb in the present tense: "She *says* that you *may* try"; "She *said* that you *might* try."

cancel out   Omit the *out*. This wordy expression is often used, perhaps by analogy with *cross out* or *strike out*.

cannot help, cannot help but   The first of these expressions is preferable in such statements as "I *cannot help* talking about my trip." The *but* should be omitted since its addition can result in a double negative: Use *cannot help* and *can but*.

can't hardly   Omit the *not*. (I *can* hardly hear you.) *Can't hardly* is a double negative. The expression, however, appears frequently in the speech (but hardly the writing) of well-educated persons in all walks of life.

capital, capitol   The first of these words may be employed in all meanings except that of "a building." A *capitol* is an edifice, a building. (He raised new *capital* for the company. The sightseeing bus passed the state *capitol*. Sacramento is the *capital* of California.)

case   This word (other than indicating the forms of pronouns and nouns) has many vague meanings. *Case, phase, factor, instance, nature, thing* are prime examples of jargon. *To case*, in the sense of "examine carefully," is slang. Don't use *case the joint* in standard English.

common, mutual   The former means "belonging to many or to all." *Mutual* means "reciprocal." (Airplanes are *common* carriers. Our respect and love were *mutual*.) Avoid the redundancy of this kind of statement: "He and I entered into a *mutual* agreement."

compare, contrast   *Compare* is used to point out likenesses, similarities (used with the preposition *to*), and to examine two or more objects to find likenesses or differences (used with the preposition *with*). *Contrast* always points out differences. (The poet *compared* his lady *to* a wood thrush. The teacher *compared* my paper *with* Henry's and found no signs of copying. In *contrast* to your work, mine is poor.)

complement, compliment   *Complement* implies something that completes. (This jewelry will *complement* your dress.) A *compliment* is flattery. (Beulah enjoyed the *compliment* paid to her.)

contact, contacted   Each of these words has perfectly proper uses, but as business terms they have been overworked. Possible substitutes are *communicate with, call, call upon, telephone*.

continual, continuous   In some uses these words are interchangeable. A subtle distinction is that *continual* implies "a close recurrence in time," "in rapid succession," and that *continuous* implies "without interruption." (The *continual* ringing of the doorbell bothers me. The ticking of the watch was *continuous*.)

contrast   See *Compare, contrast*.

convince, persuade   The former means "to overcome the doubts of." *Persuade* implies "influencing a person to an action or belief." (I am *convinced* that you are right and you have *persuaded* me to help you.) *Convince to* is not idiomatic. (*Wrong:* I convinced him to see the play. *Right:* I persuaded him to see the play. I convinced him that the play was worthwhile.)

council, counsel   *Council* means "an assembly," "a group." (This is a *council* of citizens.) *Counsel* is both a noun and a verb and means "advice" or "to advise." (The physician gave me expensive *counsel*. The manager will *counsel* fast action by the board of directors.)

cute   This is an overworked and somewhat vague word that generally expresses approval. Probably *charming, clever, attractive, winsome, piquant, pleasing, vivacious*, or one of a dozen other adjectives would come nearer the meaning you have in mind.

data   This word was originally the plural of the Latin *datum* and means "facts and figures from which conclusions may be drawn." Purists consider the word to be plural and use it with a plural verb, but its use with a singular verb is becoming more widespread. (*These* data *are* not reliable. *This* data *is* not reliable.)

des' ert, desert', dessert'   These three words involve problems in spelling, pronunciation, and meaning. The first, with accent on the first syllable, means "barren ground." (The *desert* is 100 miles wide.) *Desert* (with accent on the second syllable) means "to abandon." (Don't ever *desert* your true friends.) *Dessert* (note the double *s*) is the "last course of a lunch or dinner." (Apple pie is his favorite *dessert*.)

different from, than, to   *Different than* and *different to* are considered colloquial by some authorities, improper and incorrect by others. Even so, these idioms have long literary usage to support them, and certainly they are widely used. No one ever objects on any grounds to *different from*. Use *different from* and be safe, never sorry.

disinterested, uninterested   The former means "unbiased," "not influenced by personal reasons." *Uninterested* means "having no interest in," "not paying attention." (The minister's opinion was *disinterested*. I was completely *uninterested* in the play.) As a colloquialism, a somewhat inexact one, *disinterested* is often used in the sense of "uninterested," "indifferent."

disregardless   See *Irregardless, disregardless*.

disremember   An illiteracy. Never use this word in standard English.

done, don't   The principal parts of this verb are *do, did, done*. *Done* is frequently used incorrectly as the past tense of *do*. (We *did* [not *done*] our work early today.) *Don't* is often used incorrectly for *doesn't*. (It doesn't [not *don't*] make much difference to me.)

due to   Some authorities label this phrase "colloquial" when it is used to mean "because of." Nevertheless, it is widely used in this sense by capable speakers and writers. Purists prefer such expressions as *owing to, caused by, on account of*, and *because of*. If you wish your English to be above any possible criticism, avoid using *due to* as a preposition. (Tension there was *caused by* [not *due to*] racial unrest that had been building for decades.) Most important, remember that *due to the fact that* is a wordy way of saying the short and simple word *since*.

each . . . are   *Each*, even if not followed by *one*, implies "one." Any plural words used in modifying phrases do not change the number. (Each *is* [not *are*] expected to contribute *his* or *her* time. *Each one* of you *is* a fraud.)

either . . . or, neither . . . nor   The former means "one of two."

Neither means "not one of two." *Or* is used with *either, nor* with *neither*. The use of *either . . . or* and *neither . . . nor* in coordinating more than two words, phrases, or clauses is sanctioned by some dictionaries but not by others. (*Either* of you *is* satisfactory for the role. *Neither* the boys *nor* the girls wished to dance.)

emigrate, immigrate   The former means "to leave"; the latter means "to enter." (Our janitor *emigrated* from Poland in 1938. Many people have tried to *immigrate* to this country in the last decade.) The corresponding nouns, *emigration* and *immigration*, are similarly distinguished in meaning.

enthuse   This word is a formation derived from "enthusiasm." Most dictionaries label *enthuse* as colloquial, although it is shorter and more direct than preferred locutions such as *be enthusiastic about* or *become enthusiastic over*. Even so, the word is greatly overused and somewhat "gushy"; do not use it in formal English.

envelop, envelope   The verb *en-vel' op* (accent on the second syllable) means "to cover," "to wrap." (Fire will soon *envelop* the entire block.) En'-vel-ope (accent on first syllable) is a noun meaning "a covering." (Put a stamp on this *envelope*.)

except   See *Accept, except*.

farther, further   These words are interchangeable in meaning, but unusually precise writers and speakers prefer *farther* to indicate space, a measurable distance. *Further* indicates "greater in degree, quantity, or time" and also means "moreover" and "in addition to." (We walked two miles *farther*. Let's talk about this *further*.)

feature   As both verb and noun, *feature* is an overworked colloquialism in the sense of "emphasize" or "emphasis." *Feature* is slang in the expression "Can you *feature* that?" meaning, presumably, "Can you imagine that?"

feel   This useful word appears in several colloquial and dialectal expressions. In standard English avoid using *feel of* (for *feel*), *feel like* (for *wish to, desire*), *feel up to* (for *feel capable of*).

fewer, less   Both of these words imply a comparison with something larger in number or amount. Although *less* is widely used in place of *fewer*, particularly in informal writing and in speech, the distinction between them seems useful. *Fewer* applies to number. (*Fewer* horses are seen on the streets these days.) *Less* is used in several ways: *less* material in the dress, *less* coverage, *less* than a dollar. (The *less* money we have, the *fewer* purchases we can make.)

figuratively   This word means "metaphorically," "representing one thing in terms of another," "not literally." (*Figuratively* speaking, you acted like a mouse.) See *Literally*.

firstly, secondly   These words are acceptable, but most skilled users of the language prefer *first* and *second* because they are just as accurate and are shorter. *First of all* is a wordy expression.

foreword, forward   A *foreword* is a preface or introduction. *Forward* suggests movement onward. (That book needs no *foreword*. The crowd surged *forward*.)

formally, formerly   The first term means "in a formal manner," "precisely," "ceremonially." The latter means "in the past." (The defendant bowed *formally* to the judge. Betty was *formerly* an employee of that company.)

former, latter   *Former* and *latter* refer to only two units. To refer to a group of more than two items, use *first* and *last* to indicate order.

fort, forte   *Fort* means an "enclosed place," a "fortified building." *Forte* means "special accomplishment or ability." (The Indians burned the settlers' *fort*. Her *forte* is playing the violin.)

free from, free of   The former is idiomatically correct. *Free of* is considered either colloquial or dialectal.

free gratis   *Gratis* means "without payment," "free." Use either *free* or *gratis*, not both.

funny   A common and useful word but one that is vastly overworked. Its use to mean "strange," "queer," "odd," "remarkable" is considered colloquial. Its primary meaning is "humorous" or "comical."

further   See *Farther, further.*

genius, genus   The former refers to great ability. (Bach was a man of *genius*.) *Genus* refers to class or kind. (What is the *genus* of this plant?)

good, well   The former is an adjective with many meanings: a *good* time, *good* advice, *good* Republican, *good* humor. *Well* functions as both adjective and adverb. As an adjective it means "in good health," and as an adverb it means "ably" or "efficiently." (I feel *well* once again. The sales force worked *well* in this campaign.)

got, gotten   The principal parts of *get* are *get, got, got* (or *gotten*). Both *got* and *gotten* are acceptable words; your choice will depend upon your speech habits or on the rhythm of the sentence you are writing or speaking. *Got* is colloquial when used to mean "must," "ought," "own," "possess," and many other terms. (I *ought* [not *got*] to go.) See *Have got to.*

gourmand, gourmet   These words have to do with eating, but they are different in meaning. A *gourmand* is a large eater. (Diamond Jim Brady was a *gourmand*, often eating for three hours at a time.) A *gourmet* is a fastidious eater, an epicure. (As a French chef, he considers himself a *gourmet*.)

graduate   This word has several meanings, all of which are in some way related to marking in steps, measuring. Idiom decrees that one *graduate from* (not *graduate*) a school.

gratis   See *Free gratis.*

guess   See *Calculate, reckon, guess.*

hang, hung   The principal parts of *hang* are *hang, hung, hung.*

However, when the word refers to the death penalty, the parts are *hang, hanged, hanged*. (The draperies are *hung*. The murderer was *hanged*.)

have got to   A colloquial and redundant expression for "must," and so on. (I *must* [not *have got to*] do my laundry today.) (See *got, gotten*.) *Have* is a useful verb and appears in many expressions we use constantly. In standard English we should avoid using such expressions as *have a check bounce, have cold feet, have a lot on the ball, have it in for someone*. In these expressions the *have* is only partly responsible for the colloquialism.

healthful, healthy   These words are often used interchangeably, but *healthful* means "conducive to health"; *healthy* means "possessing health." In other words, places and foods are *healthful*, people and animals are *healthy*. (I wonder whether she is a *healthy* person because she lives in a *healthful* climate.)

hopefully   In the meaning of "let us hope" or "it is to be hoped," the use of *hopefully* is debatable. Preferably do not use the word in a sentence such as "*Hopefully*, we shall have finished our work by then."

human, humane   The word *human* refers to a person. Some especially careful or precise writers and speakers do not use the word alone to refer to man as man; they say or write *human being*. However, the practice of using the word alone as a noun has a long and respectable background. *Humane* means "tender," "merciful," "considerate." (His treatment of the prisoners was *humane*.)

hunch   This word has acceptable meanings as both verb and noun. In the sense of "a premonition or feeling that something is going to happen," it is informal and should be avoided in standard English.

i.e., e.g., viz., N.B., P.S.   These and many other abbreviations commonly appear in writing. Although abbreviations are not recommended for formal writing, many of them are useful shortcuts. For "that is" we use the abbreviation *i.e. E.g.* is an abbreviation meaning "for example." *Viz.* is an abbreviation meaning "namely." *N.B.* stands for Latin *nota bene*, meaning "note well." *P.S.* is the abbreviation for "postscript"; *P.SS.* stands for "postscripts."

if, whether   In standard English, *if* is used to express conditions; *whether*, usually with *or*, is used in expressions of doubt and in indirect questions expressing conditions. (*If* it doesn't snow, we shall go [simple condition]. We have been wondering *whether* we would reach our sales quota [doubt]. I asked *whether* the doctor had arrived [indirect question].)

immigrate   See *Emigrate, immigrate.*

imply, infer   To imply is to suggest a meaning hinted at but not explicitly stated. (Do you *imply* that I am not telling the truth?) To *infer* is to draw a conclusion from statements, circumstances, or evidence. (After that remark, I *infer* that you no longer agree.)

impractical   See *Unpractical.*

in, into   The former is used to indicate motion within relatively narrow or well-defined limits. (She walked up and down *in* her room for an hour.) *In* is also used when a place is not mentioned. (The airplane came *in* for a landing.) *Into* usually follows a verb indicating motion to a place. (When Marion strode *into* the room, everyone fell silent.)

in back of   This phrase is colloquial for "behind." However, *in the back of* and *in front of* are considered standard terms, although both are wordy. *Behind* and *before* are shorter and nearly always will suffice. (*Behind* [not *in back of*] the office was the storeroom. *Before* [or *in front of*] the house was a tree.)

in regards to   Omit the *s* in *regards*. Better yet, substitute *concerning* or *about* for the entire phrase; one word is usually more effective than three.

in search for, in search of   Both of these expressions are commonly used, but the latter is the preferred idiom.

individual   See *Party, person, individual.*

inferior than, to   The former is not standard idiom; the latter is. (This oil is *inferior to* [not *than*] that.)

ingenious, ingenuous   *Ingenious* means "talented," "resourceful," or "tricky." (This is an *ingenious* computation device.) *Ingenuous* means "innocent," "frank," or "naive." (Sally is an *ingenuous* little girl.)

inside of, off of, outside of   The *of* in each of these expressions is superfluous. (*Inside* [not *inside of*] the barn the horses are eating hay. The boy fell *off* [not *off of*] his tricycle.) When *inside* and *outside* are not prepositional, the *of* should be included: The *outside of* the house, the *inside of* the tent.

irregardless, disregardless   Each of these words is an illiteracy. That is, neither is a standard word and neither should be used under any circumstances, formal or informal. The prefixes *ir-* and *dis-* are both incorrect and superfluous in these constructions. Use *regardless*.

is, was, were   Parts of the verb *to be*. It may help you to remember that *is* is singular in number, third person, present tense. (He [or *She* or *It*] *is* in the room.) *Was* is singular, first or third person, past tense. (I [or *He* or *She* or *It*] *was* in the room.) *Were* can be either singular or plural, second person in the singular and all three persons in the plural, and is in the past tense. (*You* [both singular and plural] *were* in the room. We [or *You* or *They*] *were* in the room.) The two most frequent errors in using *to be* are employing *was* for *were*, and vice versa, and using *is* in the first or second person instead of in the third, where it belongs.

is when, is where   These terms are frequently misused, especially in giving definitions. Grammatically, the fault may be described as using an adverbial clause in place of the noun phrase or clause that is called for. "A subway *is where* you ride under the ground" can be improved to "A subway *is* an electric railroad beneath the surface of the streets." "Walking *is when* you move about on foot" can be improved to "Walking *is the act of* [or *consists of*] *moving* about on foot."

kind of a, sort of a   In these phrases the *a* is superfluous. Logically, the main word (which can be *kind, sort,* or *type*) should indicate a class, not one thing. (*What kind of* [not *what kind of a*] party is this?) Although *kind of* and *sort of* are preferred in this construction, these same phrases are often used colloquially to mean "almost," "rather," "somewhat." (She was *rather* [not *kind of*] weary. Martha was *almost* [not *sort of*] resigned to going.)

later, latter   The spelling of these words is often confused. They also have different meanings. *Later* refers to time. (He arrived at the office *later* than I did.) For *latter,* see *Former, latter.*

lead, led   These words show the confusion our language suffers because of using different symbols to represent one sound. *Lead* (pronounced *lēd*) is the present tense of the verb and causes little or no difficulty. *Led* (pronounced like the name of the metal) is the past tense and is often misspelled with *ea.* (*Lead* the blind man across the street. She *led* the blind man across the street yesterday.)

learn, teach   Standard English requires a distinction in meaning between these words. (I'll *learn* the language if you will *teach me.*) *To learn* someone something is an illiteracy.

least, lest   The former means "smallest," "slightest." The latter means "for fear that." (He did not give me the *least* argument. Give me your picture *lest* I forget how you look.)

leave, let   Both words are common in several idiomatic expressions implying permission, but *let* is standard whereas *leave* is not. (*Let* [not *leave*] me go with you.)

legible, readable   These terms are synonymous in the meaning of "capable of being deciphered or read with ease." *Readable* has the additional meaning of "interesting or easy to read." (Your handwriting is *legible.* This book is *readable.*)

lend   See *Loan, lend.*

less   See *Fewer, less.*

lest   See *Least, lest.*

liable   See *Apt, liable, likely.*

literally   This word not only is overused but also is confused with *figuratively.* It is an antonym of the latter and really means "not imaginatively," "actually." See *Figuratively.*

loan, lend   Many careful writers and speakers use *loan* only as a noun (to make a *loan*) and *lend* as a verb (to *lend* money). Because of constant and widespread usage, *loan* is now considered a legitimate verb to be avoided only in strictly formal English.

loose, lose, loss   *Loose* means "not fastened tightly." (This is a *loose* connection.) *Lose* means "to suffer the loss of." (Don't *lose* your hard-earned money.) *Loss* means "a deprivation," "a defeat," "a reverse." (The coach blamed me for the *loss* of the ball.)

lots of, a lot of, a whole lot   These terms are colloquial for "many," "much," "a great deal." The chief objection to their use is that each is a vague, general expression.

lousy   This word actually means "infested with lice." It is constantly used as a slang expression, however, to mean "dirty," "disgusting," "contemptible," "poor," "inferior," and "well supplied with" (as in "*lousy* with money"). Use it in only the most informal of informal conversations. You can startle or impress your friends by using *pediculous.*

luxuriant, luxurious   The former term refers to abundant growth; *luxurious* pertains to luxury. (The undergrowth was *luxuriant.* The furnishings were *luxurious.*)

mad   This short and useful word has many acceptable meanings such as "insane," "frantic," and "frenzied." Most authorities consider *mad* to be colloquial when it is used to mean "angry" or "furious." (I was *angry with*—or *furious with*—[not *mad at*] him.)

may   See *Can, may, might.*

maybe, may be   The former means "perhaps." (*Maybe* you will finish your task early today.) *May be* (two words) is used to express possibility. (It *may be* going to snow today.)

memorandum   This word, which is of Latin origin and means "short note" or "record of events," has two plurals, both acceptable in standard English: *memoranda, memorandums.* Abbreviations are *memo* (singular) and *memos* (plural).

might of   An illiteracy. (If you had asked, I *might have* [not *might of*] accompanied you.) See *Would of.*

moral, morale   As an adjective, the former has a meaning of "good," "proper." (Frances' *moral* code was high.) *Morale* refers to a condition, state of being, or attitude. (The *morale* in this office is excellent.)

most, almost ·   *Most* is the superlative of *many* and *much* and means "greatest in amount, quality, or degree." *Almost* means "very nearly," "all but." *Most* is colloquial when used for *almost.* (He has *almost* [not *most*] finished his assignment.)

must   As a noun, this word is no longer considered slang by most authorities, but it is tiresomely overused to mean something essential or necessary, as in "This movie is a *must.*"

neither . . . nor   See *Either . . . or.*

nice   This is a word with many meanings, including "agreeable," "pleasant," "attractive," and "delightful." Its overuse indicates the need for more specific substitutes.

no place, nowhere   The former is a perfectly sound phrase (There's *no place* like home), but in standard English it cannot be a synonym for *nowhere.* (She could find her purse *nowhere* [not *no place*].) Be certain to spell *nowhere* correctly; *nowheres* is as much dialectal as *no place.*

O, oh   The former is usually part of a vocative (direct address), is normally capitalized, and is rarely followed by any mark of punctuation. *Oh* is an interjection, may be followed by a comma or exclamation point, and is capitalized according to the usual rules. (*O* Mickey! You don't really mean that. Yet, *oh,* what hatred we had for him! *Oh,* what a chance!)

off of   See *Inside of.*

O.K.   This everyday term is colloquial or business English for "all right," "correct," "approved." It is occasionally spelled *OK, okay, okeh*. The terms *oke* and *okeydoke* are slang. For the debatable origin of *O.K.*, see any standard dictionary.

outside of   See *Inside of.*

overuse of "so"   *So* is correctly used as a conjunctive adverb with a semicolon preceding, and it is frequently used between independent clauses with only a comma before it. The chief objection to *so* in such constructions is simply overuse. In constructions like those below, *so* can often be replaced by *therefore, thus, accordingly,* and the like, or predication may be reduced.

Ineffective: The bridge was out on Route 8, *so* we had to make a long detour on Highway 20.

Improved: Since the bridge was out on Route 8, we had to make a long detour on Highway 20.

In correcting the overuse of *so,* guard against a worse error, that of using another conjunctive adverb with a comma before it and thus writing an unjustifiable comma splice: The bridge was out on Route 8, *therefore* we had to make a long detour on Highway 20. [Use a semicolon or a period.]

Sometimes *so* is misused when the writer means *so that* or *in order that:*

Ineffective: Do people want the legislators to spend more money *so* they themselves can pay higher taxes?

Improved: Do people want the legislators to spend more money *in order that* they themselves can pay higher taxes?

paid, payed   *Paid* is the past tense and past participle of the verb *pay*. (He *paid* all his bills promptly.) *Payed* is used only in the sense of to *pay* out a cable or line. (He *payed* out the anchor line slowly.)

party, person, individual   Except in telephone and legal language, *party* implies a group and should not be used to refer to one person except in a colloquial sense. *Individual* refers to a single, particular person. As nouns, *individual* and *person* are synonymous. As an adjective, *individual* means "single," "separate," and is therefore unnecessary and repetitious when used to modify *person* or when "each" has been used. Both *individual person* and *each individual member* are wordy.

passed, past   The former is the past tense of the verb *to pass;* in its use as a verb, the latter is the past participle. (The car *passed* us at 70 miles per hour. Your troubles are now *past.*) *Pass* is not only a verb; it is also a noun. In one or the other of these two categories, it appears in many expressions that are either colloquial or slangy, among them *a pretty pass, make a pass at, pass out, pass up, pass the buck.*

personal, personnel   The former means "private," "individual." (The employer granted me a *personal* interview.) *Personal* is a much overused word. Perhaps because we wish to belong, to show a close relationship with someone, we say or write such sentences as "He is a *personal* friend of mine." The *personal* should be omitted. *Personnel* means "a body of persons," usually a group employed in any work, establishment, enterprise, or service. (The *personnel* of this firm was [or possibly *were*] carefully chosen.)

plan on going, plan to go   Both of these expressions are in everyday use, but the former is considered colloquial and idiomatically not so sound as *plan to go.*

principal, principle   The former means "a sum of money" or "a chief person." As an adjective, *principal* means "main" or "chief." *Principle* is always a noun meaning "a governing rule or truth," "a doctrine." (The *principal* of that school was a man of *principle*.)

prior than, prior to Both terms are in common use but only the latter has the sanction of accepted idiom.

proposition A mathematical term colloquially much overused for *affair, offer, project, undertaking, proposal,* and similar words.

quiet, quit, quite *Quiet* means "still" or "calm." (It was a *quiet* meeting.) *Quit* means "to stop," "to desist." (Did you *quit* working?) *Quite* means "positively," "entirely." (I am *quite* certain there is a burglar in the house.)

quite a This phrase is colloquial when used to mean "more than." In standard English, avoid using such phrases as *quite a few, quite a bit,* and *quite a party.*

raise, raze, rise *Raise* means "to elevate," "to lift." (Please *raise* your eyes and look at me.) *Raze* means "to tear down." (The wreckers will *raze* this building.) *Rise* means "to get up." (When the chairman enters, everyone should *rise.*) Strictly, the word *raise* is never a noun; a few purists therefore consider it colloquial to refer to a *raise* in wages. When referring to bringing up children, *rear, raise,* and *bring up* may all be used. *Rear* is preferred in this connection, although *bring up* is also standard; *raise* is colloquial. To *raise Cain, raise the roof, raise a rumpus,* and *raise the devil* are all slang. *To get a rise out of* someone or something is also slang.

real In the sense of "really" or "very," *real* is an impropriety. (Are you *really*—or *very*—[not *real*] certain of your figures?) Adverbial use of *real* is, however, increasing steadily.

reason is because In standard English, the construction beginning "the reason is . . ." is followed by a noun or a noun clause usually introduced by *that.* Yet we often hear such a sentence as "I couldn't go; the *reason was because* I had to work." In spite of its form, the construction introduced by *reason was* is a noun clause rather than an adverbial one. But such a use should appear only in colloquial speech; standard writing requires "I couldn't go; the *reason was that* I had to work."

reason why   A redundant expression. Omit *why* and, in most constructions, also omit *reason.* "The *reason why* I like this job is the salary I get" can be improved by writing "I like this job because of the salary."

reckon   See *Calculate, reckon, guess.*

refer, refer back   *Refer* means "to direct attention" or "to make reference"; therefore, *back* is superfluous. (Please *refer* [not *refer back*] again to my statement.) The same kind of faulty diction is evident in *repeat again* and *return back.*

repeat again   See *Refer, refer back.*

respectfully, respectively   The former means "in a respectful manner." (My detailed statement is *respectfully* submitted.) *Respectively* means "severally" or "in specified order." (*Farewell, au revoir,* and *auf Wiedersehen* are ways of saying goodbye in, *respectively,* English, French, and German.)

return back   See *Refer, refer back.*

rise   See *Raise, raze, rise.*

said, same, such   As an adjective, *said* is used in legal writing but is considered to be jargon in standard English. Unless you're a lawyer (or a lawyer's secretary), avoid such expressions as *said party, said person,* and *said proposal. Same* as a pronoun is also characteristic of legal and business use. Lawyers may insist upon its retention, but business people in general and you in particular should avoid such expressions as "check enclosed in payment for *same." Such* may be an adjective, an adverb, and a pronoun—all with standard uses. It is considered colloquial, however, when used in place of a demonstrative. (I could not tolerate *that* [not *such*].) *Such* is also colloquial when used as an intensifier. (She is a *very* [not *such a*] charming person.)

saw, seen   The principal parts of *to see* are *see, saw, seen. Seen* is improperly used as the past tense; *saw* is incorrect as the past participle (I *saw* [not *seen*] you yesterday. I *have seen* [not *have saw*] you every day this week.)

sensual, sensuous   The former refers to gratification of bodily pleasures or appetites. *Sensuous* suggests the appeal of that which is pleasing to the senses. (In his abandon he indulged in every *sensual* excess he could imagine. He loved the *sensuous* music.)

set   See *Sit, set.*

shall, will   Distinctions in the use of *shall* and *will* have largely broken down. A few careful writers (and even fewer speakers) still observe them, but most of us make no effort to choose between them—except for using *shall* in questions (*Shall* I leave now?). The almost forgotten rule is this: Use *shall* in the first person and *will* in the second and third persons to express simple futurity. (We *shall* leave.) (You [or He or She] *will* go.) For emphasis, to express determination, command, intention, or promise, use *will* in the first person and *shall* in the second and third persons. (I *will* speak, no matter what the result may be. You *shall* speak—meaning "you *must* speak.")

should of   See *Would of.*

should, would   In general, use *should* and *would* according to the rules for *shall* and *will* (which see). The following may be helpful: (1) *Should* is used to express obligation (I *should* read more than I do); expectation, a corollary of obligation (They *should* be here by this time); condition (If he *should* speak, listen carefully); and simple future, first person only (I *should* like to go). (2) *Would* is used to express habitual action (He *would* walk in the woods every day); condition, after a conditional clause (If the weather were good, he *would* walk in the park); determination (He *would* do it, no matter how much we protested); wish or desire (*Would* I had gone with you); and simple future, second and third persons only (He said that he *would* go). If the governing verb is in the past tense, use *would* to express futurity, as above. If the governing verb is in the present tense, use *will:* "She *indicates* that she *will* help us."

sit, set   *Sit*, predominantly an intransitive verb, not requiring an object, has the meaning of "to place oneself." *Set,* predominantly a transitive verb, requiring an object, means "to put" or "to place." (*Set* the book on the table and come *sit* here.) *Set* used for *sit* in the meaning shown is dialectal or an impropriety. However, both words have several special meanings. For example, *set* has an intransitive use: The sun *sets* early tonight.

so   See *Overuse of so*.

so as   See *As*.

sort of a   See *Kind of a*.

stationary, stationery   The former means "having a fixed or unmoving position." (This rock is *stationary*.) *Stationery* means "paper for writing." (This is new *stationery*.)

statue, stature, statute   A *statue* is a sculptured likeness. (This is a *statue* of Robert E. Lee.) *Stature* is often used figuratively (a man of moral *stature*). A *statute* is a law. (This *statute* forbids kissing in public.)

sure   This word is used as adjective or adverb, but it is colloquial in the sense of "surely," "certainly," "indeed." (He was certainly [not *sure*] angry with the police officer.) *Sure* is also colloquial in such expressions as *sure enough* (meaning both "certainly" and "real") and *sure-fire* (meaning "certain to be successful"). See *Be sure and*.

tasteful, tasty   The former means "having or showing good taste, sense, or judgment." *Tasty* means "flavorful," "savory," "having the quality of tasting good." (The reception was a *tasteful* affair and the food served at it was *tasty*.) *Tasteful* for *tasty* is in rare or archaic use; *tasty* for *tasteful* is colloquial.

their, there, they're   These simple and common words cause much difficulty, but they are easy to keep straight. *Their* is a possessive pronoun. (This is *their* house.) *There* means "in or at that place." (Were you *there* when she arrived?) *They're* is a contraction of *they are*. (We are disappointed because *they're* not coming.)

then, than   These words are often confused in writing and some-times in pronunciation. *Than* is a conjunction used in clauses of comparison. (He worked better today *than* he did yesterday.) *Then* is an adverb of time. (We *then* went to a restaurant.)

to, too, two   Correct use of these words is a matter of careful spelling. *To* is a preposition (*to* the store) and the sign of an infinitive (*to* work). *Too* is an adverb meaning "also" or "over-abundance of." (We *too* are working, but Jack is *too* lazy to get up.) *Two* is the number after *one*. (The *two* men were *too* tired *to* go.)

try and, try to   The correct idiom is *try to*. However, *try and* is in everyday use and has been for a century. Standard English would have you write "*Try to* [not *try and*] finish your work early."

uninterested   see *Disinterested*.

unique   This word means "having no like or equal" and ex-presses absoluteness, as do words such as *round, square*, and *perpendicular.* Logically, therefore, the word *unique* cannot be compared; something cannot be "more unique," "less unique," "more round," "less round." If a qualifying word such as *nearly* is used, the illogicality is removed. "This is the *most unique* painting in the museum" is not standard, but "This is the *most nearly unique* painting" is.

unpractical, impractical, impracticable   The first two of these terms are interchangeable, although *impractical* is considered by some writers as being more formal. Each means "not practi-cal," "lacking practical usefulness or wisdom." *Impracticable* means "not capable of being carried out, used, or managed." (The piccolo player was a good man but thoroughly *impractical*. The manager considered my plan *impracticable*.)

used to, used to could   In the phrase *used to*, the *d* is often elided in speaking so that it sounds like *use to*. In writing, the *d* must be included. *Used to could* is an illiteracy; write *used to be able*.

very　*Very*, like *so*, *surely*, *too*, *extremely*, *indeed*, has been so overused that it has lost some of its value as an intensifier. Use these words sparingly and thoughtfully; consider whether your meaning isn't just as emphatic without them: "You are [very] positive about the matter." *Very* is used colloquially to qualify participles; formal use has adverbs like *much* or *greatly*. Do not substitute *plenty* or *mighty* for any use of *very*.

Colloquial:　I was *very annoyed* with myself.
Formal:　　I was *much annoyed* with myself.
Colloquial:　I am *very torn* between the desire to speak my mind and the desire to keep out of trouble.
Formal:　　I am *greatly torn* between . . .

well　See *Good, well.*

whether　See *If, whether.*

who, whom　The former is the nominative case; the latter, the objective. When in doubt, try as a memory device the substitution of *he* or *she* for *who* and *him* or *her* for *whom*, since the proper use of *he* or *she* and *him* or *her* is more easily recognized: "I wonder *who* [or whom?] I should invite." "I should invite *him* or *her*." Therefore: "I wonder *whom* I should invite."

who's, whose　The former is a shortened form of *who is.* (*Who's* ahead in the office pool?) *Whose* is the possessive case of *who.* (*Whose* toes did I step on?)

will, would　See *Shall, will; Should, would.*

-wise　This suffix has many standard uses and appears in such fully acceptable words as *clockwise* and *sidewise*. Unfortunately, it has been greatly overused in recent years and appears in scores of awkward and strained neologisms: *ideawise, travelwise, saleswise, timewise.*

worst kind, worst sort, worst way　Slang terms for *very much, greatly, intensely*, and the like.

would　See *Should, would.*

would of, could of, might of, should of　These terms are all illiteracies probably resulting from attempts to represent what is pronounced. In rapid and informal speech, that is, *would have (would've)* has the sound of *would of.* In each phrase, *have* should replace *of.*

you all   In the sense of "all of you," this phrase has a recognized and standard plural meaning. When used to refer to one person, it may be considered either dialectal or an illiteracy.

you know   This is a tiresomely overused expression, a conversational filler that really adds nothing to most statements.

7

GUIDE TO CORRECT
SENTENCE STRUCTURE

We think in words and speak and write in sentences. Such a statement is not entirely accurate, but it implies that by the use of words we phrase sentences that are tied together to make up a complete piece of writing. A sentence is the link—the only link—between a thought and full development of that thought. Like all links, it is important.

If one's sentences are awkward, vague, or faulty, the primary purpose of writing has been defeated. A major step to better writing is finding out what a sentence is and discovering what faults in structure and function are most likely to keep it from being complete, clear, direct, and communicative.

A usable definition of a sentence is that it is "one or more words conveying to the reader a sense of complete meaning." The word (or group of words) normally, but not always, has a subject and predicate. The subject may be expressed or it may be understood and not expressed. Either subject or predicate may be understood from the context.

Remember that the foregoing statements refer to *grammatical* completeness. In one sense we do not have a complete thought until we have read or written a series of sentences. A pronoun in one sentence may take its meaning from an antecedent in another. Such words as *thus, these, another*, and *again*, and such phrases as *for example* and *on the other hand* frequently show that the thought about to be presented in a new sentence is related to the thought in a preceding sentence or paragraph.

When we say, then, that a sentence conveys a "sense of complete meaning" to the reader, we do not imply that we can dispense with its context (the statements that precede or follow it). We mean only that we have a group of words so ordered as to be *grammatically* self-sufficient. For example, the statement, "He took command on July 3, 1775," is grammatically complete. It has a subject, the pronoun *he*, and it has a verb, *took* (took command). In this sense the entire statement is complete and must be begun with a capital letter and followed by a period. So far as total meaning is concerned, however, we need other sentences to tell us that *he* refers to George Washington and that the command he assumed was that of the Continental Army in the War of the American Revolution.

The study of grammar may be of little value in itself. To be able to say "A sentence is a group of words containing a single, complete thought, or a group of closely related thoughts" is valueless in writing grammatically correct sentences unless the terms of the definition are understood, unless comprehension of the functions of parts of speech, of various kinds of sentences, gives meaning to that definition. To learn the parts of speech, to distinguish simple, complex, and compound sentences—such additions to our knowledge represent wasted effort until we see such knowledge operating on the sentences which we write or speak. We will then see why the study of grammar is of little value in itself, but we will see more than that—we will find ourselves writing sentences that are grammatically correct and will know *why* and *how* we do so.

To learn to phrase good sentences, basic units of thought, is a worthwhile achievement. It has been said that the simple declarative sentence is the greatest achievement of the human intellect.

SENTENCE INCOMPLETENESS

Henry David Thoreau once wrote: "A sentence should read as if its author, had he held a plough instead of a pen, could have drawn a furrow deep and straight to the end." In writing, it is all too easy to begin a sentence well enough but to waver, pause, go off the path, and fail to complete what has been started.

The word *sentence* can mean "a stated opinion." By this definition, all words, or groups of words, which "make sense" to your reader or listener can be called sentences. But remember these two requirements for a *complete* sentence: (1) It must have both a subject and a predicate (verb) which actually appear or are clearly implied (understood); and (2) it must not begin with a connecting word such as *although, as, because, before,* and *while* unless an independent clause follows immediately in the same construction.

This is a complete sentence: "Dick has bought a new jacket." Omit *Dick* (subject) or *has bought* (verb) and not enough remains to make a full sentence. Also, substituting for *has bought* a compound participle such as *having bought* produces an incomplete statement: "Dick having bought a new jacket." If a word such as *although* precedes *Dick*, the sentence is incomplete for another reason: The clause, "Although Dick has bought a new jacket," expresses an idea, but it depends on some other statement and is not capable of standing alone. If you don't like Dick, you might write: "Although Dick has bought a new jacket, he still looks like a jerk."

A Phrase Is Not a Sentence

A phrase is only part of a full sentence. It should be attached to, or should be expressed within, the sentence of which it is a part. Or the phrase should be made complete in itself by adding what is needed, usually a subject, or verb, or both.

> *Incorrect: Winter being mild last year.* I had to start mowing the lawn weeks earlier than usual.

> *Correct: Winter was mild last year*, and I had to start mowing the lawn weeks earlier than usual.

A Dependent Clause Is Not a Sentence

Adverbial and adjective clauses can never stand alone; they always *depend* upon something else for completeness. Correcting a dependent clause fragment often involves no change in wording; sometimes, changing a capital to a small letter and a period to a comma or to no mark at all will correct the error. Sometimes, you may prefer to make a dependent adverbial clause into an independent clause by omitting a subordinating conjunction and make an independent clause of an adjective clause by changing the relative pronoun to a personal one.

> *Incorrect:* I had no money for the trip. *When suddenly Jack paid me what he had borrowed.* (Adverbial)
> *Incorrect:* Sue lived in Akron for five years. *From which her family moved to Atlanta.* (Adjective)

> *Correct:* I had no money for the trip. Suddenly Jack paid me what he had borrowed.
> *Correct:* Sue lived in Akron for five years, from which her family moved to Atlanta.

Avoid Starting a Sentence with One Construction and Then Stopping or Shifting to Another

An unfinished or incomplete sentence results when a writer begins a statement and then shifts thought and construction, keeps adding words, yet stops before he or she has given meaning to the opening words. Or the writer may start with an independent clause but then add an unfinished statement which he or she forgets to coordinate with the first independent statement. In correcting such unfinished constructions, the writer should determine carefully what is missing and then supply it, in proper grammatical elements.

> *Incomplete:* An old woman in the apartment, who, because she had become progressively lame, was forced to use a cane and then to be confined to a wheelchair.
> *Improved:* An old woman in the apartment, who, because she had become progressively more lame, was forced to use a cane and then to be confined to a wheelchair, asked the landlord to install a telephone in her kitchen.

> *Incomplete:* I thought that preparing dinner for eight guests

would be a simple matter, but after deciding on a menu and shopping for the food, being very careful to stay within my budget, and then spending hours over a hot stove that burned the lima beans and three of my fingers.

Improved: I thought that preparing dinner for eight guests would be a simple matter, but after deciding on a menu and shopping for the food, being very careful to stay within my budget, and then spending hours over a hot stove that burned the lima beans and three of my fingers, I realized that a dinner party is a formidable undertaking.

Now you know that a major fault in sentence structure is incompleteness. And yet it should be noted that some statements convey a full thought without employing an actual or implied subject or verb. Such expressions as *Hello, Good-bye, Of course, But to continue,* and *Never again* make clear statements. Sentence fragments appear in stories, novels, and plays because they reflect normal conversation. But in writing sentences, remember that none is complete unless it fully and clearly transmits to your reader a complete thought or a closely knit group of thoughts.

THE COMMA SPLICE

Every sentence should end with a period, question mark, or exclamation point. But that is not the entire problem. You not only should make certain that sentences punctuated as sentences are complete, but that they appear one at a time.

When thoughts stray from or dart ahead of writing, you may find that, instead of setting down full sentences one at a time, you are joining, or splicing, with a comma statements that should be separated by a period or linked by a semicolon, a colon, or a conjunction *and* a comma. Such comma splices, considered faulty in both punctuation and in sentence construction, are serious flaws because the reader cannot determine where one sentence ends and the next one begins.

Comma splices, or "comma faults," occur in several forms:

1. Two statements which are not grammatically related but which are related by content.

2. Two related statements, the second of which begins
   with a personal pronoun whose antecedent is in the
   first.
3. Two related statements, the second of which begins
   with a demonstrative pronoun or adjective (*that, this,
   those, these, such*).
4. Two statements, the second of which contains, or begins
   with, a conjunctive adverb (*however, then,* and so on).

In order of the faults given above, consider these comma
splices:

A meeting of the committee is scheduled for tonight, many
   important items are on the agenda.
The physician examined the patient carefully, she did not say a
   word.
Drive carefully when you near the bridge, this is very narrow.
I was late for the lecture, however, Mr. James did not scold me.

The common splice error can be corrected in several ways:

1. Use a period after the first statement and a capital letter
   at the beginning of the second.
2. Use a semicolon between the statements.
3. Subordinate one of the statements and retain the
   comma.
4. Insert a conjunction between statements, or as a substitute for the conjunctive adverb, and retain the comma.

Each of the comma splices illustrated above can be corrected in
more than one of the four ways shown. For instance, the first
"sentence" may be revised as follows:

A meeting of the committee is scheduled for tonight. Many
   important items are on the agenda.
A meeting of the committee is scheduled for tonight; many
   important items are on the agenda.
A meeting of the committee has been scheduled for tonight,
   and many important items are on the agenda.

In rewriting "comma splice sentences," be careful to avoid a series of short, choppy sentences. Also, do not try to show a causal (cause and effect) relationship when in fact it does not really exist.

An occasional comma splice can be both suitable and stylistically valid. Many writers and professional editors carefully avoid all comma splices of whatever kind, but a case can be made for using a comma in such constructions as these:

I worked, I struggled, I failed.
That is Alice, this is Betty.
We are not going to the library, we are going to a movie.

THE FUSED SENTENCE

A fused sentence is one in which two independent and distinct statements are "blended." That is, separate statements are run together with no marks of punctuation between them. Consider these two sentences:

The Depression deepened its hold on American business thousands of men lost their jobs and breadlines became a common sight.
When he left the Army, Herbert took up horseracing this activity is often called the Sport of Kings.

Judged by grammatical standards, each of these "sentences" contains two independent and distinct statements that can be written separately. If the writer decides the two statements are sufficiently related in thought, he or she may choose to connect them more closely with punctuation which is not terminal.

The Depression deepened its hold on American business. Thousands of men lost their jobs and breadlines became a common sight.
When he left the Army, Herbert took up horseracing. This activity is often called the Sport of Kings.
When he left the Army, Herbert took up horseracing, often called the Sport of Kings.

In correcting a fused sentence, do not fall into the trap of the comma splice. Use of a comma may be a less grave error than using no punctuation at all, but that is debatable. Note this sentence:

We lived in Madison two years ago, our house was in the center of town.

Using a comma after *ago* is incorrect. One of the four methods by which a comma splice may be corrected should be applied to the correction of a fused sentence:

We lived in Madison two years ago. Our house was in the center of town.

We lived in Madison two years ago; our house was in the center of town.

We lived in Madison two years ago, and our house was in the center of town.

When we lived in Madison two years ago, our house was in the center of town.

WORDS IN ORDER

Some languages are highly inflected. That is, the endings of nouns, adjectives, adverbs, and verbs in such languages are varied, and it is easy to identify their relationships to each other and to other words in a sentence. The English language is not highly inflected. Words in an English sentence have meaning largely because of their position: They mean one thing in one position, another in another, and have little meaning at all in still another position. Many experts contend that the true basis of English grammar is word order.

Note how the meaning of "My *first* husband's job was in market research" changes when the position of *first* is shifted: "My husband's *first* job was in market research." "I was invited to a party *tonight*" has a meaning different from that of "I was *tonight* invited to a party."

Here are some rules to follow: (1) Related words should be kept together; (2) words should not be misplaced and allowed to dangle; (3) words that belong together should not be needlessly separated.

Misplaced Modifiers

A word that describes, limits, or "modifies" another word should be so placed that the relationship between the two is unmistakable. When a modifier is placed so that it could as readily modify the word or phrase preceding it as the word or phrase immediately following, it is said to "look two ways," or to be a "squinting" modifier. In the sentence "The boy who is delivering our newspaper *currently* needs a haircut," there is ambiguity: Is the boy who needs a haircut in current possession of the delivery chore, or is the official delivery boy in current tonsorial distress?

To clear up the confusion, you should revise. One way to do this is to add *certainly* after *currently.* In this way, you indicate that the adverb *currently* modifies *is delivering,* and the adverb *certainly* applies to *needs.* Another method is to move the modifier and include it with the material it modifies—transfer *currently* to a position between *who* and *is,* or (if such is the writer's intention) to a position following *haircut.* If the resulting sentence is still awkward, rewrite it.

Or consider this sentence: "The person who can do this *well* deserves praise." *Well* may modify either *can do* or *deserves.* You should revise. One way to clear up the confusion is to add *certainly* after *well.* Now the adverb *well* modifies *can do,* and the adverb *certainly* applies to *deserves.*

Take another example: "The repairman who does his work quietly *from the point of view of the housewife* is worthy of praise." The "squinting" italicized phrases should appear at the beginning or end of the sentence, which will still be wordy and awkward but at least understandable.

Words such as *only, even, hardly, not,* and *scarcely* require careful placing. They are associated with the word or phrase immediately following or immediately preceding. In the sentence "He *hardly* has enough money for the purchase," *hardly* may be thought to modify "has"; actually, it is probably intended to modify "enough." To remove any possible doubt, revise the sentence to read "He has *hardly* enough money for the purchase."

Here is a sentence containing eleven words: *Only the foreman*

told me to finish the job before noon. In it the word *only* can
appear in every position from one through eleven: The *only*
foreman told me . . . , the foreman *only* told me . . . , the foreman
told *only* me . . . , and so on. The position of *only* will provide
eleven somewhat different meanings for the sentence. (Note that
placing it in the sixth position causes a split infinitive, perhaps not
a very sound idea.)

The position of phrases and clauses can also provide confusion.
It is not likely that writers of the following expressed what they
meant to say:

Last month the Capitol was closed for alterations to all visitors.
(*To all visitors* should appear after *closed;* the resulting sentence
will be no gem, but at least confusion will disappear.)

The preacher discussed everyday affairs and people whom you
and I know *as simply as a little child.* (Place the italicized phrase
after *discussed* or at the beginning of the sentence.)

Dangling Modifiers

Any misplaced word, phrase, or clause dangles in the sense that it
hangs loosely within a sentence. The word another word or group
of words is intended to modify should never be taken for granted;
it should be expressed and it should be placed so that your readers
can easily make the intended association.

The term *dangling* applies especially to verbal phrases and
elliptical clauses, the correct position of which depends upon
logical, careful thinking.

Sentences containing dangling verbal phrases may be corrected
in three ways: (1) by expanding the verbal phrase to a dependent
clause; (2) by supplying the substantive (noun or pronoun) the
dangling phrase *should* modify; (3) by placing the construction so
near the supplied substantive that no confusion is possible.

Incorrect: Walking down the aisle, the curtain rose. (Participial
  phrase)
Incorrect: To play tennis well, a good racquet is needed. (Infinitive phrase)

Incorrect: By exercising every day, your health will improve. (Gerund phrase)

Correct: While we were walking down the aisle, the curtain rose.

Correct: Walking down the aisle, John saw the curtain rise.

Correct: We, walking down the aisle, saw the curtain rise. (This revision is no great improvement because it widely separates subject and verb.)

The two other incorrect sentences given may also be improved by one of the three methods suggested. Most of us don't mind making an error, but we do dislike being thought incoherent or ludicrous, both of which these sentences definitely are.

When a verbal phrase is used to denote a general action rather than a specific one, it is *not* considered a dangling modifier: "*Considering everything*, his suggestion was reasonable."

Dangling elliptical clauses create a related problem. *Ellipsis* means "an omission," "something left out." An elliptical clause is one without a subject, or verb, or both; it dangles unless the implied (understood) subject is the same as that of the main clause.

Incorrect: When 19 years old, my grandfather died.

Incorrect: While working last night, the lights went out.

Incorrect: Before thoroughly warmed up, you should not race a motor.

To correct such confused sentences, insert in the dangling clause the needed subject and verb, or change the subject (or subject and verb) in the main clause.

When I was 19 years old, my grandfather died.

When 19 years old, I grieved because my grandfather had died.

While I was working last night, the lights went out.

Before it is thoroughly warmed up, you should not race a motor.

You should thoroughly warm up a motor before you race it.

SPLIT CONSTRUCTIONS

Separating, or splitting, closely related parts of a sentence is not always incorrect. But splitting verbs in a verb phrase, the two parts of an infinitive, and a preposition and its object often results in awkwardness and lack of clarity. Whenever possible, keep logically related elements together.

Split Infinitive

When a word, phrase, or clause comes between the sign of the infinitive, *to*, and a verb, the construction is called a *split infinitive*. Reputable speakers and writers occasionally split an infinitive; consequently, this error is no longer considered as grave as it once was. Also, on rare occasions, you must split an infinitive to make clear and exact what you have in mind. For example, in this sentence, "Martha wants *to really see* Tod in person," moving *really* to any other place in the sentence would change the meaning or weaken the effectiveness of the sentence.

Normally, however, no sound reason exists for putting an adverb or phrase or other group of words between *to* and a verb. "He requested us to *as soon as possible* leave the building" would be clearer and more natural if the italicized words were moved to the end of the sentence.

Separating the Parts of a Verb Phrase

Splitting an auxiliary verb and a main verb is rarely effective or natural. Consider the following sentences:

The speaker *has*, although one would hardly believe it, *been* lecturing for over an hour.
This was the recording we *had* before we left Chicago *heard* so often in discotheques.
He *has*, to my great surprise, *sung* very well.

By bringing together the words in italics, the sentences become more clear and direct:

Although one would hardly believe it, the speaker *has been* lecturing for over an hour.

This was the recording we *had heard* so often in discotheques before we left Chicago.

To my great surprise, he *has sung* very well.

Subject and Verb, Preposition and Object

Separation of such elements is occasionally justifiable. But in awkward and generally ineffective sentences like the following, the italicized elements should be brought together:

Jack, as soon as he heard the question, *raised his hand*. (Subject and verb)

Mabel crept *into*, although she was terrified, *the frail canoe*. (Preposition and object)

Coordinate Elements

Two coordinate phrases or two coordinate dependent clauses should not be widely separated. Because of their approximately equal weight, they should be brought together and their relationship indicated by the appropriate coordinating conjunction:

Ineffective: Although he was conscientious on the job, he could not win a promotion, *although he performed many extra duties*.

Effective: Although he was conscientious on the job and *although he performed many extra duties*, he could not win a promotion.

Ineffective: Unless the blizzard lets up, we cannot make it to the mountain lodge, *unless the roads are passable*.

Effective: Unless the blizzard lets up, and *unless the roads are passable*, we cannot make it to the mountain lodge.

LOGICAL SENTENCES

Seeing to it that sentences are complete, properly punctuated, and with their words in order constitute three major steps toward better writing. Unfortunately, that is still not enough. Because we don't always think, or think carefully, we can and do construct sentences that violate common sense and logic.

You can expect your readers to give careful attention, but you should not expect them to untangle mixed and involved constructions or to correct your mistakes in thinking.

An illogical construction involves a grouping of words that (1) is contrary to reason, (2) violates some principle of regularity, (3) fails to make good sense, (4) omits an important word or words, (5) adds an element which has no grammatical function, (6) substitutes a dependent clause functioning as one part of speech for another.

These six kinds of mixed and illogical structures can be examined under several headings.

Omission of a Necessary Verb

In both speaking and writing, we often omit words without necessarily being illogical or unclear. "He always has worked hard and always will [work hard]" is understandable without the bracketed words. But it is doubtful that the following sentence could be considered complete: "The floor is swept and the dishes washed." In this sentence, *is* is understood to accompany *washed*. But *dishes is washed* is wrong. We should write: "The floor is swept and the dishes *are* washed."

"I never have and probably never will write good letters." (The word *written* should be added after *have*.)

Omission of Other Essential Words

If a necessary article, pronoun, conjunction, or preposition is omitted, your meaning will not be clear or, worse, may be misinterpreted.

"The Chairman and Chief Executive received us." (This sentence may mean that one person is both Chairman and Chief Executive. If you mean to indicate two people, add *the* after *and*.)

"I have interest and regard for your work." (Add *in* after *interest*.)

"She asked that question be repeated." (Add another *that* before *question*.)

Omission of Words in a Comparison

Doubtful: He is so wealthy.
Doubtful: Your report was the greatest success.
Doubtful: His feet are bigger than any boy in town.

Clearer: He is so wealthy that he never needs to think about money.
Clearer: Your report was the greatest success of any received thus far.
Clearer: His feet are bigger than those of any other boy in town.

Mixed or Double Comparison

A confused construction may occur when you try to include two comparisons in the same statement. Good usage permits a double comparison in the same sentence but only when the second appears after the first has been completed.

Illogical: The Battle of Stalingrad was *one of the greatest if not the greatest* single conflict of all time.

Preferable: The Battle of Stalingrad was *one of the greatest* single conflicts of all time, *if not the greatest*.

Confusing Blends

Certain blends may creep into anyone's writing. *Regardless* and *irrespective* are good words but are often faultily blended into *irregardless*. *In spite of* and *despite* may be illogically blended

into *despite of*: "*Despite of* what you say, I am not convinced."
Blending *where* (meaning *at* or *in which*) with *at which* results in
expressions such as "*Where* does she live *at?*" and "The town
where I live *in.*"

Double Negatives

Everyday speech is filled with expressions such as "haven't
scarcely" and "can't help but." These are forms of what is called
the *double negative*, two negative terms in the same statement.
The double negative was used repeatedly by Chaucer, Shakespeare, and many other great writers of the past. It still appears
regularly in correct French. Double negatives in English today,
however, are considered out of style and unacceptable.

You are not likely to write, or often hear, such expressions as "I
didn't see nobody" and "I didn't get none." You should avoid such
commonly used and less obviously illiterate expressions as "I did
not have but two," "one can't help but," "not scarcely enough,"
and "not hardly any."

Misuse of Dependent Clauses

Dependent clauses function as parts of speech; to substitute an
adverbial clause for a noun clause is as illogical as to use an adverb
in place of a noun.

> *Dubious:* Because she had *no new dress* was the reason Joy
>   stayed at home.
> *Dubious:* Eleanor noted *where the paper says* that it will snow
>   tonight.
> *Correct:* Joy stayed at home *because she had no new dress.*
> *Correct: That she had no new dress* was the reason Joy stayed at
>   home.
> *Correct:* Eleanor noted *that the paper says* it will snow tonight.

Using an adverbial clause in place of a noun or noun phrase is as
illogical as using it for a noun clause. *When, where,* and *because*
clauses are chief offenders in this form of illogicality:

Dubious: Stealing *is when* (*is where*) one takes the property of another without permission and with stealth.

Dubious: My high fever was *because* I was in a weak condition.

Clear: Stealing is taking the property of another without permission and with stealth.

Clear: Stealing is the act of taking the property . . .

Clear: My weak condition caused my high fever.

Clear: That I was in a weak condition was the cause . . .

A noun clause, not a complete sentence, should be the subject or object or complement of *is* and *was*. A quotation may be the subject or complement of *is* and *was:* " 'When I have fears that I may cease to be' is a line from Keats' famous poem." Ordinarily, however, you should convert a sentence into a noun clause (or, rarely, a noun phrase) in this construction.

Illogical: I had lost my nerve was the reason I did not try.

Illogical: Fred's only hope is he will get his paycheck today.

Improved: The reason that I did not try was that I had lost my nerve.

Improved: Fred's only hope is that he will get his paycheck today.

Improved: Fred has only one hope: getting his paycheck today.

CONSISTENT SENTENCE STRUCTURE

Consistency in a sentence means that its various parts are similar and in agreement and should remain so unless there is good reason for shifting them. This "rule" consists of avoiding shifts in tense, subject and voice, number, class or person of pronouns, figures of speech, and mood. Keeping all these elements consistent is not difficult but does require a little thought and care.

Be Consistent in Tense

Tense indicates the time of a verb (past, present, future). A careless writer is likely to shift from past to present time or from present to past or back and forth between the two. Consider this passage:

"Jill *was walking* briskly along the sidewalk when suddenly a Honda *turned* the corner. It *careens* wildly down the street, twisting as if its rider *is* unconscious. Jill *leaped* to one side."

The writer began with the past tense: *was walking* and *turned*. He then shifted to the present tense: *careens* and *is*. Finally, he reverted to the past tense: *leaped*. To be consistent (that is, avoid shifts in tense), *careens* should be *careened* and *is* should be *were* or *was*. Or, of course, the entire passage could be put into the present, in which case it would start with *is walking* and never shift to the past.

Be Consistent in Subject and Voice

Voice is a term in grammar which indicates whether the subject is acting (active) or being acted upon (passive). In general, the active voice is more effective than the passive; however, adhering to the use of either one removes a major cause of shifts in subject. Ordinarily, one should have a single subject in a sentence and should use only one voice.

Faulty: The diesel engine burns little kerosene, and Ed says it is completely reliable.

Faulty: As you sail across the harbor, channel markers can be seen.

Improved: Ed says that the diesel engine burns little kerosene and is completely reliable.

Improved: As you sail across the harbor, you can see channel markers.

Be Consistent in the Use of Number

Frequent mistakes in the use of number are careless switchings from plural nouns to singular nouns, or singular to plural, or failing to make pronouns agree in number with their antecedents.

Faulty: I enjoyed an ice cream soda, but *they* tend to make me fat.

Faulty: If men really try their best, *he* is bound to succeed.

Faulty: If boys treated Grandmother with respect, she would surely respect *him.*

Improved: I enjoy an ice cream soda, but *it* tends to make me fat.

Improved: If men really try their best, *they are* bound to succeed.

Improved: If boys treated Grandmother with respect, she would surely respect *them.*

Avoid Shifting the Class or Person of Pronouns

A shift in pronoun reference violates the rule that pronouns and antecedents must agree in person. The most common occurrence of this fault is shifting from the third person to the second.

"If *one* tries hard enough, *you* will usually succeed." (*One* is an indefinite pronoun in the third person; *you* is a personal pronoun in the second person. The sentence should read: "If *you* try hard enough, *you* . . ." or "If *one* tries hard enough, *he.* . . ."

Be Consistent in Using Figures of Speech

Figures of speech—that is, words used not in their literal sense but for the images they suggest—are occasionally effective and vivid. However, guard against sudden switches from literal to figurative speech and switches from one figure to another:

"That foreman is a cold fish who always has an axe to grind."

Before we pass judgment on the foreman, we must answer a question: What use has a fish for an axe? This is a clearer statement:

"That disdainful foreman always has a selfish motive."

Be Consistent in the Use of Mood

Mood (sometimes spelled *mode*) is a grammatical term indicating the style or fashion of a verb. Mood suggests the state of mind or the manner in which a statement is made: a fact, a request, a command, a probability, a condition. English has three moods:

indicative (He *has come* to see us); *imperative* (*Come* here at once); and *subjunctive* (Suppose he *were* to come).

Do not needlessly shift from indicative to imperative or subjunctive or mix their use. The sentence "Last spring I *would play* tennis every morning and *swam* every afternoon" should read "Last spring I *would play* tennis every morning and *would swim* every afternoon," or "Last spring I *played* tennis every morning and *swam* every afternoon."

UNIFIED SENTENCES

Unity means "oneness," "singleness of purpose," "being united or combined as one." In writing, unity implies that every sentence should contain a single thought or a group of closely related thoughts. Making sentences unified is an aid in keeping the writer settled on the track and the reader focused on what is being conveyed.

Unity has little to do with length; a long sentence may be unified and a short one not. This long sentence forms a unit of thought: "Although Lee liked her fellow employees, especially Mary Ellen and Harvey, she was tired of working and decided to resign and marry Henry." But this short sentence lacks unity: "Mary Ellen was a good worker, and she had a friend named Henry."

Sentence unity is violated in two principal ways: (1) putting too many details into one sentence and (2) placing unrelated ideas together.

Rambling Sentences with Too Many Details

Here are two rambling sentences containing excessive detail. Each has been rewritten to indicate how such sentences can be made more unified:

Faulty: He was reared in Southport, a village in Connecticut, which has only about 1,000 inhabitants, but which has a famous yacht club, three churches, an excellent public library, several tree-lined residential streets, and a good motel, being located just off U.S. Highway 95.

Faulty: As I grew older, my desire to play basketball grew also, and when I entered high school I was too small to play my first two years of school, being only five feet tall, so I had to sit on the bench, but later in high school I began to grow, and before I graduated my senior year I was playing center on the first team, for I had grown 13 inches in two years.

Improved: He was reared in Southport, Connecticut, a village of about 1,000 inhabitants which is located just off U.S. Highway 95. Southport has several tree-lined residential streets, an excellent public library, a motel, three churches, and a famous yacht club.

Improved: Although my interest in basketball had grown with the years, I discovered upon entering high school that my physical growth had not kept pace with my desire to play. For two years, my five-foot frame occupied the bench. That before I graduated I was playing center on the first team I contend is due to a genuine, if familiar, surprise: in the years between I had grown 13 inches.

Unrelated Ideas in the Same Sentence

You can achieve unity in a sentence containing unrelated ideas by showing some evidence of relationship or by subordinating one idea. If the ideas are not closely related and relationship cannot logically be indicated, place them in separate sentences. If no relationship is evident, omit one of the ideas.

Faulty: His brother was a tall man, and he was a good fisherman.

Improved: His brother, a tall man who loved the sea, was a good fisherman.

Improved: His brother was a tall man. He was also a good fisherman.

CONCISE SENTENCES

Nearly everyone uses more words than necessary. This overuse is especially noticeable in conversation, but many written sentences are guilty of the same fault. Careful attention to sentence structure will usually result in a wholesale removal of words that add little or nothing to meaning or effectiveness. Much of the most memorable writing the world has ever known is short, sharp, and word-hungry.

Wordy Phrases and Expressions

It is a sound rule never to use two words where one will do or twenty words where ten will serve. A speaker was once asked whether certain rules should be observed. He could have said "Yes." Instead he replied: "The implementation of sanctions will inevitably eventuate in repercussions." A recent governmental pamphlet contained this monstrous sentence: "Endemic insect populations cause little-realized amounts of damage to forage and timber." What did the writer mean? Probably "Native insects harm trees and grass more than we realize."

Such writing is of course gobbledygook: inflated, pompous, and wordy. You may never be guilty of writing such highflown sentences as these, but it is likely that your work does contain numerous wordy expressions. Study the following list and check your own sentences to see how many of them appear:

REDUCE THESE	TO THESE
advance planning	planning
after the conclusion of	after
as a result of	because
at this point in time	now
by means of	by
by the time	when
come in contact with	meet
due to the fact that	since (due to)
during the time that	while

REDUCE THESE	TO THESE
get in touch with	telephone (write, meet)
hurry up	hurry
in accordance with	by
inasmuch as	since
in case	if
in connection with	with
in order to	to
in regard to	about
in the event that	if
in the month of April	in April
in this day and age	today
in view of the fact that	since
it has come to our attention that	(begin with the word following *that*)
it is interesting to note that	(begin with the word following *that*)
I would appreciate it if	please
of great importance	important
on condition that	if
provided that	if
under date of May 5	of May 5
with the exception of	except

The foregoing list is only a sampling of hundreds of wordy expressions that could be named. Comb sentences carefully to see what can be eliminated without real loss. For example, you will find that "there is" and "there are" sentences are customarily wordy: "In this building there are five elevators that await inspection" can do quite well without "there are" and "that." Cutting out unnecessary words can become an interesting game, a game that will increase the effectiveness of your writing.

As a further aid in detecting wordiness, study this additional list of wordy expressions:

absolutely essential	entirely eliminated
around about that time	few (many) in number
audible to the ear	final end (outcome)

backup
call up on the phone
choose up
Christmas Eve evening
combine together
complete monopoly
completely unanimous
connect up with
consensus of opinion
cooperate together
cover over
each and everyone
endorse on the back
most unique
most unkindest
necessary need
personal friend
recur again
reduce down
repeat again
resume again
return back

first beginnings
four-cornered square
from whence
important essentials
individual person
join together
long length
loquacious talker
many in number
more better
more older
more perfect
more perpendicular
revert back to
rise up
separate out
(a) short half-hour
small in size
talented genius
this afternoon at 4 P.M.
this morning at 8 A.M.

Reducing Predication

Reducing predication means decreasing the number of words used to make a statement. Consider these suggestions:

1. Combine two short sentences into one.

    From: He was a mechanic in a repair shop. He specialized in carburetor adjustment.

    To: He was a garage mechanic, specializing in carburetor adjustment.

2. Reduce a compound sentence to a complete or simple sentence.

    From: Sarah Bernhardt was for many years an excellent actress, and everyone admired her talent.

To: Everyone admired the talent of Sarah Bernhardt, who
               was for many years an excellent actress. *or*

To: Everyone admired the talent of Sarah Bernhardt, for
               years an excellent actress.

3. Reduce a clause to a phrase.

From: a haze that resembled the color of smoke
To: a haze the color of smoke

4. Reduce a phrase to a single word.

From: a haze the color of smoke
To: a smoke-colored haze

5. Reduce two or more words to one.

From: a foreman in the department of shipping
To: a shipping foreman

Unnecessary Details

Using unnecessary details is known as *prolixity.* A prolix sentence
obscures or weakens the main idea.

Wordy: Last winter the squash tournament was won by Barry
   Stebbins with a racquet he had purchased two months before
   from a friend of his who had bought a new one made of catgut
   and who sold Barry his old one for $8.50.
Improved: Last winter the squash tournament was won by
   Barry Stebbins with a racquet he had bought from a friend
   for $8.50.
Still better: Last winter Barry Stebbins won the squash tournament with a second-hand racquet.

Useless Repetition

The needless repetition of an idea without providing additional
force or clearness is called *tautology.* This flaw is obvious in the
following sentence: "This entirely new and novel innovation in
our program will delight our TV viewing audience; it has just

been introduced for the first time and will cause pleasure to many people who will be watching."

> *Faulty:* Peggy was anxious for Jack to succeed and eager that he do so.
>
> *Faulty:* In all necessary essentials the work is completed and finished.

> *Improved:* Peggy was eager for Jack to succeed.
>
> *Improved:* In all essentials the work is completed.

Brevity has been called the "soul of wit." It is more than that: it is an indispensable aid in writing effective sentences. Using no unnecessary words is hardly an attainable goal, but eliminating most useless, space-consuming, time-wasting words and expressions constitutes a major step toward better writing.

EXERCISES IN CORRECT SENTENCE STRUCTURE

Sentence Recognition

In each of the numbered passages below, printed here without internal punctuation, you are to count the sentences. Some of the passages are incomplete (sentence fragments). Use a capital letter to indicate that the passage contains: *A*—one sentence; *B*—two sentences; *C*—three sentences; *D*—four sentences; *E*—no sentence (a sentence fragment).

1. Ever since primitive man decided it was easier to raise his own meat than to go out and hunt wild game there have been herdsmen and farmers who have had to build fences which moreover had to be maintained.
2. Fence building and fence repairing whether they concern stone walls living thorn hedges rail fences barbed wire or electric barriers to be installed and kept in good condition.
3. About the time young Abraham Lincoln was splitting oak and walnut logs into rails for "worm" fences middle western farmers began to hear of a small thorny

tree native to the Arkansas River region that could be grown in dense hedges to enclose horses cattle sheep and hogs because the Osage (Wazhazhe or "war people") Indians inhabited that region it was called the Osage Orange.

4. The Osage Orange is a medium-sized tree occasionally it reaches 50 feet in height and two feet in diameter it has glossy simple leaves they are about twice as long as broad.

5. The twigs armed with many straight stout sharp thorns about three-quarters of an inch long and orange-brown in color.

6. The large wrinkled orange-like green fruit four or five inches in diameter as well as the leaves and twigs contain a milky juice that is quite bitter commonly known as "hedge apples" these heavy and hard fruits are used by boys as missiles for mimic warfare and other purposes they are not edible.

7. The only tree of its kind in the world although it is distantly related to mulberries and figs and silkworms feed as readily on its leaves as on those of the mulberry.

8. Some of these trees have yellowish male flowers which bear pollen that is carried by bees to other trees with greenish female flower heads the ones which produce the "oranges."

9. Growing well on many kinds of soil throughout most of the United States sprouts from roots or shoots grown from seed or cuttings in nurseries are planted in one or two rows several inches apart where a hedge fence is wanted once or twice a year these are trimmed to form a dense hedge about four feet high and two feet wide the "whips" or sprouts being sometimes planted at an angle to create an interwoven lattice-like fence.

10. If farmers neglect the trimming the hedges grow rapidly to become havens for birds and other wildlife the trees so produced however are valuable as posts for wire fences because Osage Orange is more durable in

the soil than any other wood many such fences having lasted more than 50 years without a single rotten post since they occupy and shade too much valuable cropland most such overgrown hedges have been removed in recent years.

Fragments, Comma Splices, Fused Sentences

In each pair of sentences, one is faulty. Faulty sentences are of three kinds: (1) sentence fragments, (2) comma splices, (3) fused sentences. Find the faulty sentences in the numbered items and on a separate sheet rewrite each in an acceptable form. Then indicate the nature of your revisions by a capital letter to show that the item contains: *A*—a sentence fragment that could be best corrected by changing the form of one word (changing a participle to a finite verb, for example); *B*—a sentence fragment that could be best corrected by joining it to the preceding or following sentence (with appropriate changes in punctuation and capitalization); *C*—a sentence fragment that could be best corrected by rewriting (to make its structure complete); *D*—a comma splice (to be corrected by changing the punctuation or by inserting a connective word); *E*—a fused sentence (to be corrected by inserting appropriate punctuation or by inserting a connective word).

1. I was wrong in thinking the ice was thick enough to skate on, it was not. Fortunately the water was not very deep, and I scrambled ashore without much trouble.
2. Insurance statistics prove that women drive more safely than men. However, it will take more than statistics to convince me, in fact I just don't believe it.
3. It turns out you were right I forgot to return the book to the library. But I seldom make such mistakes, and I can't imagine how it happened.
4. The natives had a kind of lie-detector test, in which the suspected culprit was required to chew dry rice. The theory being that a bad conscience prevents or slows the flow of saliva.

5. An electric dryer is cheaper to buy than a gas dryer, however, it is more expensive to operate. So the salesman told me, at any rate.

6. Contrary to common belief, a bent stick always breaks first on the inside of the curve, not the outside. Because the tensile strength of wood is much greater than its compressive strength.

7. The use of silver rather than paper dollars was until recently common in the western states, especially for games of chance. "Iron dollars," as the old-timers called them.

8. People tend to hum or whistle tunes that were popular when they were about 20 years old. And are seldom conscious of doing so.

9. Ben and Sam often quarreled violently then they would make up and act as if nothing had happened. After I got to know them I decided that they were just putting on a show, the customers having no suspicion of their intention.

10. A very interesting speech, whatever you may think of the opinions expressed. But most of the audience, I believe, came away unconvinced.

Word Order and Dangling Elements

Each of the numbered sentences below is faulty, either in the order of words or in the way in which modifiers are attached to the remainder of the sentence. Find the faulty sentences and on a separate sheet rewrite each in acceptable form. Then, for each item, write a capital letter to show that the sentence contains: A—a word or phrase so placed as to give the sentence two or more meanings; B—separated parallel elements giving the sentence an awkward effect; C—a split construction: the separation of words that come together in normal speech patterns; D—a dangling modifier, although the thing modified is named in the sentence; E—an elliptical dangling modifier: the thing modified is not named in the sentence.

1. I, after only a couple of days in Paris, was delighted to find my French coming back with a rush, although some of the slang baffled me, of course.
2. Fish are easy to catch in these waters when using the right bait.
3. After the first week, Professor White almost knows every student in his class.
4. Traveling by air all the way, the trip around the world was completed by Mallard in only eight days.
5. Although not trusting by nature, I gave Vic the loan because he seemed to be in dire want, although I didn't know him very well.
6. The woods were at last left behind, and, looking westward, an unbroken expanse of prairie sloped down to the river.
7. If I'm not imposing on your time, I'd like to take a look at the old Hackett house this afternoon, if you're willing to go with me.
8. I took hold of the sharp-finned fish that was struggling on the line with my bare hands.
9. We were stuck in the expressway jam for half an hour, and, while fuming helplessly in the line of cars, the airplane took off without us.
10. To play your best game, you have only to firmly keep in mind that your opponent is just as nervous as you are.

Parallelism and Word Order

Most of the numbered sentences below contain faults. Some sentences are acceptably constructed. For each sentence, write a capital letter to indicate that in order to make the sentence acceptable, you would have to: A—insert a necessary word or words; B—take out a superfluous word or words; C—change the form of one or more verbs or verbals; D—change the order of the words; E—do nothing: the sentence is acceptable as it stands. If so instructed, rewrite each faulty sentence on a separate sheet.

1. The problem these days is found not so much in choosing a college as gaining admittance to the college chosen.

2. Fired up by the hope that Father would be vastly impressed (and perhaps disposed to reward me accordingly), I swept the basement, cleaned out the garage, and then I carried all the trash to the alley.

3. In the debate on Latin American policy, he said that either we must gamble on supporting the non-Communist Left or reconcile ourselves to alliances with military dictatorships.

4. Working on my stamp collection is in my opinion much more interesting than to watch television.

5. The most reliable sources of humor, as every jokesmith knows, are surprise at incongruity, the release of forbidden impulses (such as cruelty), and irreverence toward custom or authority.

6. Expressways not only cost far more than improved public transportation but often create more problems than they solve.

7. The referee tossed the coin, acted out the usual choices of the opposing field captains, and the all-important game was under way.

8. It is well to invest in a variety of enterprises rather than putting all your eggs in one basket.

9. Either one has to be 65 or blind in order to claim an extra personal exemption.

10. In navigation, finding your latitude is vastly easier than to determine your longitude, which depends upon knowing exactly what time it is somewhere else.

Coordination and Subordination

Rewrite in *three* sentences these *seven* sentences:

1. A patient swallowed a pill.
2. It contained only a little milk sugar.
3. He had been told it was a powerful drug.

4. Within ten minutes he was suffering severe reactions.
5. His lips swelled.
6. His skin broke out.
7. Other patients also displayed physical reactions after taking the same pill.

Illogical Constructions

Each numbered sentence below may contain one of the following faults: (1) an illogical construction (a faulty sentence plan or two sentence plans blended together); (2) an undesirable shift in person, number, tense, or voice; (3) a pronoun to which the reference is vague or missing. Some sentences are acceptable as they stand. For each sentence, write a capital letter to indicate that in order to correct the sentence you would: A—insert a necessary word or take out a superfluous word; B—change the wording to effect consistency (correct an undesirable shift in point of view); C—rework the sentence to make the reference of a pronoun clear or correct; D—change the basic plan of the sentence so that its parts are logically united; E—do nothing: the sentence is acceptable as it stands. If so instructed, rewrite each faulty sentence on a separate sheet.

1. Just as Martin thought he had paid off his month's debts, they sent him another bill.
2. My chief criticisms of your story are that it has too little narrative interest and too many lush descriptions.
3. The subject which you are best in, you are likely to spend the most time on it.
4. When I serve my time in the Army, I hope they send me to Hawaii.
5. This is probably the only large city which you can pass between extremes of wealth and poverty by walking only a block or row.
6. We were much put out to discover that the boys had got into the refrigerator and drank almost all the Cokes before the party started.

7. In this editorial it says that the first principle of foreign policy is to refrain from doing what is clearly wrong.

8. One of the chief causes of rigidity in international relations is that every government becomes the prisoner of its own propaganda.

9. The tourist can now cross the Straits in a few minutes by bridge, whereas they often used to wait hours for a ferry.

10. The winter I won both the skating and skiing trophies was my greatest athletic achievement.

Conciseness

Most of the sentences below contain deadwood of one kind or another that should be cut out or trimmed. Some sentences are already about as concise as they can be made. On a separate sheet, rewrite each wordy sentence in acceptable form. Then write a capital letter to indicate that you have made the sentence more concise by: *A*—taking out something that repeats an idea already expressed; *B*—taking out a qualifying tag that adds no real information or interest; *C*—reducing a predication to a phrase or word; *D*—doing nothing: the sentence is already concise.

1. The information that has been put together in this report should be immediately given to the sales department.

2. In this modern world of today, we are subject to many pressures unknown to our ancestors.

3. To me, this magazine contains an excess of advertising over other printed matter.

4. The most widespread and long-continuing use of competitive civil-service examinations occurred in the old Chinese Empire.

5. In the early sixties, intercollegiate athletics became not much more than an appendage, so to speak, of commercial television.

6. It was obvious to everyone that Violet resembled her maternal grandmother on her mother's side.

7. One of the reasons it took Odysseus many years to get home was that ships were then so rigged that they could sail only with a favoring wind.

8. Frankly, if I were in the situation that you are in, I would give the boss a piece of my mind and let him do whatever he liked about it.

9. Dixon turned out to be an abominable cook, and by the end of the week we had more or less decided to take turns at the job and give him something else to do.

10. The Schmidt camera, which combines the reflective and refractive principles and which was invented only a few years ago, is the first basic innovation in telescope design since the eighteenth century.

ANSWERS TO EXERCISES

Sentence Recognition

1. A	3. B	5. E	7. E	9. B
2. E	4. D	6. C	8. A	10. C

Fragments, Comma Splices, Fused Sentences

1. D	3. E	5. D	7. C	9. E
2. D	4. A	6. B	8. B	10. C

Word Order and Dangling Elements

1. C	3. A	5. B	7. B	9. D
2. E	4. D	6. E	8. A	10. C

Parallelism and Word Order

1. A	3. D	5. E	7. A	9. D
2. B	4. C	6. E	8. C	10. C

Coordination and Subordination

A patient swallowed a pill that contained only a little mild sugar. He had been told that it was a powerful drug, and within ten minutes he was suffering severe reactions: his lips swelled and his skin broke out. Other patients also displayed physical reactions after taking the same pill.

Illogical Constructions

1. *C*	3. *D*	5. *A*	7. *C*	9. *B*
2. *E*	4. *C*	6. *B*	8. *E*	10. *D*

Conciseness

1. *C*	3. *B*	5. *B*	7. *D*	9. *B*
2. *A*	4. *D*	6. *A*	8. *C*	10. *C*

8

GUIDE TO CORRECT
PUNCTUATION AND
MECHANICS

Correct, clear, effective writing is impossible without proper punctuation. Our thoughts—and the relationships of our thoughts—are dependent upon punctuation for their clear transmission to readers. Actually, punctuation originally developed because, without it, written language was unable to indicate or reproduce certain definite and clear qualities of speech. We can always tell, for example, from a person's voice whether he or she is making a statement or asking a question. But in writing we would not know which sentence made a statement and which asked a question unless we saw a period at the end of one and a question mark terminating the other. We also know that a pause, or a rising inflection, means something in speech.

These and other meanings and qualities in speech are reproduced in writing by certain marks of punctuation. In addition, since English is not a highly inflected language, the essential meaning of a sentence and the relationships of its parts are revealed primarily by word order. But word order is flexible, and punctuation is required to show or to suggest the grouping of words and phrases in a sentence which conveys meaning.

Punctuation is an integral (or organic) part of writing. You cannot indiscriminately sprinkle your writing with punctuation marks and expect it to be fully understood. To be sure, punctuation usage varies with individual writers, but certain basic principles remain steadfast. These principles may be called "descriptive rules," since they have been formulated from hundreds and thousands of examples of punctuation as applied by reputable authors and, much more importantly, by professional editors and type compositors. When we have enough examples of one use of a certain mark of punctuation, we state this as a general principle or rule, beginning it thus: "Use the . . ." or "*Always* use the. . . ." When most of our examples agree: "The mark is *usually* used . . ."; when examples are insufficient to make a generalization: "The mark is *occasionally* used. . . ." Correct punctuation permits individuality only to the extent that communication of thought from writer to reader is aided, not impeded.

What is usually considered correct punctuation is about as fixed in usage as is correct spelling, and for a similar reason. Our punctuation usage is based upon the practice of editors and compositors who normally follow one or more of a group of standardized books of rules; spelling practices, too, are made rigid by the same professional groups relying upon standard guidebooks and dictionaries.

The most important marks of punctuation are these:

.	Period	,	Comma
?	Question mark	;	Semicolon
!	Exclamation point	:	Colon
—	Dash	" "	Double quotation marks
-	Hyphen	' '	Single quotation marks
'	Apostrophe	( )	Parentheses

The use, misuse, and overuse of each of these marks are discussed in the pages that follow. In addition, other items involving punctuation and the mechanics of writing are also discussed: *italics, capital letters, brackets, abbreviations,* and *numbers.*

END STOPS

An *end stop* is a mark of punctuation used at the end of a sentence. Sometimes also referred to as *terminal marks,* end stops are a period, question mark, or exclamation point. More than 95 percent of all sentences end with a period, regardless of where they appear or who writes them. But the other two end stops have special, limited uses.

1. Use a period at the end of a declarative sentence:
   His trip began with a ticket for speeding.
   Dick prefers winter to summer weather.

2. Use a period after most abbreviations:

   Mr. and Mrs. Richard Soule
   Mary E. Bisacca, M.D. (b. 1905, d. 1960)
   Oct. 15; Ariz.; bbl.; Ave.; St.; P.M.

3. Use three spaced periods to indicate an intentional omission. Such periods, called *ellipses* or *ellipsis periods* or the *ellipsis mark,* indicate an omission of one or more words within a sentence or quotation. If the omission ends with a period, use four spaced periods:

   Some books are to be tasted, others . . . swallowed, and some few . . . chewed and digested.
   The day wore on from sunrise to late afternoon. . . .

4. Use a period before a decimal, to separate dollars and cents, and to precede cents written alone:

   5.26 percent $4.38 $0.65

5. Use the exclamation point to end a forceful interjection or to indicate surprise or vigorous emotion:

   So you have really decided to go!
   What an incredibly rude remark!
   May I ask you—please!—to help me now.

6. Use a question mark at the end of every direct question:

   Does Ninki really love Henry?
   You said—did I understand you?—that you were ill.
   Pat asked, "May I go with you today?"

7. Use question marks to indicate a series of queries in the same sentence or passage:

> Are you going? Is your sister? John? Mimi?
> Do you remember when car windshields opened to let in the breeze? When men wore garters? When grandmothers were elderly?

Distinguish the Purposes of End Stops

1. Use a period, not an exclamation point, after a mildly imperative sentence:

> "Take your time and work carefully."

2. Use a period, not a question mark, after an indirect question:

> "Please tell me what he said and how he said it."

3. Use a period, not a question mark, after a polite request or only superficially interrogative sentence:

> "May I have your hat" is an expression more often prompted by courtesy than by curiosity.

Do Not Overuse End Stops

1. Do not use a period at the end of a title.
2. Do not use the period to punctuate sentence fragments.
3. Avoid using a question mark enclosed in parentheses to indicate doubt, uncertainty, or a humorous meaning.
4. Use the exclamation point sparingly. The emotion, surprise, or command expressed should be strong to warrant the exclamation point. Writing dotted with exclamation points is a form of immaturity. Also, an exclamation point after a long sentence looks silly; most of us don't have sufficient breath to exclaim more than a few words at a time.

THE SEMICOLON

The semicolon is entirely a mark of separation, or division; that is, it is never used to introduce, enclose, or terminate a statement. It is a stronger mark than the comma, signifying a greater break or longer pause between sentence elements. But it is weaker than the period and other terminal marks (question mark, exclamation point) and cannot be used to end a sentence. Its use indicates that two or more statements are not sufficiently related to require commas, but are too closely related to justify being put in separate sentences separated by a terminal mark.

1. Use the semicolon to separate independent clauses not joined by a simple conjunction:

> Laughter is not at all a bad beginning for a friendship; it is far the best ending for one. (Oscar Wilde)
> Life is very short and very uncertain; let us spend it as well as we can. (James Boswell)
> A little neglect may breed mischief: for want of a nail the shoe was lost; for want of a shoe the horse was lost; for want of a horse the rider was lost. (Benjamin Franklin)

2. Use the semicolon to separate independent clauses joined by a conjunctive adverb.

Conjunctive adverbs, special kinds of adverbs which can also be used as conjunctions, include *also, anyhow, as a result, besides, consequently, for example, furthermore, hence, however, in addition, indeed, in fact, instead, likewise, meanwhile, moreover, namely, nevertheless, otherwise, similarly, still, then, therefore, thus.*

> We regret that we have sold all of the shirts in blue; *however,* we have the same style in white.
> Dorothy's brother is a busy boy; *in fact,* he works harder than she does.
> She ran a high fever for three days; *then* she admitted defeat and let her brother summon a doctor.

He expected a reward for his diligent efforts on behalf of the party; *instead,* he was punished.

3.   Use the semicolon between independent clauses which are lengthy or contain internal punctuation:

Many paperback books, especially the cheapest ones, are so hastily and economically thrown together that they soon rip apart; however, with proper care, such as we should give all books, even the cheapest ones can be preserved for a time.

Success, so some maintain, requires intelligence, industry, and honesty; but others, somewhat fewer in number, insist that only personality and contacts really count.

4. Use the semicolon to separate phrases and clauses of considerable length and also series of words in which complete clarity is desired:

The ones chosen to represent the office were Lisa Black, president of the debating society; Jack Smoak, varsity baseball captain; and Gene Toale, active in dramatics.

Do Not Overuse the Semicolon

The semicolon has its special uses and should be employed only in the situations described in preceding sections. Like other marks, it should not be inserted aimlessly nor should it be overused. Especially avoid using semicolons in the following ways:

1. To set off phrases or independent clauses unless for specific situations mentioned above. The semicolon really has the same function as a period: It indicates a complete break and marks the ending of one thought and the beginning of another. A fairly safe rule: no period, no semicolon.

Phrases and dependent clauses cannot be set off by periods and thus cannot be marked by semicolons.

Faulty: Since Mary wants to go with us; we must revise our plans. (The opening dependent clause should be followed by a comma, not a semicolon.)
Being aware of the high cost of living; I am sympathetic to your predicament. (The opening participial phrase requires a comma at the end, not a semicolon.)

2. To introduce statements or lists. The semicolon is not a mark of introduction, such as are, for example, the colon, dash, and comma, and should never be used for this purpose.

Faulty: His goal is simple and direct; to make the team.
Here is what you need; health, money, and ambition.
Dear Sir; Dear Mrs. Woods; Gentlemen;

Substitute a colon for each semicolon above; however, a dash *could* be used in the first and second illustrations, and a comma could appear in the third group of illustrations.

3. To indicate a summary.

Faulty: Sweeping, dusting, mopping; these were my household chores. (Use a colon or dash, not a semicolon.)

THE COLON

The colon is a mark of expectation or addition. Its primary function is to signal the reader to "watch for what's coming." That is, it signals to the reader that the next group of words will fulfill what the last group promised. What does come after the colon is usually explanatory or illustrative material which has been prepared for by a word, or words, preceding the colon.

Major uses of the colon are to introduce lists, enumerations, tabulations; to introduce a word, phrase, or even a to-be-emphasized clause; to precede an example or clarification of an idea suggested before the colon; to introduce a restatement of a preceding phrase or clause; to introduce a formal quotation; to spell out details of a generalization.

1. Use the colon to introduce a word, phrase, or clause, or after an introductory statement which shows that something is to follow.

> Only one other possibility remains: to travel by bus.
> This is my problem: where do I go from here?
> Do this before you leave: buy traveler's checks, check your passport, have your smallpox vaccination.
> There are three lovely little girls in that family: Jocelyn, Virginia, and Helen.

2. Use the colon to separate introductory words from a long or formal quotation which follows.

> Deems Taylor concluded his article on Richard Wagner with these words: "The miracle is that what he did in the little space of seventy years could have been done at all, even by a great genius. Is it any wonder that he had no time to be a man?"

The Colon as a Separating Mark in Special Situations

1. In business letters, the salutation is separated from the body of the letter by a colon: Dear Mr. Clark:; Dear Sir:; Gentlemen:; My dear Mr. Swan:.

It is customary to place a comma after the salutation of a friendly or personal letter (Dear Ginny,), but the colon is not so formal a mark as to repulse friendship. Use either a comma or a colon after the salutation in such letters.

2. Titles and subtitles of books may be separated by a colon: *Education for College: Improving the High School Curriculum; The English Novel: A Panorama.*

3. Hour and minute figures in writing time may be separated by a colon: 8:17 P.M.; 3:26 A.M.

4. Acts and scenes of plays may be separated by a colon: Shakespeare's *Twelfth Night*, II:v.

5. Chapters and verses of the Bible may be separated by a colon: John 3:16.

6. Volume and page reference may be separated by a colon: *The History of the English Novel*, V:83.

7. A publisher's location and name may be separated by a colon: *New York: HarperCollins.*

8. In stating proportions, both a single colon and double colon may be used: 2:4::4:8 (two is to four as four . . .).

Do Not Overuse the Colon

The colon is a useful mark adding clarity to writing, but it should be employed to accomplish only the purposes mentioned. Used in other constructions, the colon becomes both obstructive and intrusive.

1. Do not place a colon between a preposition and its object: I am fond of: *New York, Washington,* and *Miami.* (There is no need for the colon or any other mark of punctuation after *of.*)

2. Do not place a colon between a verb and its object or object complement:
   He liked to see: *TV plays, movies,* and *baseball games.* (Use no mark of punctuation after *see.*)
   She liked a number of activities, such as: *dancing, cooking,* and *swimming.* (Use no mark of any kind after *such as.*)

THE DASH

The dash is an emphatic mark of punctuation most often used to indicate a sudden interruption in thought, a sharp break, or a shift in thought. It has been called "the interruption, the mark of abruptness, the sob, the stammer, and the mark of ignorance." This colorful definition implies that the dash is a vigorous mark which has emotional qualities and which may be misused.

Some other mark of punctuation can always be substituted for a dash. It does have functions roughly equivalent to those of a comma and, moreover, resembles a terminal mark of punctuation (period, exclamation point, question mark) in certain situations. However, a dash lends a certain air of surprise or emotional tone on occasion and, if used sparingly, is a device for adding movement, or a sense of movement, to writing. But it is rightly called a "mark of ignorance," since some writers use it indiscriminately and far too often.

1. Use a dash to introduce a word or group of words you wish to emphasize:

   There is only one other possibility—to leave at once.
   There is only one thing he needs for his complete happiness—love.

   A colon also could be used in such constructions as these; the dash adds emphasis, vigor, and a tonal quality of emotion.

2. Use the dash to indicate a break or shift in thought:

   I think—no, I am positive—that you should stay.
   Here is a fuller explanation—but perhaps your students will not be interested.
   She is the most despicable—but I should not say more.

   Breaks or shifts in thought and the use of dashes to indicate them should both be rare.

3. Use a dash to indicate omission of letters and words and to connect combinations of letters and figures:

May–August (May to or through August)
He lived in that city 1988–1991.
Joe Pear is a pilot on the New York–Chicago run.
The First World War, 1914–1918, was fought to end all wars.
Selectman B—— was an excellent orator.
We were in one d—— of a spot when we landed.

A hyphen (-) might be substituted in typing or handwriting in each of the examples above except the last two, where a double dash could also be used.

4. Do not use a dash in expressions such as those above when the word *from* or *between* appears:

From May to (or through) August (not *From May–August*)
Between 1956 and 1963 (not *Between 1956–1963*)

5. Use dashes to set off strongly distinguished parenthetical material:

My advice—if you will pardon my impertinence—is that you apologize to your friend.

My brother is not afraid—he is a surgeon, you know—of performing the most delicate operation.

I was pleased—delighted, I should say—to hear your news.

She was aware—she must have known—that the proposal was hopeless.

THE COMMA

Because the comma serves so many different purposes it is one of the most widely used of all punctuation marks. Its varied and distinct uses make it by far the most troublesome of the marks; in fact, comma usage varies so greatly that only a few rules can be considered unchanging. But this mark of punctuation, more than any others, can and does help to clarify the meaning of writing. Its overuse and misuse also obscure meaning more than the misapplication of any of the other marks. If you can master the uses of the comma—or even the basic ones—no other mark can hold any terrors for you.

As has been noted, the comma is a relatively weak mark as compared with the period, semicolon, and so on. It shows a brief pause, less complete separation than other marks. Always used within a sentence, it serves several purposes: to introduce, to separate, to enclose, to show omission.

Commas to Introduce

1. Use a comma to introduce a word, phrase, or, on occasion, a clause.

    > Only one other possibility remains, to leave town.
    > I had an important decision to make, whether I should drop out of school or borrow the money and continue.
    > I have need of only two things, money and more money.

    The colon may substitute for the comma in each of the above examples.

2. Use a comma to introduce a statement or question which is preceded by a mental question or musing aloud.

    > I wondered, should I tell Mother the whole story?
    > I thought, you're in real trouble now.
    > I told myself, you can do this as well as anyone.

3. Use a comma to introduce a short quotation.

    > Jack said, "I'll never say that again."

    If the "he said" or its equivalent follows the quotation, it is separated from it by a comma, provided a question mark or exclamation point is not demanded:

    > "I'll never say that again," said Jack.

    If the "he said" or its equivalent is inserted between the parts of a quotation, it is enclosed by commas—provided one part is dependent:

"I'll never say that again," said Jack, "unless I lose my temper."

When the quotation being introduced is long or formal, the colon replaces the comma.

Make a careful distinction between quotations which are really quotations of speaking or writing and quoted material which is the subject or object of a verb or material stressed by quotation marks, such as titles, slang, and special word use. As examples of such special uses, observe the following:

"Make haste slowly" is the motto that came to my mind.
The usual remark is "May the better man win."
When Patrick Henry thundered "Give me liberty or give me death," he contributed a great catch phrase to the world.
"Itsy-bitsy" is not the exact phrase to use for "very small."

Commas to Separate

1. Use the comma to separate independent clauses joined by such conjunctions as *and, but, yet, neither, nor, or.*
   This principle is one of the most frequently used and illustrated in English writing. This frequency accounts for considerable flexibility in application.
   If the clauses are short, the comma may be omitted before the conjunction. This brings up the question "How short is short?" If each independent clause consists of only subject and predicate, or of three or four words each, then they are obviously short and the comma may be omitted:

   The rains came and the rivers rose.
   In the final judging, Mary did not win nor did Jane.

   Fairly long clauses are sometimes written without a comma between them if their connection is particularly close or if the subject of both clauses is the same:

Henry read the assignment over hurriedly and then he began a more careful rereading of it.

2. Use a comma to separate an introductory modifying phrase or adverbial clause from the independent clause which follows:

Before John started on his trip, he made a careful plan of his itinerary.
If I arrive first, I'll wait for you in the library.
After thinking about it, he decided to go.

Many introductory adverbial clauses are simply transposed elements. Inserted in their natural order, they may or may not have commas, depending upon meaning. Inserted elsewhere, they are enclosed by commas:

After you arrive on the campus, various meetings will be held to help orient you.
Various meetings, after you arrive on the campus, will be held to help orient you.

When the adverbial clause follows the independent clause, omit the comma if the adverbial clause is necessary to complete the meaning of the sentence:

Paul works because he has no other way to live.

3. Use commas to separate words, phrases, and clauses in a series.

You will find Graham around somewhere: in the living room, in the basement, or out in the garden.
She whispered, she muttered, but finally she shouted.
I have brought my textbook, my notebook, and some paper with me.
Stop, look, and listen.

One kind of series is represented by A, B, and C—three or more words, phrases, or clauses, with an appropriate pure conjunction joining the last two members.
Some writers omit the comma before the conjunction and

use A, B and C. Since greater clearness is frequently obtained by the use of the comma before the conjunction, present practice favors the comma.

Another kind of series is represented by A, B, C—three or more words, phrases, or clauses, with no conjunctions. Commas are used after each member except *after* the last, unless the clauses are all independent:

This store sells newspapers, magazines, books on weekdays only.

Do not use commas separating members of a series, unless emphasis is desired, when a conjunction is used to join each pair:

I have read nothing by Swift or Milton or Poe.
I have thought and pondered and reflected and meditated—and I still don't know what to do.

4. Use a comma to separate two or more adjectives when they equally modify the same noun.

I bought an old, dilapidated chair and a new, ugly, badly faded rug.

When the adjectives are not coordinate, commas are omitted:

The old oaken bucket was covered with wet green moss.

Notice that a comma is never used to separate the last adjective from the noun.

Sometimes there may be doubt, as in "an old, dilapidated chair" above. Then you must use your judgment in deciding, for it is sometimes difficult to determine whether the adjectives are coordinate or not. Several tests, although not infallible, may help. One way of testing is to insert the coordinate conjunction *and* between the adjectives; if the *and* fits, use a comma when it is omitted, otherwise not. Another test: Does the first adjective modify the idea of the second adjective and the noun? If so, the adjectives are not coordinate. Also, if one of the adjectives describes shape or material or color, the adjectives are probably not coordinate.

5. Use a comma to separate contrasted elements in a sentence. Such contrasted elements may be words, phrases, numbers, letters, or clauses:

> Your misspelling is due to carelessness, not to ignorance.
> Books should be kept on the table, not on the floor.
> My lucky number is 7, not 5.
> Psmith begins his name with a *P*, not an *S*.
> The harder it snowed, the slower they drove.

6. Use a comma to separate words or other sentence elements that might be misread.

Constructions in which commas are needed to prevent misreading are usually questionable or faulty. If it is possible, rephrase such sentences to eliminate awkwardness and to increase clearness. At times, however, a comma is essential to clarify meaning:

> Outside, the house needs a coat of paint; inside, the walls need replastering.
> The day after, a salesman called with the same product.
> In 1988, 984 persons volunteered.
> Instead of a hundred, thousands came.
> Last week I was in bed with a cold, and my mother took care of me.

7. Use a comma, or commas, to separate thousands, millions, etc., in writing figures.

> The deficit may reach $7,985,000,000 this year.
> In this contest 6,811 entries have been received.

Commas are used with all numbers of four or more digits except years, telephone numbers, and house numbers:

> In the fall of 1985 my sister was born.
> My number is 255-1229.
> The Tomlins have sold their home at 4977 Wood Street.

Commas to Enclose

1. Use commas to enclose parenthetical words, phrases, or clauses.

    A fairly adequate test of a parenthetical expression is this: It may be omitted without materially affecting the meaning of the sentence or, frequently, though not always, its position in the sentence may be shifted without any change in meaning.

> *However,* we do not disagree too much.
> We do not, *however,* disagree too much.
> We do not disagree too much, *however.*
> We must, *on the other hand,* discuss every aspect of the problem.
> I believe, *if anyone should ask my opinion,* that action should be postponed.

    Parenthetic elements vary in intensity, and you show by punctuation their relative strength. Some expressions are so weak that they require no punctuation.

2. Use commas to enclose inserted sentence elements.

    Inserted sentence elements—emphatic, suspending, or transposed expressions—are somewhat similar to parenthetical words, phrases, and clauses. *Emphatic* expressions are set off because the writer indicates that he or she considers them emphatic. *Suspending* expressions interrupt or retard the movement of the sentence, holding important information until near the end of the sentence. *Transposed* expressions, like *I believe, I think, it seems to me, I suppose, you see,* and, frequently, adjectives following their nouns, are out of their normal order and require punctuation not used in normal word order. Such inserted expressions are frequently more essential to the thought of the sentence than purely parenthetical material, but they are nonrestrictive in function.

He did not make that statement, *as you will see if you read more carefully,* and I am certain that he did not mean it to be misunderstood. (Emphatic)

This is a good novel, *not only because it contains plenty of action,* but because it fully develops three characters. (Suspending)

Action, *I believe,* should be postponed. (Transposed)

3. Use commas to enclose nonrestrictive phrases and clauses.

Phrases and clauses are *nonrestrictive* when they do not limit or restrict the word or words modified, whereas phrases and clauses are *restrictive* when they limit the word or words modified. Observe what the same clause does in each of the following sentences:

Augusta, *which is the capital of Maine,* has a population of 21,680.

The city *which is the capital of Maine* has a population of 21,680.

In the first sentence, the omission of the italicized clause does not materially change the meaning of the sentence; its purpose is to give added information. In the second sentence, the same clause is necessary; it identifies, it tells which city (the capital of Maine). The clause in the first sentence is *nonrestrictive,* and it is set off from the remainder of the sentence by commas; the clause in the second sentence is *restrictive* and is not enclosed by commas.

The principle of restrictive and nonrestrictive phrases and clauses should become clear if you will carefully note comma usage in the following sentences:

Chapter 8, *which tells of the rescue,* is well written.

The chapter *which tells of the rescue* is well written.

The car *that you saw* was a sports model.

The books, *those that I own,* are all by American authors.

The man *my brother met in Chicago* has traveled widely.

Engelbert Summerfield, *whom my brother met in Chicago,* has traveled widely.

4. Use commas to enclose absolute phrases.

An absolute phrase, a group of words having no grammatical relation to any word in the sentence, consists of a noun and a participial modifier, the latter being sometimes omitted but understood:

> *The task having been finished,* we started on our return trip.
> I went to the first desk, *my application (held) in hand,* and asked for Mr. Stump.
> We needed a fourth member for our club, *Ellen having moved to another town.*

5. Use commas to enclose words in apposition.

A word in apposition is a noun or pronoun (word or phrase) identifying in different words a preceding noun or pronoun. Usually the appositional word or phrase is explanatory and therefore nonrestrictive. When the appositional word or phrase limits or restricts meaning, then the commas are omitted:

> My father, a *physician,* has just retired from active practice.
> This is Mr. Law, *our newly elected president.*
> *Richard the Lion-Hearted* was a famous English king.
> Carl Martin, *our supervisor,* was a considerate man.
> My task, *to compose a short story,* seemed hopeless.
> *The river Ohio* is beloved of song writers.

6. Use commas to enclose vocatives.

A vocative is a noun, pronoun, or noun phrase used in direct address. That is, a vocative indicates to whom something is said. A vocative may appear at various positions within a sentence:

> *Mr. Brown,* will you speak next?
> I am proud, *Mother,* of what you have accomplished.
> Will you please, *sir,* speak more distinctly?

We are assembled, *ladies and gentlemen,* to discuss an important problem.

7. Use commas to enclose initials or titles following a person's name.

Abbett, R. H., Abner, W. G., and Adams, B. R., head the list of names.
John Eddy, M.D., and Robert Morgan, D.D., are the featured speakers on the program.
The son of James Adams, Sr., is listed as James Adams, Jr., on our records.

8. Use commas to enclose places and dates which explain preceding places and dates.

Harry left on May 10, *1984,* to go to Akron, *Ohio,* for an interview.
He lives in Ogden, *Utah,* having been transferred there from Newt, *Ohio.*

The second comma must be used when the state follows town or city and when the year follows both month and day. When only month and year are used, the use of commas around the year is optional: use two or do not use any.

In the date line of a letter, punctuation is optional. It was formerly common practice to write *July 7, 1992;* increasingly popular is the form *7 July 1992.* Both are acceptable. For clarity, always separate two numerals; where a word intervenes, the comma may be omitted if you prefer.

Commas to Indicate Omission

1. Occasionally, use a comma to avoid wordiness or faulty repetition.

Most sentences which require a comma to make clear that something has been left out are poorly constructed and should be rephrased. In rare instances, however, using a comma to show omission helps to avoid wordiness:

Mary collects stamps; Eliza, coupons; Lois, money.
A decade ago she was young and beautiful; only 6 years later, old and ugly.
In this room are 23 children; in that one are 34.
In this room are 23 children; in that, 34. (The comma replaces the words *one are*.)
He takes himself seriously, others, lightly.

Use No Unnecessary Commas

Modern punctuation usage omits many commas that were formerly used; therefore, be able to account for each comma in your writing. A comma must be *needed* for sense construction, clearness, or effectiveness. Avoid using the comma needlessly to separate closely related sentence elements.

Some of the most common misuses or overuses of the comma are discussed in the following "do not use" statements.

1. Do not use a comma to separate a subject from its predicate or a verb from its object or complement. No comma is needed in any of these sentences:

    We asked to hear the motion reread.
    I found that driving was not so hard after all.
    To do satisfactory work is my aim.

2. Do not use a comma before the indirect part of a quotation. No comma is needed in this sentence:

    The speaker asserted that he stood squarely for progress.

3. Do not use a comma indiscriminately to replace a word omitted.

    The word *that* in an indirect quotation; the word *that* in introducing other noun clauses as objects, and the relative pronouns *who, whom, which, that* are frequently omitted in informal writing; they should not be replaced by commas. In "Jack replied, he would return next week," the comma is incorrectly used for *that*; in "The man, I met was a friend of a friend of mine," *whom* should replace the comma. "She thought, that man was dead" should be written "She thought that that man was dead." In such constructions both comma and pronoun can be omitted.

4. Do not use a comma before the first or after the last member of a series:

> We went swimming in a cool, clear, smooth-flowing, river.
> Avoid a mixture of, red, yellow, green, blue, and brown paints.
> The red, white, and blue flag waved in the wind.

Omit the last comma in the first sentence, the first comma in the second.

5. Do not use a comma between two independent clauses where a stronger mark of punctuation (semicolon, period) is required.

> Confusion is always caused by this misuse, sometimes called the "comma fault" or "comma splice." Use a period or semicolon in place of the comma in such a statement as this:

> My mother told me to be home early, I told her I couldn't.

6. Do not use a comma, or pair of commas, with words in apposition that are actually restrictive.

> The following italicized words really limit, identify, or define; they should not be enclosed with commas:

> Goya's painting *The Shooting* is one of his greatest.
> My cousin *Dorothy* is a lovely person.
> Zeno *of Elea* was a follower of Parmenides.

7. Do not use a comma in any situation unless it adds to clarity and understanding.

> Comma usage is slowly growing more and more "open" and less and less "closed." In the following sentences every comma can be justified, but each could equally well be omitted since clarity is not affected in the slightest degree:

> After the movie, Joe and I went home, by taxicab, because we wanted, at all costs, to avoid subway crowds.

Naturally, the last thing you should do, before leaving work, is to punch the time clock.

The most frequently used and most important for clarity of all marks of punctuation are commas. Use them when necessary to make your meaning clear; avoid using them when they slow down thought or interrupt or make your writing look as though you had used a comma shaker.

THE APOSTROPHE

The apostrophe, a mark of punctuation and a spelling symbol, has three uses: to indicate omission of a letter or letters from words and of a figure or figures from numerals; to form the possessive (genitive) case of nouns and of certain pronouns; to indicate the plural of letters, numerals, symbols, and certain abbreviations.

1. Use an apostrophe and *s* to form the possessive case of a noun (singular or plural) not ending in *s:*

   women, women's   office, office's
   children, children's   horse, horse's

2. Use an apostrophe to form the possessive case of a plural noun ending in *s:*

   ladies, ladies'   days, days'
   boys, boys'   students, students'
   heroes, heroes'   horses, horses'

3. Use an apostrophe alone or an apostrophe and *s* to form the possessive of singular nouns ending in *s:*

   James Jones, James Jones' (*or* Jones's)
   Keats, Keats' (*or* Keats's)
   She liked Francis' looks and Burns' (*or* Burns's) poems.

4. In compound nouns add the apostrophe and *s* to the last element of the expression, the one nearest the object possessed.

somebody else's coat	my mother-in-law's car
Queen Mary's crown	the office manager's chair
Mr. Clinton's aide	the editor-in-chief's pen

5. Use an apostrophe to show that letters or figures have been omitted.

didn't (did not)	wasn't (was not)
isn't (is not)	he's (he is)
can't (can not)	don't (do not)

The most misspelled short and simple word in the English language is reflected in this use of the apostrophe. *It's* means "it is" and can never be used correctly for *its* in the possessive sense. "When a skunk lifts *its* tail, that is a sign *it's* frightened." Before writing *i-t-s* think whether or not you mean "it is."

6. Use an apostrophe and *s* to indicate the plurals of numerals, letters, and words considered as words:

Don't overuse *and's*, *but's*, and *for's* in your writing.
He has trouble making legible *8's*.
My cousin spent the last half of the *1950's* in Korea.

7. Never use an apostrophe in forming the plural of nouns and the possessive case of personal and relative pronouns:

The Smiths [not *Smith's*] are coming home tomorrow.
Correct: *ours, yours, his, hers, its, theirs, whose*
Incorrect: *our's, ours', your's, yours', his', her's, it's, their's, theirs', who's* (unless you mean *who is*)

QUOTATION MARKS

Quotation marks, both double (" ") and single (' ') are marks of enclosure for words, phrases, clauses, sentences, and even paragraphs and groups of paragraphs. By definition, *quotation* means repeating (or copying) what someone has said or written. *Quotation marks* are a device used principally to indicate the beginning and end of material so quoted. These marks, often called *quotes*, consist of two (or one) inverted commas at the beginning (*open-quote*) and two (or one) apostrophes for closing a quotation (*close-quote*). On a standard typewriter keyboard, single and double quotation marks are the same at beginning and end.

1. Use quotation marks to enclose every direct quotation and each part of an interrupted quotation:

   "Dinner will be served at seven," replied Barbara.
   "Father," I said, "may I have the car this evening?"

2. In dialogue use a separate paragraph for each change of speaker:

   Larry was dressing for tennis when Bill walked into the room.
   "What's up?" Bill asked. He walked over to the sofa in the corner and sat down.
   "Game with Sue at noon," Larry replied. "But I was up so late last night that I think I'll be awful."
   "Well, who was your date?"
   "Sue," Larry replied sheepishly.

3. If a direct quotation extends for more than one paragraph, place quotation marks at the beginning of each paragraph but at the end of only the last.

4. Use quotation marks to enclose words with a widely different level of usage:

   The Mayor of our town, in my opinion, is a "stuffed shirt."
   The policeman "lit into" me as if I had committed a major crime; when he finished, I "lit out" in a hurry.
   The person who has "had it" so far as all religion is concerned looks with impatience on the role that religion has played in man's progress toward self-mastery.

5. Use quotation marks to enclose chapter headings and the titles of articles, short stories, and short poems.
   When both chapter heading and book are mentioned, or title of article (story, poem) and magazine, book and magazine names should be indicated by italics (underlining):

For such information consult the chapter "Private Preparatory Schools" in the *American Educational Directory*.

Some humorous theatrical experiences are discussed in Jean Kerr's article "What Happens Out of Town" in a recent issue of *Harper's Magazine*.

The book *The Togetherness of Words* has many interesting chapters. The one with the oddest title is called "Varieties of English: Simian, Syntactic, Sensible, and Superb."

6. Use single quotation marks to enclose a quotation within a quotation:

"Tell me," Father asked Mother after the wedding, "whether the bride said, 'I promise to obey.'"

Our instructor said, "When you say, 'I'll bring in my paper tomorrow,' I expect it to be turned in tomorrow, not sometime next week."

On the rare occasions when it is necessary to punctuate a quotation within a quotation within a quotation, the correct order is double marks, single marks, double marks. If you need more than this, rephrase your sentence before you lose your reader entirely:

The teacher next said, "This student asked, 'What did the teacher mean when she said, "Sue, be there on time tonight"?'"

Place Quotation Marks Correctly with Reference to Other Marks

1. The comma and the period *always* come *inside* quotation marks. This rule never varies and applies even when only the last word before the comma or period is enclosed.
2. A question mark, exclamation point, or dash comes *outside* quotation marks unless it is part of the quotation. A single question mark comes inside quotation marks when both the nonquoted and quoted elements are questions.
3. The semicolon and colon come *outside* quotation marks.

Are you thoroughly confused by now? Perhaps these illustrations will help:

"I need your help now," she said. "I need it more than ever."

Some praised the performance as "excellent," and others thought it was only "fair."

Did she say, "I have enough money"?

She asked, "Have I enough money?"

What is meant by "dog eat dog"?

Our play was obviously a "bust"!

"The play was a 'bust'!" our coach exclaimed.

Read E. B. White's "Walden"; it is, I think, his best essay.

Look up the following in "A Glossary of Famous People": Theodore Roosevelt, Woodrow Wilson, Charles E. Hughes.

THE HYPHEN

The hyphen is a mark of separation used only between parts of a word. Paradoxically, its most frequent use is unification, bringing together two or more separate words into a compound word which serves the purpose of a single part of speech. The hyphen, therefore, is more a mark of spelling than of punctuation, to indicate that two or more words or two or more parts of one word belong together.

One Word, Hyphenated Compound, or Two Words

Use your dictionary to determine whether a word combination is written as a compound with a hyphen, as one word written solid, or as two separate words.

Compounds are also treated under the sections on spelling, but in the interests of ready reference they are discussed here, too.

Many compounds are written solid, many are written with a hyphen, and many are written either with a hyphen or as two words, depending upon meaning. However, the present-day tendency is to avoid using hyphens whenever possible. Seven groups, or classes, of words ordinarily require hyphens:

1. Two or more words modifying a substantive and used as a single adjective: *soft-spoken, ocean-blue, wind-blown, trans-Andean, ever-rising.*
2. Words of a compound noun: *mother-in-law, go-between, fellow-citizen.*
3. Compound words, usually, when *self, ex, half,* or *quarter* is the first element: *self-control, ex-president, half-truth, quarter-share.*
4. A single capital letter joined to a noun or a participle: *B-flat, H-bomb, S-curve, T-shaped, U-turn.*
5. Elements of an improvised compound: *make-believe, know-it-all, never-say-die.*
6. Compound numerals from *twenty-one* through *ninety-nine.*
7. Compounds formed from the numerator and denominator of fractions: *four-fifths, one-thousandth.*

Word Division

Occasionally, at the end of a longhand or typewritten line, a long word must be divided. Avoid such division if you possibly can, and do not divide the word if it is the last one on the page. When division is necessary, follow these directions:

1. Place the hyphen at the end of the first line, *never at the beginning of the second.*
2. Never divide a monosyllable. Five- to seven-letter one-syllable words like *breath, death, ground, thought,* and *through* cannot be divided. Write the entire monosyllable on the first line; if this is not possible, carry the whole word over to the next line.
3. Divide words of more than one syllable between syllables, but avoid dividing one-letter syllables from the remainder of the word, as well as any unpronounced *ed* in one- or several-syllable pronunciations. Undesirable: *a-bout; i-talics; man-y; ask-ed; dress-ed; attack-ed.*
4. When in doubt about correct syllabication, consult your dictionary in order to divide words properly. Several simple suggestions, however, apply to many words:

a. Prefixes and suffixes can be divided from the main words (but see 3, above).

b. Compound words are divided between their main parts.

c. Two consonants are usually divided.

PARENTHESES

Parentheses are curved punctuation marks principally used to enclose incidental explanatory matter in a sentence. Such material is important enough to be included but is not intended to be a part of the main statement and often has no direct grammatical relationship to the sentence in which it appears. Marks of parenthesis (or *parentheses*) signal to the reader what a speaker means when he or she says "By the way," or "Incidentally," or something similar.

You may set off incidental (parenthetical) material by commas, dashes, or marks of parenthesis. Each of these marks is acceptable for this purpose. Your choice will usually depend upon the closeness of the relationship between the material inserted and the remainder of the sentence. No specific rule can be stated, but commas are ordinarily used to enclose parenthetical material closely related in thought and structure to the sentence in which it occurs. Dashes enclose parenthetical material which more abruptly breaks into the sentence or may be used in a somewhat informal style. Parentheses are used to enclose material more remote in thought and structure or material that runs to some length or may itself contain internal punctuation, such as commas.

1. Use parentheses to enclose material only remotely connected with its context:

   These directions (I am certain they are accurate) should be thoroughly studied.
   If you find any strawberries (surely they must be plentiful now), please bring me some.

2. Use parentheses to enclose numerals or letters indicating divisions:

He left hurriedly for several reasons: (*a*) poor health, (*b*) lack of money, (*c*) dull companions, (*d*) a job in the city.

3. Use parentheses to enclose sums of money when accuracy is essential:

Her grocery bill was fifty-four dollars ($54.00).
The retail price is forty cents (40¢) per pound.

Sums of money repeated for accuracy and enclosed in parentheses occur most often in business writing and in legal papers. Ordinarily, you need not resort to this device; either words or numerals will suffice.

4. Avoid using parentheses to enclose question marks and exclamation points to express doubt or irony.

Doubt and irony can usually be expressed more forcefully in other ways. Do not use a question mark as a lazy excuse for not finding out exact information:

Paul is in good shape; he needs to lose only (!) forty pounds.
This baby was born on June 22 (?) last year.
The ambitious candidate boasted in a modest (?) way and never raised his voice above a gentle (?) roar.

BRACKETS

A bracket is one of two marks (brackets are always used in pairs) used primarily for the purpose of enclosing material that is not part of a quoted passage. That is, brackets are editorial marks used to enclose comments, corrections, or additions to quoted material. The mark is often used in professional and academic writing but has limited use elsewhere. Brackets should never be confused with marks of parenthesis, which have entirely different uses. Parentheses are used to enclose your own parenthetical material; brackets are used solely to set off matter inserted by you in someone else's writing which you are quoting.

1. Use brackets to enclose a comment inserted in a quoted passage:

"On the first float rode the Homecoming Queen [Miss Jane Gaston], her attendants, and her escort."

"In March of that year [1957] Cameron wrote his first book."

If you are quoting a person who has made an error, or what you consider an error, you can add the correction and enclose it in brackets. If you do not wish to make the correction but merely to call attention to it, you may use the Latin word *sic*, which means "thus," and enclose it in brackets:

"Milton portrays Satan as a fallen angle [*sic*] of tremendous size."

2. Use brackets to add to a quoted passage:

"He was fined £100 [$240] for the violation."

"Later in the poem," the lecturer continued, "he [Jim Dooley] is killed."

"They [the Indians] were not any more at fault than their adversaries [the cavalry]," the speaker concluded.

The advertisement read: "These sweaters [Fisherman's knit, Scandinavian design] were designed by Ceil Allen."

ITALICS

In longhand and typewritten copy, certain words and groups of words should be underlined to correspond to the conventions of using italic type. These conventions, however, have never been standardized, and the use of italic type varies widely from publication to publication.

To a printer, italic type means letters with a slope to the right which look quite unlike the so-called roman type ordinarily used. To a reader, italic type indicates that some word or group of words has been singled out for emphasis or other distinction.

As a careful and thoughtful writer, you are urged to employ italics (underlining) in the specific situations cited below and quotation marks in other constructions.

Certain Groups and Classes of Words

1. Titles of books and magazines:

   The Quest for Security, The Return of the Native, Harper's Magazine, True

2. Titles of plays, operas, long poems, and motion pictures:

   Oliver! (play), *Carmen* (opera), *The Song of Hiawatha* (long poem), *Casablanca* (motion picture)

3. Names of ships, trains, and aircraft:

   the *United States* (ship), the *City of Philadelphia* (train), the *Spirit of St. Louis* (aircraft)

4. Names of newspapers:

   Chicago Tribune, The Buckhannon Record

   Some teachers and style manuals suggest not italicizing the name of the city or the definite article in the title of a newspaper: the Bridgeport *Post;* the New York *Times.* But the actual title itself is always italicized (underlined).

5. Names of legal cases:

   James Smith v. *Mary Smith* or James Smith *v.* Mary Smith

6. Scientific names:

   Haliacetus leucocephalus (bald eagle), *Felis catus* (an ordinary *cat* to you and me)

Foreign Words and Phrases

There is a *je ne sais quoi* quality about this painting.

The foreign student in America must work out a *modus vivendi.*

Note that thousands of words and phrases have been so thoroughly absorbed into the English language that they need no longer be italicized. Such words as these can safely be written without italics (underlining):

billet doux	mores	alias
et cetera	en route	matinee
delicatessen	carte blanche	bona fide
hors d'oeuvres	gratis	ex officio
vice versa	sauerkraut	prima facie

Items for Specific Reference or Emphasis

Never, under any conditions, keep poisonous substances in your medicine cabinets.

You should *always* sign your name to a letter.

CAPITAL LETTERS

It is impossible to state all the rules for employing capital letters in English. The appearance of capitals is widespread; usage is not fixed and unchanging; exceptions occur for almost every "standard" rule of capitalization. For example, the latest printing of the *U.S. Government Printing Office Style Manual* devotes thirty-seven pages to the use of capitals—and thoughtfully adds a blank page on which one presumably may make notes of exceptions and variations.

Despite the confusion which exists about capital letters, the basic principles involved are somewhat clearer than they were at the turn of the century. In general, books, magazines, and especially newspapers are employing fewer and fewer capitals than formerly. A glance at a book or newspaper of a century or two ago will clearly indicate this trend.

Capital letters are also treated in the sections on spelling, but repetition here is for emphasis.

1. Capitalize the first word of every sentence, including every quoted sentence:

> Are you going to the movies tonight?
> Our congressman said, "Don't miss seeing that movie."

2. When only a part of a direct quotation is included within a sentence, it is usually not begun with a capital letter:

The accident victim said that he felt "badly shaken," but he refused hospitalization.

3. Capitalize the first word of every line of poetry:

"And we are here as on a darkling plain,
Swept with confused alarms of struggle and flight
Where ignorant armies clash by night."

Matthew Arnold

Capitalize Proper Nouns

1. *Names of people and titles used for specific persons:*

    Abraham Lincoln, Franklin Roosevelt, the Senator, the Secretary, the President, Mr. Speaker, Mother, Grandfather, the Mayor

2. *Names of countries, states, regions, localities, other geographic areas, and the like:*

    Canada, France, Arizona, the Orient, the Torrid Zone, the Midwest, the Blue Ridge Mountains, the Solid South, Painted Desert, the Kanawha River, Lake Erie

3. *Names of streets:*

    Seventh Avenue, Bronson Road, Cherry Lane

4. *Names of the Deity and personal pronouns referring to Him:*

    Jesus Christ, the Almighty, God, Heavenly Father, Jehovah, Him, Thy, His

5. *Names for the Bible and other sacred writings:*

    Book of Psalms, Bible, Gospels, the Scriptures, the Koran

6. *Names of religions and religious groups:*

    Roman Catholicism, Episcopalian, Moslem, Protestantism, Unitarian

7. *Names of the days and the months (but not the seasons):*

Sunday, Monday, etc.; January, February, etc.; winter, spring, summer, fall, autumn

8. *Names of schools, universities, colleges:*

Salem High School, Cornell University, Virginia Military Institute, Wesleyan College

9. *Names of historic events, eras, and holidays:*

Civil War, Cenozoic era, Stone Age, Renaissance, Veterans Day, Yom Kippur

10. *Names of races, organizations, and members of each:*

Eskimo, Negro, Aryan, University Club, American League, New York Mets, an Odd Fellow, a Boy Scout

11. *Vivid personifications:*

Destiny, the Angel of Death, the New Frontier, the Nutmeg State, Star of Fortune

12. *Trade names:*

Pepsi Cola, Bon Ami, Mr. Clean, Frigidaire

Capitalize all words except prepositions, articles, and conjunctions in the titles of books, plays, magazines, and musical compositions:

Antony and Cleopatra, The Blue Danube Waltz, Better Homes and Gardens, Man Will Prevail, Ten Modern Masters.

Do not capitalize prepositions, conjunctions, and articles except at the beginning or end of the title or unless they consist of five or more letters: *The Taming of the Shrew, Caught Between Storms, Mr. Pim Passes By.*

ABBREVIATIONS

Abbreviations, shortened forms of words and phrases, help save time and space. In addition, proper use of abbreviations avoids the needless spelling out of often repeated phrases and words, a practice which annoys some readers. Coming across spelled-out items such as "Mister Jones" and "Mistress Adams" would be distracting and bothersome to most modern readers.

As a general rule, spell out all words and phrases that would be puzzling if abbreviated and abbreviate correctly all terms that are frequently encountered and readily understood in shortened form.

In the following list, some abbreviations are acceptable in any style of writing, some only in informal writing, and some probably should not be used at all because they may cause confusion. For example, the abbreviations *Mr.* and *Mrs.* are acceptable at all times; the abbreviations *c.* and *ct.* (for cent or cents) are suitable only in informal writing; the abbreviation *civ.* probably should not be used on any occasion since it can stand for civics, civilization, civies (civilian clothes), and civil (as in civil engineer).

Names and titles: Capt., Rev., Ph.D., Mr., Mrs.
School subjects: bot., lit., Fr.
Addresses: Ct., Dr., Pl., St., Ter.
Calendar divisions: Wed., Sept., in the '40's
Measurements: A.M., P.M., in., bu., lb.
Money: $, dol., c., ct.
Geographic names: Conn., St. Charles, N.Y.C., U.S.A.

The recommendation to use a period after most abbreviations is clear and normally should be followed. However, you should note exceptions to this rule, as follows:

Special forms: ABC, UNICEF, TV, PAL
Shortened forms: phone, ad, lab, exam
Ordinal numbers: 4th, 6th, 9th
Nicknames: Ben, Ted, Ned, Al, Liz, Meg
Contractions: can't, aren't, doesn't, wasn't

NUMBERS

Since exact and unchanging rules for representing numerals cannot be cited, it is preferable to adopt a general system and to use it consistently. In arriving at a formula that will cover most of your uses of numerals, remember these generally accepted principles:

1. Never begin a sentence with an actual numeral.
2. Use words for numbers between one and ninety-nine.
3. Use figures for words above ninety-nine.
4. When a number can be expressed in not more than two words, write it in words.
5. When a number can be expressed in no less than three words, use figures.
6. Arabic numerals are generally preferable to Roman numerals.

Familiarizing yourself with these six principles, which are usually but not always consistent, will save you much trouble.

Words to Represent Numbers in Special Cases

1. Isolated numbers less than 10:

   We can choose one of five magazines to read.
   At least two women should be chosen for alternates.

2. Indefinite expressions or round numbers (figures are also acceptable, however):

   The mid-twenties was a frantic, mad era in this country.
   We have a hundred cows and six hundred pigs on our farm.
   or
   We have 100 cows and 600 pigs on our farm.
   If he lives to be a million, he will still be a bore.
   This stadium will seat ten thousand people.
   or
   This stadium will seat 10,000 people.

3. One number or related numbers at the beginning of a sentence:

Three of our officers are from out of town.
Four hundred employees were covered by group insurance.

4. Numbers preceding a compound modifier containing a
figure:

Now we need six ¼-inch strips of canvas.
Our tent is supported by two 8-foot poles.

5. Fractions standing alone:

This cardboard is one-eighth inch thick.
I live about one-fourth of a mile from the school.

Figures to Represent Numbers in Special Cases

1. Isolated numbers of 10 or more:

The amount is 10 times what it was in 1988.
Only 23 persons attended the service at the church.

2. Dates, including the day or the day and the year:

My birth date was July 21, 1953.
Please report for work on August 1.

3. House, room, telephone, and zip code numbers:

I live at 1607 Ravinia Road, Columbus, Ohio; my telephone number is 532–2784.
Send your request to 3 Park Street, Rutland, Vermont
10570.

4. Highway and comparable numbers:

On this set we cannot get Channel 3.
We took U.S. Highway 91 to Milford.

5. Measurements:

The white lines on a football field are 5 yards apart.
The parcel-post package weighed 5 pounds and 10
ounces.
The rows were planted 3 feet apart.

6. Time:

> 9 A.M., 3:46 P.M., half past 6.
> 10 o'clock (not 10 o'clock A.M. or 10 o'clock *in the morning*.)
> 8 years 3 months 25 days; 3 hours 15 minutes 8 seconds.

7. Percentage:

> The interest rate is 5%.
> 10 percent, one-half of 1 percent, 4¼ percent bonds.

8. Money:

> $4.55, $0.50, 50 cents, $6 per bushel, 35¢ apiece

9. Chapters and page numbers:

> Chapter 6, p. 483, pp. 20–32, p. 1654

EXERCISES IN CORRECT PUNCTUATION AND MECHANICS

Periods and Related Marks

Each entry in the pairs below may contain a mistake in the use of periods, question marks, or exclamation points. Use a capital letter to indicate that of the two sentences: A—the first only is acceptable; B—the second only is acceptable; C—both are acceptable; D—neither is acceptable.

1. Will you please refer to the Simmons file for the requested information. As I prepared to drive away, Father asked me if I hadn't forgotten something?
2. Mrs Ethel Richardson agreed to serve as secretary at the meeting. The skid marks measured 18 yd. 2 ft. 4 in.
3. NASA announced a delay of the moon shot because of overcast skies. As soon as Porter arrived, he asked us if we had bought our diving equipment.
4. "Many provisions . . . for governmental intervention

in the economy, once regarded as startling and dangerous, have now come to be commonplace and routine . . ." The FRB announced a rise in the bank discount rate of 5.5 percent.

5. The title of his paper, "The Can-Opener Culture," seemed to me too comprehensive for a short essay. On your way out, would you please post this letter for me?

6. How many times have I asked you not to slam that door! Just as Bert had said, there was a good record player in the cabin, but his record collection contained nothing but—ugh!—country music.

7. Instead of addressing the letter to Mr. Henry Tripp, 1256 So. Euclid Ave., you would show your correspondent more respect by spelling out the address fully. A frequent and well-intended social query—haven't you lost some weight lately?—can never actually be pleasing, since it implies that the hearer was too fat before or is too thin now.

8. How can we make you comfortable? Something to eat? A magazine? Television? Or would you like just to be let alone? She was always asking her guests if they didn't believe in extrasensory perception?

9. Did the Weather Bureau say it will rain today? Isn't that a pity?

10. Will you kindly let me know as soon as Emerson returns to his office. You expect me to meet her plane at 2:30 AM? Impossible!

Semicolon, Colon, Dash

Each item below begins with a correct sentence; you are to rewrite it as directed. Use a capital letter to indicate that the shift from the original to the rewritten sentence requires you to: *A*—insert, or change a mark to, a semicolon or semicolons; *B*—insert, or change a mark to, a colon or colons; *C*—insert, or change a mark to, a dash or dashes; *D*—take out one of the marks above, or change it to a comma; *E*—keep the same punctuation as in the original.

1. The facts of her childhood were hardly ideal: she was born into poverty, abandoned at the age of six, and reared in an orphanage. [Take out *she was.*]
2. At high school he starred in all the sports offered: football, basketball, and track. [Take out *all the sports offered.*]
3. Now listen to this carefully: send word to me at once if the drill brings up any gravel or even coarse sand from the well. [Put *now listen to this carefully* after *me.*]
4. The wind had veered to the east and raised a scattering of whitecaps on the bay; a canoe crossing looked too dangerous to try. [Change *had* to *having.*]
5. Not all people, it has been found, can roll the tip of the tongue into the shape of a tube; this ability, being hereditary, cannot be acquired by practice—nor does it appear to be good for anything, for that matter. [Insert *and* after *tube.*]
6. A cat when lapping up milk cups its tongue backward, not, as many suppose, forward, in a rapid series of dipping and raking motions; this fact is one of the curious revelations of high-speed photography. [Take out *this fact is.*]
7. You can hardly be a success in politics without being your own convinced disciple, but the reverse proposition is unfortunately not true. [Change *but* to *however.*]
8. The accident occurred at 12 minutes after three in the afternoon. [Put the time in numerical and abbreviated form.]
9. The army expects of its rank and file one thing above all, and that is obedience. [Take out *and that is.*]
10. Because of a rainy spell construction was halted for a week, so we were free from Monday through Friday. [Change *so* to *consequently.*]

Commas to Introduce or to Separate

Each item below begins with a correct sentence; you are to rewrite it as directed. Make only changes required by directions. Use a capital letter to indicate that the rewritten sentence, compared with the original, has: *A*—lost a mark of punctuation; *B*—gained a mark of punctuation; *C*—changed one mark of punctuation to another (for example, a comma to a semicolon); *D*—more than one change in punctuation; *E*—the same amount and kind of punctuation as before. *Example:* As soon as I get home from work, I will wash the car. [Start the rewritten sentence with the words *I will.*] *Explanation:* The rewritten sentence reads: I will wash the car as soon as I get home from work. [A comma has been *lost*, so the answer is *A*.]

1. I have arranged your interview with Adderley, and I will take you to see him on Monday. [Take out the second *I.*]
2. I have arranged your interview with Adderley, and he will see you on Monday. [Take out *and.*]
3. Adderley is the only man you have yet to interview. [Start the sentence: *There is only one man whom you.*]
4. Arrowheads were often made of obsidian (volcanic glass) in the absence of metal. [Start the sentence: *In the absence.*]
5. Yesterday the Sioux City stockyards reported taking in 400 cattle and 300 sheep. [Multiply each figure by 10.]
6. He still owes more than $600. [Multiply the figure by 100.]
7. Willow bark contains various amounts of salicylic acid and was long used as an analgesic before the discovery of aspirin. [Insert *it* after *and.*]
8. "Should I really trust him with the secret?" I wondered aloud. [Start the sentence with *I wondered* and take out *aloud.*]
9. Let me know as soon as the undercoat is dry, and I will finish painting the car. [Start the sentence: *As soon as.*]

10. "For all I know," he said, "I may drive the old car for another year." [Change *For all I know* to *I haven't decided yet.*]

Commas to Enclose or Set Off

Each item below begins with a correct sentence; you are to rewrite it as directed. Make no changes except those required by the directions. Write a capital letter to indicate that the rewritten sentence, compared with the original, has: *A*—lost one comma; *B*—lost two commas; *C*—gained one comma; *D*—gained two commas; *E*—the same amount of punctuation as before.

1. My uncle Harvey is a policeman. [Insert *maternal* after *My.*]
2. Mr. Vertigo Spinn
   Churn Agitators, Inc.
   1313 Rolls Avenue
   Centrifuge, Ohio
   [To this address add the zip code number *43606.*]
3. The announced lineup for Tuesday's game had James Carter at second base and Alvin Carter in left field. [Insert the phrase *no relation* after *Alvin Carter.*]
4. The new name in the lineup for Tuesday's game was J. Carter. [Put Carter's initial *after* the surname.]
5. Mr. Larkin called while you were out, and in a very bad temper, too. [Insert *you may as well know* after *and.*]
6. The course in English composition is not addressed to a specific and generally agreed-on subject matter. [Insert *like physics or chemistry* after *not.*]
7. I had to stay home that afternoon and supervise the Two Demons, as we call the twins, Mother having decided to get her hair done. [Start the sentence: *Mother having decided.*]
8. The giant panda is not a bear or, for that matter, closely related to any familiar animal. [Insert *as many suppose* after *not.*]

9. There is an association with members on both sides of the Atlantic whose sole purpose is to rescue the reputation of King Richard III from the calumnies of Tudor-minded historians. [Insert *an earnest and active one* after *association*.]

10. In this statement Mr. Tompkins has raised a question that deserves our earnest consideration. [Change *has* to *you have*.]

Restriction and Nonrestriction

Each item below begins with a correct sentence; you are to rewrite it as directed. Make no changes except those required by the directions. Write a capital letter to indicate that the rewritten sentence, compared with the original, has: *A*—lost a comma; *B*—lost two commas; *C*—gained a comma; *D*—gained two commas; *E*—the same number of commas as before (possibly none).

1. A boat which leaks may be dangerous. [Change *A* to *John's*.]

2. The members of the senior class, who were wearing caps and gowns, were enjoying the mingled feelings of pride and absurdity usual on such occasions. [By the management of punctuation alone, make it clear that some members of the senior class were not wearing caps and gowns.]

3. About a century ago, a lawless class of young bloods (called "scorchers") who burnt up the streets on high-wheeled bicycles were the subject of angry editorials. [Insert *at speeds as high as 15 miles per hour* after *bicycles*.]

4. I did not call on the Haskins just because Miriam was staying with them. [Make it clear that the speaker did *not* call on the Haskins.]

5. The men of the first group who had already crossed the creek signaled for the others to follow them. [Make it clear that *all* the men of the first group had crossed the creek.]

6. More than half the people who take up the doctor's time, it is said, have nothing specifically discoverable wrong with them. [Change *people* to *patients*.]

7. The protein-deficiency diseases which afflict the populations of many backward countries are often caused by lack of a single amino acid, lysine. [Change *The protein-deficiency diseases* to *Diseases associated with underconsumption of proteins*.]

8. Protein-deficiency diseases are often caused by lack of an amino acid, lysine, which is abundant in meat but scanty in some cereals. [Put *lysine* at the end of the sentence.]

9. Since Howard arrived, nobody at our summer hotel has lacked amusement, for he is infinitely diverting. [Put *since Howard arrived* after *amusement*.]

10. Since prices have increased along with them, recent increases in wages may not mean additional purchasing power. [Shift the words preceding the comma to the end of the sentence.]

Quotation Marks and Related Marks

Each sentence below may contain a mistake in the use of quotation marks, italics, or some other mark. Write a capital letter to indicate that in the sentence: A—quotation marks are missing, superfluous, or misplaced with respect to accompanying punctuation; B—italic indicators are missing or superfluous; C—some other mark or letter is missing or superfluous; D—a wrong mark is used (for example, italics instead of quotation marks); E—none of these: the sentence is acceptable as it stands.

1. There's a favorable review of "The Nylon Jungle," an Italian movie now featured at the Araby Theatre, in today's Chicago *Spectator*.

2. "In those days," she said, "you had to send the children to school in Switzerland in order to qualify as a member of the *haut monde*."

3. With an expression of intense hauteur, she said, "Do

you really imagine that eating pie a la mode is the custom of all Americans"?

4. "Who was it," he asked, "that said, 'People will give
   up making war only when it comes to be regarded as
   vulgar.'?"

5. She replied, "I think it was Oscar Wilde;" then after a
   pause, "however, I'd better look it up to make sure."

6. Interviewed aboard the Queen Elizabeth at his de-
   parture, the Prince said, "Americans are very clever
   people; they can understand my English but I can't
   understand theirs."

7. Paraphrasing William James, he said, "If you want to
   kick a bad habit, you should enlist pride in support of
   will power by announcing the decision publicly."

8. "Different as they look," said Professor Fitts, "the
   words sporran and purse are etymologically related."

9. The popular aphorism "nice guys finish last" is attrib-
   uted to Leo Durocher.

10. "Are you absolutely sure," demanded the prosecutor,
    "that you heard the woman cry, 'It was Gerald—I *saw*
    him!'?"

Marks of Enclosure

Each sentence below may contain a mistake in the use of parentheses, brackets, or punctuation associated with them (a comma
used with a parenthesis). Write a capital letter to indicate that the
sentence: *A*—lacks a necessary mark or marks; *B*—has a superfluous mark or marks; *C*—uses a wrong mark or marks (some
other mark[s] should have been used); *D*—misplaces a mark or
marks with respect to accompanying punctuation or text; *E*—is
acceptable as it stands.

1. It's an interesting coincidence that these years of political jitteriness [the middle 50's] abounded also in
   sightings of saucers from outer space and other un-
   identified flying objects.

2. Professor White's exploits as a secret courier during

World War II were recounted in an earlier issue of the same magazine [see January 26, 1958].

3. "It was with genuine regret," wrote the General, "that I then lay (*sic*) down the burdens of command."

4. Mrs. Hawkins is the recognized dictator of our little town's society (this is the same person, believe it or not, whom you knew in high school as Mary Trotter.)

5. Pentwater, Michigan, once a lumber shipping center and one of the busiest ports on the lake, is now a quiet resort community.

6. The short stories of Saki (Hector Hugh Munro), are among the wittiest ever written.

7. Writes Professor Bloch: "There can be little doubt that the Whig aristocracy of the eighteenth century led the best *all-around* [my emphasis] life ever enjoyed by any class anywhere."

8. "When Monroe uttered his famous Doctrine in 1822 (actually 1823), he can have had but little idea of the interpretations that subsequent administrations would put on it."

9. I know exactly where we left the car; it was just opposite a little shop with the sign, I'm not likely to forget it, "Antiques and Junque."

10. Although Timmy accepted my veto of his plan to trap old Mr. McDowell in an elephant pit, (I said it might break his neck), I could see that he privately regarded my objection as frivolous and cowardly.

Mechanics

Each sentence below may contain a mistake in the use of hyphens, apostrophes, capitals, abbreviations, numbers, or special marks such as the acute accent, circumflex, or cedilla. A "wrong mark" in the key listed below includes also the wrong form, such as a capital instead of a small letter, a spelled-out number instead of an Arabic figure, and so on. Write a capital letter to indicate that the sentence: A—lacks a necessary mark or marks; B—has a superfluous mark or marks; C—uses a wrong mark or form (some other should have been used); *D*—misplaces a mark or marks; *E*—is acceptable as it stands.

1. May'nt we come in now?
2. We visited the Trent's last night.
3. Among teen-agers, a passion for nonconformity can co-exist comfortably with passive submission to the mores of the clique or gang.
4. I told my Mother I would be home early.
5. There were 4 absentees on Monday.
6. The lowest temperature recorded for this day was on January 12th, 1940.
7. Professor Clark is preeminent in his field.
8. The President appoints the members of the cabinet.
9. It was an easily-forgotten novel.
10. Senora Madura was accompanied by her husband, the Ambassador.
11. He secured a loan at the rate of five and one-half per-cent.
12. Examples of highly visual writing are easily found in Keat's poetry.
13. You should be more self-reliant and not take second hand advice.
14. The store specializes in boys' and womens' wear.
15. Thucydides' history of the Peloponnesian war is fascinating reading.
16. I finally figured out that he was my ex-brother-in-law's first cousin.
17. The Secretary stated in a hearing of the Senate Foreign Relations Committee that he had no ready-made solutions of our problems in the East.
18. According to Simmons' report, twenty-two cartons are missing.
19. Most under-developed countries lie south of the Tropic of Cancer.
20. Afterwards Father asked me where I had picked up such half-baked ideas.

ANSWERS TO EXERCISES

Periods and Related Marks

1. *A*	3. *C*	5. *D*	7. *C*	9. *A*
2. *B*	4. *B*	6. *C*	8. *A*	10. *A*

Semicolon, Colon, Dash

1. *B*	3. *C*	5. *E*	7. *A*	9. *C*
2. *D*	4. *D*	6. *C*	8. *B*	10. *A*

Commas to Introduce or to Separate

1. *A*	3. *B*	5. *E*	7. *B*	9. *B*
2. *C*	4. *B*	6. *B*	8. *D*	10. *C*

Commas to Enclose or Set Off

1. *D*	3. *E*	5. *D*	7. *E*	9. *D*
2. *E*	4. *C*	6. *D*	8. *D*	10. *D*

Restriction and Nonrestriction

1. *D*	3. *E*	5. *D*	7. *D*	9. *A*
2. *B*	4. *C*	6. *E*	8. *A*	10. *E*

Quotation Marks and Related Marks

1. *D*	3. *A*	5. *A*	7. *A*	9. *E*
2. *E*	4. *C*	6. *B*	8. *B*	10. *E*

Marks of Enclosure

1. *C*	3. *C*	5. *E*	7. *E*	9. *C*
2. *E*	4. *D*	6. *E*	8. *C*	10. *B*

Mechanics

1. *D*	5. *C*	9. *B*	13. *A*	17. *E*
2. *B*	6. *B*	10. *A*	14. *D*	18. *C*
3. *E*	7. *E*	11. *C*	15. *C*	19. *B*
4. *C*	8. *C*	12. *E*	16. *E*	20. *E*

9

GUIDE TO CORRECT

SPELLING

Correct spelling is essential for intelligent communication. It is taken for granted and expected at all times. Yet many people realize their writing sometimes contains spelling errors, and they are embarrassed by doubts and fears about the correct spelling of difficult words. Distraction, confusion, and misunderstanding result from errors in spelling. Therefore, no one should be satisfied with anything less than perfection.

Perhaps you are one of those people who feel disturbed by their spelling errors and have enough of a spelling conscience to do something about it. Or perhaps you are among those who doubt their ability to master this difficult subject. You may have tried many times and failed. If so, is there any hope for you?

The answer is that if you really have a desire to learn to spell perfectly you can, provided:

1. You can pronounce such words as *accept* and *except* so that they will not sound exactly alike.
2. You can look at such words as *sad* and *sand* and in a single glance, without moving your eyes, detect the difference between them.
3. You can sign your name without looking at the paper on which you are writing and without even consciously thinking about what you are doing.
4. You can tell your friend Bill from your friend Sam by a mere glance.

5. You can learn a simple rhyme, such as "Old King Cole was a merry old soul. . . ."
6. You can remember that a compliment is "what *I* like to get."
7. You can learn the alphabet, if you do not know it already.
8. You can equip yourself with a reliable desk dictionary.
9. You can learn what a syllable is and proofread your writing syllable-by-syllable.
10. You have normal intelligence, here defined as the ability to read and write simple English and keep out of the way of speeding automobiles.

If you can honestly meet these ten provisions, you can learn to spell *without ever making a mistake.* If you can pass Number 10 and only three or four of the others, you can still double your spelling efficiency. It's worth trying, isn't it?

YOU AND THE PROBLEM OF SPELLING

The one thing demanded of all who have had educational advantages is that they be able to spell. In your daily work or in social situations you may not need to be able to add a column of figures. Few people will care. Not often will you be thought stupid if you don't know the dates of historical events—say, the Battle of Waterloo. Your knowledge of economics can be nil. You may not know the difference between an oboe and an ibis, an atom and a molecule. But if you can't spell, you're in trouble. Rightly or wrongly, fairly or unfairly, misspelling is the most frequently accepted sign of illiteracy.

Why is this? You can argue that the ability to think clearly is far more important than spelling. So are clear expression of thoughts, an attractive personality, and demonstrated ability in one's job. The fact remains that incorrect spelling is heavily penalized in our society—so heavily that it keeps people from getting jobs they want or prevents them from moving up to better positions. Inability to spell gives people complexes just as much as unsureness about grammar or proper methods of dress and social behavior.

The main reason for this somewhat illogical reliance on spelling as an index of intelligence and literacy is that correct spelling is the one fixed and certain thing about our language. The overwhelming majority of English words are spelled in only one way; all other ways are wrong. The accepted system *is* accepted. It is the system in which our business communications, our magazines, our newspapers, and our books have been written for generations.

This uniformity applies to no other aspect of our language. You can vary your choice of words as much as you please. You can write sentences which are long or short and punctuate them in various ways. In most circles you can split an infinitive or use a double negative and not be penalized. But you can spell a word in only one correct way. In a rapidly changing world this substantial uniformity is understandably attractive to many people, particularly to those who are good spellers.

Even where alternative spellings are possible, only one will be thought correct for a given piece of writing. For example, both *telephone* and *phone* are commonly used, the latter a colloquial form of *telephone*. Your employer or the editor for whom you are writing may insist on *telephone*, and that full spelling will then be the right one. Both *theater* and *theatre* are correct spellings, but you would probably use the former in the United States and the latter in England.

One might argue logically that many wrong spellings are "better" than the right ones since they "show" the word more clearly. *Wensday* more clearly reveals the sound of the word than does *Wednesday*. But logic and common sense will not help; in Old English *Wodnes daeg* was the day of the god *Woden*, and the *d* has remained. Spelling is frequently a matter of conforming not to logic but to custom and tradition.

If enough people make a "mistake" in punctuation, or grammar, or the meaning of a word, that "mistake" becomes acceptable usage. This is a scientific fact of language. Through the years our language has changed, and will change, in its idioms, its vocabulary, its pronunciation, and its structural form. Change is the essential, inevitable phenomenon of a living language, as it is of any living organism. But this observation, this law, does not yet apply to the spelling of English words.

For many generations, spelling practice has been supported by sentiment, convention, prejudice, and custom. This is strong support, since each of us can think of many other activities similarly reinforced. The world is largely ruled by sentiment. A hundred, a thousand, observances are based only upon convention. Think briefly of the clothes people wear, table manners, office etiquette, and you will see the point. If sentiment, convention, and custom were removed from our social order, our way of living would be altered beyond recognition.

If English spelling were much more illogical than it is, the problem might be solved. Then no one could spell correctly; all of us would be bad spellers together. But enough people have learned to spell correctly to make things difficult for those who can't. This is the situation today, and we must make the best of it.

At some time in the distant future, correct spelling may be thought unimportant. Until that time, we can take comfort in realizing that spelling, like every other activity of the human mind, *can* be learned. It will have to be if we are to free ourselves from the doubts and frustrations that diminish our self-confidence when we write. It will have to be if we wish to "get ahead," to be socially acceptable, to be considered educated and literate.

TACKLING THE PROBLEM

Nearly every spelling authority who has written on the subject has presented some sure-fire approach to the problem of poor spelling. All other methods are wrong; this is the only true one. And the method *has* worked—for some people. For others it has been a flat failure. There was nothing especially wrong with the method except that it did not allow for the fact that people differ. They differ in sex, color, and personality—and they differ in ways of learning. The system by which A learns easily and quickly may work poorly for B or may not work at all. There is no one guaranteed method for everyone, but some plans for studying spelling are sounder than others. Actually, spelling is sometimes "taught" in such a fashion as to preclude any possibility of real success. Before explaining the six approaches recommended in this book, we should review a few facts about people and the learning process.

Our minds operate in accordance with certain principles. We may call them *laws* if we wish, although reputable experimental psychologists would hardly do so. For instance, you have probably long since found out that you can remember something which is important to you. You can remember it so well, so clearly, that you think you could never forget it. You also realize that you can conveniently fail to remember things you wish to forget—dental appointments, for example.

Incentive, then, or a strong motive to remember, will facilitate memory. And a good memory will aid the process of learning. Thus, the task of learning to spell will come easier to you if you bear in mind the practical value to be gained and discipline yourself to study and practice.

The mental process most important in word study is the ability to form mental pictures, or *mental images* as they may be called. These images are of several types. For example, each of us can form some sort of visual image when a suggested idea calls up in our minds a picture. When the word *church* is suggested to you, you immediately "see in your mind" a picture of the object named. So do I, although your visual image and mine may differ. Almost any object—automobile, child, office manager, snow—will summon up for you, and for everyone, some sort of visual image.

This power of visualization is far stronger in some people than in others. You may know every detail about your bedroom and yet not be able to see it in your mind's eye. Many of us have lapses in our powers of visualization. Therefore, the suggestion set forth later, that you "mentally see" words, may or may not be helpful to you. If it isn't, some other approach will make more sense. It's no discredit not to have visual memory, although it is true that this mental process can be trained. You probably can close your eyes and, without difficulty, see your own signature. But you may not be able to "see" any of the words you persistently misspell. If so, try another approach.

When a suggested idea summons up a memory of what the object sounds like, we have an *auditory* (hearing) image. Some of us can, and some cannot, "mentally hear" the sounds named in "the bark of a gun," "the popping of hot fat," "the song of a lark," "the laughter of children." Being auditory-minded is not especially helpful in learning to spell, unless we are also visual-minded. If we are both, the sounds of a few words can be compared with their visual images. Some of the memory devices (*mnemonics*) suggested later depend upon this relationship.

Related to the visual image and the auditory image is the *motor* image. Motor images are connected with the use of different muscles in the body. If you are a swimmer and think of the last lap in a long race, you can summon up the feeling of weary arm and leg muscles.

How can a motor image apply to spelling? Have you ever said of the spelling of a word you have in mind: "That may not be correct. Wait until I write it"? If so, you have called upon a motor image (hand-motor memory) to aid your visual memory. Motor memory is, for some people, a powerful aid in spelling; they apparently can actually feel the motions called into play by writing. You can close your eyes and without conscious thought write your signature entirely from "feel": this is motor memory.

The more mental images you have of words, the better your spelling will become. Visual, auditory, and motor images can aid in recalling correct spellings. This fundamental principle of the human mental process has an enormously important bearing on learning to spell and explains why some methods are ineffective and wasteful. For one example, you may have tried to learn the spelling of some word by repeating its letters to yourself over and over. If you have an especially well developed "auditory memory," this method may work. But auditory images are difficult or impossible for many people to summon up. In fact, some psychologists maintain it is the least developed means of recall for most of us. Mouthing words over and over is a complete waste of time for a majority of people.

When you were in school and misspelled a word, your teacher may have required you to write it correctly ten, twenty, or a hundred times. Such drill was designed to fix the word so firmly in your motor memory that you would never misspell it again. Unfortunately, such drill can, and often does, become rote; you perform the exercise without conscious attention to what you're doing. You are expending muscular effort but not relating it to visual or auditory images. We all realize that we perform certain acts with little or no conscious attention so that we are hardly aware of the process involved: shifting automobile gears, sewing, walking, carrying food to our mouths with a fork, even reading. But learning to spell requires attention and concentration, not rote methods that have little or no relationship to forming important mental images.

Well, if these are poor methods of learning to spell, what is the most effective? First, there is no *one* best method. Learning to spell is an individual matter. What works for you may not work for your friend, and vice versa. (It's even possible, but not likely, that some people can learn to spell words by mouthing them or writing them down a hundred times.) But there are a half-dozen approaches that may be effective. One or more may work for you, depending upon your mental makeup. Almost surely, one method will be better than others for you.

These six methods, discussed fully in the sections that follow, have worked for millions of people. Each is psychologically sound: each has individual merits. But not all of them will work for you. If you can't "visualize" words (the most helpful approach for the largest number of people), don't lose heart; one of the other methods may suit your individual mental processes far better. Here, then, are the six methods:

1. Mentally see words as well as hear them.
2. Pronounce words correctly and carefully.
3. Use a dictionary.
4. Learn a few simple rules of spelling.
5. Spell carefully to avoid errors.
6. Use memory devices.

MENTALLY SEE WORDS AS WELL AS HEAR THEM

The ability to visualize words, to see them in the mind's eye, is the hallmark of the good speller. To mix some metaphors, it is one's "ace in the hole," one's "secret weapon." When a word is mentioned, a proficient speller can "see" the word in full detail, every letter standing out, as though it were written on paper, or the floor, the wall, the sky—against whatever background object he or she calls to mind. If you are a poor speller, you lack this ability to some degree. Why is this so?

Perhaps one reason is that you learned to read words as units and were not required to sound them out letter-by-letter and syllable-by-syllable. Such a method of teaching was partly a protest against the chaotic or nonexistent relationship between sound and symbol in many English words. This approach also recognized that we *do* read words as units, not as successions of letters. Possibly this "modern" method of teaching reading helped to create many poor spellers.

It is quite possible to learn the general appearance of words on flash cards and later to recognize them elsewhere. You have no difficulty in visualizing such words as *cat, hat, dog,* and *run.* But unless you have actually studied them, you may mistake *their* for *there,* or *its* for *it's,* to mention only two examples of oft-misspelled words. (Fortunately, most teachers have long since modified this new approach and now teach not only by word units but also by sounds, letters, and syllables.)

Again, your difficulty in visualizing words may have to do with your perception span. Some people can form a remarkably definite and complete impression of an entire room at a single glance; others can look at the same room for minutes on end without really "seeing" it at all. Similarly, many words contain too many letters for some people to take in at a single glance; possibly three to five letters is all they can perceive at one time. (Please remember that we are here discussing not reading but accurate and detailed mental pictures.)

If your ability to "see words in your mind" is weak and faulty, begin by dividing the words you are studying into syllables. Then you can focus on one syllable at a time (usually two to five letters) and not stretch your perception (seeing) span beyond reasonable limits. After learning to "see" each syllable separately, you can more and more easily visualize the complete word made up of separately seen units. For example, if you cannot mentally see the word *compete*, focus first on *com* and then on *pete*. When you have learned to see each unit, you can readily see them combined. If you cannot "see" the word *competitively*, try focusing on each of the individual units and then combine them: *com-pet-i-tive-ly*.

A principle of photography may be of help in this problem. What we call a snapshot is an instantaneous photograph—a picture taken with a small amount of exposure time. Other pictures require longer exposure for varying reasons. Simple words like *cat, dog, boy*, and *am* may be called snapshots—they make an instantaneous clear image on the mind. But words like *cataclysm, dogged, boycott*, and *amphibious* require longer exposure. That is, you must look at them, probably by syllables, long enough to form clear and precise mental images of them.

When you have a strong, completely established mental picture of a word, you can spell it on any occasion without hesitation or difficulty. The greatest single mistake of poor spellers is not looking at a word with enough care and time to fix it in their minds firmly and forever. Don't say that you can't do this; you already have done so with many words. You can picture and spell without hesitation many simple and even some very complex words. You can do this for your own name, for your town or city, and for the street on which you live. That is, you have looked at these words and have actually *seen* what you looked at.

Here is a good method of learning to "see" words mentally:

1. With your eyes on the word being studied, pronounce it carefully. If you don't know the proper pronunciation, consult a dictionary.
2. Study each individual letter in the word; if the word has more than one syllable, separate the syllables and focus on each one in turn.
3. *Close your eyes* and pronounce and spell the word

either letter-by-letter or syllable-by-syllable, depending upon its length.

4. Look at the word again to make certain you have recalled it correctly.

5. Practice this alternate fixing of the image and its recall until you are certain that you can instantly "see" the word under any circumstances and at any time.

Such a procedure is especially valuable when dealing with tricky words which add or drop letters for no apparent reason; which contain silent letters; or which transpose or change letters without logical cause:

explain but *explanation*
proceed but *procedure*
pronounce but *pronunciation*
curious but *curiosity*
maintain but *maintenance*
fire but *fiery*

The most frequent error in visualizing words is mistaking one for another similar to it. A *homograph* is a word identical with another and therefore causes no spelling trouble, whatever difficulty it may provide in pronunciation and correct usage. The *bow* in *bow tie* is spelled the same as the word *bow*, meaning "to bend," but differs in pronunciation and meaning.

Homonyms, however, do cause spelling trouble. They are words identical in pronunciation but have different meanings and often different spellings. If you spell *bore* when you mean *boar*, or *meet* when you mean *meat*, you have incurred homonym trouble. The only sure remedy for this type of blunder is to study such words until they and their meanings are fixed in your mind.

PRONOUNCE WORDS CORRECTLY

Just compare heart, beard, and heard,
Dies and diet, lord and word,
Sword and sward, retain and Britain,
(Mind the latter, how it's written)

Made has not the sound of bade;
Say, said, pay, paid, laid, but plaid.

These lines of doggerel amusingly demonstrate that pronunciation is not a safe guide to spelling. A system which tolerates, for example, *cough* and *through* is quite imperfect. (A frequently cited illustration is that if you use the sound of *f* as the *gh* in *enough*, of *i* as the *o* in *women*, and of *sh* as the *ti* of *fiction*, you can spell *fish* as *ghoti*.) For another example of confusion confounded, consider the sound of *ain*, the sound we have in *pain*. It can be, and is, represented by these entirely different spellings: *pane, reign, vein, campaign, champagne*. In fact, pronunciation is so unreliable a guide to spelling that you can quite logically spell *coffee* as *kauphy*, with not a single corresponding letter in the two words.

Scholars agree that there are only about 50 speech sounds in the English language, nearly all of which are used in dictionaries to record pronunciation. To express these sounds, we have only 26 letters in our alphabet and they appear in about 250 spelling combinations. Consider the sound of long *e*, the sound we have in *equal*:

1. eve
2. seed
3. read
4. receive
5. people
6. key
7. quay
8. police
9. piece
10. amoeba
11. Caesar

This is entirely illogical, isn't it? Of course. But for several reasons the situation is not hopeless.

First, not all sounds and spellings differ so much as those just cited. The examples given are designedly extreme. Actually, some relationship often exists between sound and spelling; a large number of words are spelled exactly as they sound, and many others have sounds and spellings almost alike. The words *bat, red*, and *top* are spelled as they sound to most people. Many longer words are also spelled as they sound, especially if you break them into syllables: *lone-li-ness, mem-o-ry, part-ner*, for example. The situation is not without hope.

Second, many of the words which differ most greatly in sound and spelling are those which you rarely need to use. Like almost everyone else, including good spellers, you would look up such words in a dictionary before attempting to write them; they do not have to be learned. Few people can spell, on demand, such a word as *phthisic*. They consult a dictionary, and so should you.

Third, actually *mispronouncing* words causes more trouble than does a difference between the spelling and sound of a correctly pronounced word. In other words, correct pronunciation is sometimes of little help in spelling, but *mispronouncing* often adds an additional hazard. It is probably improper pronunciation which would make you spell *Calvary* when you mean *cavalry*. *Affect* and *effect* look somewhat alike, but they do have different pronunciations as well as different meanings. A *dairy* is one thing; a *diary* is another and will be so indicated by correct pronunciation. There is some reason why, from sound, you might spell *crowd* as "croud" or *benign* as "benine." But there is no reason *except* poor pronunciation for spelling *shudder* as "shutter," *propose* as "porpose," or *marrying* as "marring."

Spelling consciousness, an *awareness* of words, depends in part on correct pronunciation. Properly pronouncing the following words will help some people to spell them correctly. Mispronouncing them will cause nearly everyone spelling trouble. Look at each word until you are fully aware of it. Pronounce it correctly, consulting your dictionary often and carefully.

The list is merely suggestive; people mispronounce so many words in so many different ways that no list can be complete. But the author has encountered faulty spellings of the words listed here and suspects that they represent fairly general mispronunciations. The first part of the following list deals with perfectly good words that have been confused. The second part reveals pronunciations resulting in nonexistent, incorrect words.

Words Confused in Pronunciation

caliber	casualty	cemetery
caliper	causality	symmetry
carton	celery	color
cartoon	salary	collar

elicit	impostor	sculptor
illicit	imposture	sculpture
errand	pastor	sink
errant	pasture	zinc
finally	plaintiff	specie
finely	plaintive	species
gig	relic	tenet
jig	relict	tenant

CORRECT	INCORRECT
garage (storage place)	*gararge*
height (distance from bottom to top)	*heighth*
imagine (to form an idea)	*imangine*
irrelevant (unrelated)	*irrevelant*
poem (literary composition)	*pome*
radio (transmission of sound waves)	*raido* or *radeo*
research (systematic inquiry)	*reaserch*
strategic (favorable or advantageous)	*stragetic*
temperature (degree of heat)	*tempreture*
tragedy (serious drama or event)	*tradegy*

Misspellings Due to Incorrect Prefix

CORRECT	INCORRECT
perform (to act, to do)	*preform*
perhaps (possibly, probably)	*prehaps*
perversely (persisting in error)	*preversely*

precipitate (to cause action)   *percipitate*
professor (a teacher)   *perfessor* or *prefessor*
proposal (a plan, scheme)   *porposal* or *preprosal*

Misspellings Due to Added Vowels

CORRECT	INCORRECT
athletics (sports, games)	*athaletics* or *atheletics*
disastrous (causing harm, grief)	*disasterous*
entrance (act or point of coming in)	*enterance*
grievous (serious, grave)	*grievious*
hundred (the number)	*hundered*
laundry (washing of clothes)	*laundery* or *laundary*
mischievous (prankish)	*mischievious*
partner (associate)	*partener*
similar (like)	*similiar*
Spanish (pertaining to Spain)	*Spainish*
umbrella (shade or screen)	*umberella*

Misspellings Due to Dropped Vowels

1. John's truck *accidentally* (not *accidently*) hit the child.
2. This is an *auxiliary* (not *auxilary*) gasoline tank.
3. The physician prescribed *beneficial* (not *benefical*) drugs.
4. The pianist gave a *brilliant* (not *brillant*) recital.
5. This harsh *criticism* (not *critcism*) is merited.
6. He is a soldier, not a *civilian* (not *civilan*).
7. She is a *conscientious* (not *conscientous*) housewife.
8. This *convenient* (not *convenent*) room is for your use.
9. John is *deficient* (not *deficent*) in his accounts.
10. Mary is an *efficient* (not *efficent*) typist.
11. Your face is *familiar* (not *familar*).

12. I seek your *financial* (not *financal*) help.
13. King Cole was a merry, *genial* (not *genal*) soul.
14. Beethoven was a man of *genius* (not *genus*).
15. Your sentence is *grammatically* (not *grammaticly*) sound.
16. The money is only *incidentally* (not *incidently*) important.
17. The chemistry *laboratory* (not *labortory*) is large.
18. I like to read good *literature* (not *literture*).
19. *Mathematics* (not *mathmatics*) deals with numbers.
20. A child is a *miniature* (not *minature*) adult.

In addition to these twenty words illustrated in sentences, check your pronunciation of the following. Some people slur over the vowels that are shown in boldface; some omit them entirely; some pronounce them with considerable stress. Pronounce each word as you normally do. If the letters in boldface are silent, or lightly stressed in your speech, you are likely to omit them from your spelling.

accuracy	delivery	misery
aspirin	family	particular
bachelor	history	privilege
boundary	lengthening	regular
considerable	liable	scenery
criminal	magazine	temperature
different	memory	victory

Misspellings Due to Dropped Consonants

Mr. Avery is an old acquaintance of mine.
The Arctic Circle is entirely imaginary.
He is a candidate for the office.
The driver was convicted of drunkenness.
He stopped school in the eighth grade.
Mac grew up in a poor environment.
February is the shortest month in the year.
He is opposed to all forms of government.
Karen is now a proud kindergarten pupil.

There are thousands of books in her library.
Sam is probably the best salesman in the company.
He purchased a large quantity of food.
Mae did not seem to recognize me.
He was a good representative for the firm.
This statement surprised me.

In addition to these illustrated words, and as a start on your additional list, pronounce each of the following as you ordinarily do. Perhaps your pronunciation will offer a clue to the cause of some of your misspellings. In each word, the "offending" consonant appears in boldface. Some of these consonants are silent or are slurred over.

accept	grandfather	recognize
authentic	handle	rhythm
column	handful	slept
condemn	hustle	soften
contempt	identical	swept
consumption	kept	tentative
empty	listen	used to
except	often	wrestle
fasten	prompt	yellow

Misspellings Due to Unstressed Vowels

academy	ecstasy	optimism
accident	excellent	peril
actor	fakir	politics
arithmetic	grammar	private
benefit	humorous	privilege
business	hunger	professor
calendar	loafer	repetition
comparative	luxury	respectable
corner	maintenance	ridiculous
democracy	martyr	separate
develop	mathematics	sofa
dilute	medicine	sponsor

discipline	murmur	terror
distress	nadir	vulgar
dollar	occur	

Misspellings Due to Silent Letters

Sounds have been dropping out of our language for many centuries, but their disappearance has affected pronunciation much more than spelling. Actually, many letters no longer pronounced in certain words persist in our spelling, for no good reason: the *l* in such words as *could, would,* and *should* has been silent for hundreds of years, but it hangs on in spelling.

The problem is compounded when we realize that the majority of the letters in our alphabet appear as silent letters in one word or another:

dead	honest	raspberry
doubt	weird	often
scene	knife	guess
handsome	salmon	answer
come	mnemonics	yacht
off	column	bough
sign	famous	

Some silent letters cause little difficulty in spelling. If you are "visual minded," you will automatically put a *k* in *knee* or a *g* in *gnat*. But other letters which are silent, or are so lightly sounded as to be almost unheard, do cause trouble. Here is a list of some common words which, in the pronunciation of most educated people, contain silent letters:

bomb	indebted	pneumatic
comb	knack	prompt
condemn	knee	psychology
crumb	kneel	thumb
daughter	knit	tomb
dough	knob	wrap
dumb	knock	wreck

eight	knot	wretch
fourth	know	wring
ghost	plumber	write

Once again, pronunciation is not a safe guide to spelling. But *faulty* pronunciation sometimes adds hazards. Pronouncing words correctly is at least a slight aid in correct spelling. Try to form clear and definite *auditory* and *visual* images of words whose pronunciation can compound spelling problems.

USE A DICTIONARY

When you are suspicious of the spelling of any word you should check it immediately in your dictionary. "Doubt + dictionary = good spelling" is a reliable formula. However, it is a counsel of perfection, one that few of us is likely always to follow. Not only that, our sense of doubt may be so great that we spend half our writing time flipping dictionary pages rather than communicating and thus grow bored and frustrated.

Also, you may have tried to look up a word in the dictionary and been unable to find it. If your visual image of a word is weak, you can frustrate yourself even more: Look for *agast* and you may give up before discovering that the word is *aghast*. You won't find *pharmacy* and *photograph* among words beginning with *f*. In fact, the confusion of sound and spelling has caused more than one reputable publishing firm seriously to consider preparing a dictionary for poor spellers. Such a dictionary would have been helpful to the man who was away on a trip and telephoned his secretary to send his gun to him at a hunting resort. The secretary could barely hear him (the connection was poor) and asked her boss to spell out what he wanted. "Gun," he shouted. " 'G' as in *Jerusalem*, 'u' as in Europe, 'n' as in *pneumonia*." Whether or not he received his *jep* is unknown; maybe she sent him a dictionary instead.

Even topnotch spellers consult a dictionary for the spelling of some words. You may not hesitate over *chiaroscuro* or *chimerical*, but you may need to look up *aficionado* or *solipsism* or *Yggdrasill*. Granting that few of us would use these words in the first place, most of us would check our doubts by consulting a dictionary each time. In addition, compound words frequently require hyphens for correct spelling; even superb spellers must look up many such words.

If you haven't done so yet, now would be a good time to get thoroughly acquainted with your dictionary. Better still, make it your friend; best of all, make it your constant companion.

Choice of a Dictionary

But you should know that there are dictionaries and dictionaries. Some, such as a pocket dictionary, are so small as to be virtually worthless save as a limited guide to spelling and pronunciation. Others, of fair size, may have been so hastily and carelessly produced that they are unreliable. Even the name "Webster" in the title is no longer a guarantee of quality because as a label "Webster" is no longer copyrighted and appears alike in the titles of both reliable and unreliable dictionaries. You should have—and if you don't have, you should buy—a dictionary you can trust.

My advice is that you secure for your own use a desk-size dictionary. You will find it a never-failing help in time of spelling trouble. Not only that: intelligent use of a dictionary can help to *prevent* trouble, too. That is, certain approaches to the vast amount of knowledge recorded in a desk-size dictionary can fix certain principles and patterns in our minds so that we do not have to consult it for, *at most*, more than 5 percent of the words we use. Certain facts about word derivations, prefixes, suffixes, plurals, apostrophes, hyphens, and capitalization can be learned easily. They will apply to large numbers and classes of words and help to improve our spelling in almost wholesale fashion. First, let's consider word derivation.

ETYMOLOGY (WORD DERIVATION)

Etymology, a word taken from Greek, means an account of the history of a given word. More particularly, etymology deals with the origin and derivation of words. Knowing what a word comes from will often help you to spell it correctly. For example, the word *preparation* is derived from the Latin prefix *prae* ("before-hand") plus *parare* (meaning "to make ready"). Knowing this, and accenting the first *a* in *parare*, may help you to spell the word correctly: *preparation*, not *preperation*.

Similarly, our word *dormitory* (a building containing sleeping rooms) is derived from the Latin word *dormitorium*. Noting the first *i* in this Latin word, and perhaps also knowing that the French word for sleep is *dormir*, may help you to spell *dormitory* with an *i* and not an *a*.

A study of etymology primarily will aid in building your vocabulary. But it also has its uses in learning to spell. Here are somewhat simplified etymological comments on a few other common words that may fix this principle in your mind and lead to further study:

1. *Calendar.* This word is descended from the Latin word for "account book," *calendarium*. Note the *a*; we frequently misspell the word as *calender* (a perfectly good word with an entirely different meaning).

2. *Consensus.* This word comes from the same Latin root as *consent* (*con* + *sentire*, to feel). Note the *s* in *sentire* and you will not spell the word *concensus*, as is frequently done.

3. *Equivalent.* This frequently misspelled word may be easier for you if you remember that it means "equal in value" and is derived from the prefix *equi* + *valere*. Accent the *val* sound in *valere* (value).

4. *Extravagance.* This word is composed of *extra* (beyond) plus the Latin word *vagans* (*vagari*, to wander). "Extravagance" is wandering beyond limits. Accent the letters *v* - *a* - *g* in the root word to insure correct spelling.

5. *Familiar.* This common word, often misspelled with an *e* where the second *a* should appear, is related to the Latin word *familia* (servants in a household).

6. *Finis.* This synonym for "end" has the same origin as the words *definite* and *finite*. Accent the "i" sound and come up with two *i*'s in this word.

7. *Medicine*. Many people tend to spell the second syllable of this word with an *e*. Its origin goes back to Latin
   medicina (*medicus*). Accent the *i* as an aid to correct
   spelling.
8. *Optimism*. This word comes to us by way of the
   French word *optimisme* (from Latin *optimus*, meaning
   "best"). Focus on the two *i*'s in *optimism*.
9. *Privilege*. From *privus* (private) plus *lex*, *legis* (law),
   this word can be remembered as "privy" (private) with
   the *y* changing to *i* plus *legal*, which fixes *leg* in *privilege*.
10. *Recommend*. This word comes from Latin *recommen-
    dare*. Think of it as *re* + *commend* and avoid that all-
    too-present double *c*.

USE A DICTIONARY: PREFIXES AND SUFFIXES

Prefixes, as we have noted, are syllables added to the beginning of
words to alter or modify their meanings or, occasionally, to form
entirely new words. For example, we add the prefix *mis* to the
word *spell* and form *misspell*.

Suffixes are syllables added at the end of words to alter their
meanings, to form new words, or to show grammatical function
(part of speech). Thus we add *ish* to *small* and form *smallish*.

The readiness with which prefixes and suffixes are tacked on to
root words in the English language is an indication of the freedom
in word formation that has characterized our language for many
centuries. For example, consider the word *recession*. This is
derived from a Latin word *cedere* (*cessus*), which has the general
meaning of "go." To this base we add the prefix *re*, which has a
generalized meaning of "back" or "again," and the suffix *ion*, an
ending which shows that the word is a noun (name of something).

Related to *recession* are many words with still other prefixes
and suffixes but all coming from a similar root, or base: *recede*,
recess, *recessive*, etc. The same root appears in *concession*, *pro-
cession*, *secession*, etc. The prefix of *recession* occurs in such
words as *reception* and *relation*. Examples like this could be
extended indefinitely.

For one final example, you can select the root word *scribe* (derived from the Latin equivalent of "to write"). From this root, you can easily form well-known words by using prefixes and suffixes:

ascribe, ascription
circumscribe, circumscription
describe, description
inscribe, inscription
prescribe, prescription
proscribe, proscription
subscribe, subscription
transcribe, transcription

A knowledge of the ways in which prefixes and suffixes are added to words will not only increase your vocabulary but also improve your spelling. However, we shall discuss here only a few common prefixes and suffixes appearing in everyday words. Those interested in these additions to words can consult any of a number of lengthy studies available in almost any library.

Prefixes

The following is a list of common prefixes which will be of considerable aid in spelling:

a-, ab- (from, away) as in *avert, absent*
ad- (toward, to) as in *adhere, adverb*
ante- (before) as in *antecedent, antedate*
anti- (against, opposite) as in *antidote, antitoxin*
con-, com- (with) as in *confide, commit*
de- (away, down) as in *decline, depressed*
di-, dis- (separation, reversal, apart) as in *divert, disappoint*
e-, ex- (out of, former) as in *elect, exclude*
hyper- (over, above) as in *hyperacidity, hypercritical*
in- (in, into) as in *induce, invert*
in- (not) as in *inexact, invalid*
inter- (between) as in *intercede, intervene*
mis- (wrong, bad) as in *misconduct, mistake*

non- (not, not one) as in *non-American, nonresident*
ob- (against) as in *object, obtuse*
poly- (many) as in *polygamy, polytechnic*
pre- (before) as in *predict, prenatal*
pro- (forward) as in *proceed, propel*
re- (again, back) as in *repay, restore*
sub- (under) as in *subscribe, submarine*
trans- (across) as in *transfer, transport*
ultra- (beyond) as in *ultramodern, ultraviolet*
un- (not) as in *unhappy, untruth*

This is a very brief list of prefixes, but they appear in a large number of misspelled words. Here are notes on the spelling of words containing a few of these prefixes:

Ad-

This prefix alters its form according to the root word to which it is attached. For example, before a root beginning *sc* or *sp*, the *d* is dropped, as in *ascent* and *aspire*. Before such letters as *c, f, g, l, n, p,* and *t,* the *d* in *ad-* is assimilated (becomes the same as the following letter): *accommodate, affix, aggression, allegation, announce, appoint, attend.*

Ante-, anti-

The first of these prefixes is of Latin origin and means "before" or "prior." *Anti-* is from Greek and means "opposite" or "against." Note these different spellings:

ante-bellum (before the war)
*ante*meridian (before noon; A.M.)
*ante*room (room before)
*ante*type (an earlier form)
*anti*biotic (defense against bacteria)
*anti*climax (contrast to preceding rise in action)
*anti*freeze (against freezing)
*anti*septic (against infection)

De-, dis-

These prefixes will cause spelling problems when you don't distinguish clearly between root words beginning with *s* and the prefixes themselves. Note these spellings:

describe (write down) *de + scribe*
despoil (strip down) *de + spoil*
dissemble (disguise) *dis + semble*
dissimilar (unlike) *dis + similar*

Remember: Only about thirty common words begin with *diss*, but ten times as many begin with *dis*. Only three fairly common words (and their derivatives) begin with *dys: dysentery, dyspepsia, dystrophy* (as in *muscular dystrophy*).

A simple rule: When the prefixes *dis* and *mis* are added to a root word beginning with *s*, neither *s* should be omitted: *dissatisfied, misstep*. When they are added to roots not beginning with an *s*, use only one *s: disappear, misfortune*.

Inter-

This prefix meaning "between" is frequently confused with *intra*, which means "inside," "within."

*inter*fere (between)
*inter*collegiate (between colleges)
*inter*state (between, among states)
*intra*mural (within the walls)
*intra*state (within a state)
*intra*venous (within a vein, veins)

Un-

When this prefix is added to a root word beginning with *n*, neither *n* is omitted:

unnamed	unneeded	unnoticed
unnatural	unnegotiable	unnumbered
unnecessary	unnoted	unnurtured

Suffixes

It would be possible to make a list of suffixes, but doing so would not in itself be much of an aid to correct spelling. For one thing, the list would have to be very lengthy; for another, many suffixes have several different meanings, others have vague or general meanings.

Only eight suffix groups cause major spelling problems. Within each group are many words that give trouble, some of the most often misspelled words in the language. Here is a brief discussion of each of the eight groups.

-Able, -ible

Even excellent spellers have occasional difficulties with these endings; they can unhesitatingly spell most words having one or the other of these suffixes, but once in a while they, too, must seek out their dictionaries.

-Able

1. The ending should usually be *able* if the base (root) is a full word: *eat + able*.

Fortunately, many of our most familiar, most used words add *able* to form adjectives. Note that if you drop *able* from each of the following you are left with a *complete* word:

acceptable	dependable	peaceable
available	detestable	perishable
avoidable	drinkable	predictable
breakable	fashionable	profitable
comfortable	favorable	readable
commendable	laughable	taxable
considerable	noticeable	workable

2. The ending should usually be *able* if the base is a full word except for lacking a final *e*: *desire + able = desirable*.

Fortunately, this group of *-able* words is not nearly so large as the preceding one. The following words illustrate the basic principle:

believable	excitable	pleasurable
debatable	excusable	sizable
describable	likable	usable
desirable	lovable	valuable

3. The ending should usually be *able* if the base ends in *i* (the original word may have ended in *y*): *enviable*.

This principle of spelling makes more sense than most spelling "rules." If it were not followed we would have a double *i* (*ii*), an unusual combination even in our weird spelling system.

classifiable	justifiable	reliable

4. The ending should usually be *able* if the base has other forms with the sound of long *a*: *demonstrate, demonstrable*.

This principle will be helpful only if you actually sound out another form (or forms) of the root word to see whether it has (or they have) the long *a* sound: *abominate, abominable; estimate, estimable*, etc.

delectable	inflammable	intolerable
durable	innumerable	irreparable
impregnable	inseparable	irritable

5. The ending should usually be *able* if the base ends in hard *c* or hard *g*.

Hard *c* is sounded like the *c* in *cat*; hard *g* has the sound of *g* in *get*. The following words illustrate this principle:

amicable	explicable	practicable
applicable	indefatigable	irrevocable

These five principles cover most of the fairly common words which have endings in *able*. But there are a few exceptions. If you wish to be able to spell all words ending with *able*, then study the following by some other method suggested in this book; rules won't help much:

affable	ineffable	portable
culpable	inevitable	potable
equitable	inscrutable	probable
formidable	insuperable	unconscionable
indomitable	memorable	vulnerable

-Ible

1. The ending should usually be *ible* if the base is not a full word.

Contrast this principle with item 1 under *-Able*. If the base is a complete word, we then add *able: mail + able = mailable*. If the base is not a complete word, we add *ible: ris + ible = risible*, and *poss + ible = possible*.

audible	feasible	negligible
conbustible	horrible	plausible
credible	infallible	terrible
edible	intelligible	visible

2. The ending should usually be *ible* if the base ends in *ns: respons + ible = responsible*.

These words illustrate this spelling principle:

comprehensible	indefensible	reprehensible
defensible	insensible	responsible
incomprehensi-		
ble	irresponsible	sensible

3. The ending should usually be *ible* if the base ends in *miss: admiss + ible = admissible*.

Comparatively few words belong in this category. Here are several examples:

| dismissible | permissible | transmissible |
| omissible | remissible | |

With roots not ending in *miss*, but closely related, are such words with *ible* endings as *accessible, compressible, irrepressible*, and *possible* (which also fits under group 1 above).

4. The ending should usually be *ible* if *ion* can be added to the base without intervening letters: *collect, collection, collectible*.

Quite a few words create such new forms by the immediate (nothing coming between) addition of *ion*. All such words form adjectives ending in *ible*; here are a few samples:

accessible	convertible	inexhaustible
collectible	digestible	reversible

You should note that this rule is tricky: If *ion* cannot be added to the root immediately (without intervening letters), the *able* ending is more likely, as in *present, presentation, presentable*.

5. The ending should usually be *ible* if the base ends in soft *c* or soft *g*.

This principle should be compared with item 5 under *-Able*. A soft *c* sounds like an *s* (force); a soft *g* sounds like a *j* (tangent). The following words contain a soft *c* or a soft *g*. Also note that, with few exceptions, the roots are not complete words.

convincible	illegible	legible
eligible	intelligible	negligible
forcible	invincible	seducible

Just as there are a few exceptions to the rules for *able* endings so are there for words ending in *ible*. The commonly used words that are exceptions are not numerous. Among those words which, by rule, should end in *able* but do not are the following:

collapsible	flexible	inflexible
contemptible	gullible	irresistible

The following words merit careful study because each is an exception to the principles discussed above:

correctable	dispensable	predictable
detectable	indispensable	

-Ally, -ly

These two suffixes are often confused by spellers with inadequate visual memories. Because these endings appear so often in commonly used words, they account for large numbers of misspellings. The same advice applies: When in doubt, consult your dictionary.

Perhaps these basic principles concerning *-ly* will also be helpful:

1. The suffix *ly* is used to form an adverb from an adjective: *poor + ly = poorly*. If the adjective ends in *l*, *ly* is tacked on to the complete root, thus producing an *lly* ending.

Here is a list of frequently used, and occasionally misspelled, adverbs:

accidentally	fundamentally	personally
actually	generally	physically
annually	incidentally	really
continually	individually	skillfully
cruelly	literally	successfully
especially	logically	truthfully
exceptionally	naturally	universally
finally	occasionally	usually

2. The suffix *ly* is added to basic words ending in silent *e*, and the *e* is retained.

absolutely	immediately	scarcely
completely	infinitely	sincerely

3. If an adjective ends in *ic*, its adverbial form ends in *ally*.

This is a simple, clear rule with only one exception: *publicly*. This word you must fix in your visual memory. Here are examples of adverbs formed from adjectives with *ic* endings:

academically	basically	lyrically
artistically	emphatically	scholastically
automatically	fantastically	systematically

The following adverbs do not completely follow the principles just enumerated. Fix them in your visual memory:

duly	only	truly
incredibly	possibly	wholly

-Ance, -ence

The suffixes *ance* and *ence* are added to root words (verbs) to form nouns: *attend, attendance; prefer, preference.*

With one exception, to be noted below, there is no uniform guiding principle to your choice of *-ance* or *-ence.* Here again, correct pronunciation is of no help. True, if you know the conjugation of Latin verbs you can form a helpful rule, but so few of us do know Latin that it's useless to state the principle. Your only safe procedure is to consult your dictionary and try to form good visual images of *-ance* and *-ence* words.

One helpful principle, and one only, is this: If a verb ends in *r* preceded by a vowel and is accented on the last syllable, it forms its noun with *ence*:

abhorrence	inference	preference
coherence	interference	recurrence
conference	occurrence	reference

Here are lists of often misspelled words ending in *ance* and *ence.* Study each until you have a total recall of its appearance.

FREQUENTLY MISSPELLED "-ANCE" WORDS

abundance	appearance	distance
acquaintance	assurance	endurance
admittance	attendance	entrance
allegiance	balance	grievance
alliance	brilliance	guidance
allowance	contrivance	instance
ambulance	defiance	insurance

FREQUENTLY MISSPELLED "-ENCE" WORDS

absence	difference	obedience
audience	eminence	patience

circumference	evidence	preference
coincidence	excellence	presence
conference	existence	prominence
confidence	experience	reference
conscience	influence	residence
convenience	innocence	reverence
correspondence	insistence	silence

-Ar, -er, -or

The suffixes *ar*, *er*, and *or* have various origins, functions, and meanings. Their most common shared meaning denotes an actor, a doer, "one who." Many thousands of English words end in *ar*, *er*, and *or*, but here again accurate pronunciation is little aid in spelling. Furthermore, no rules or principles are applicable to their correct spelling. Consult your dictionary; try to form accurate visual images.

Following are lists of *-ar*, *-er*, and *-or* words often misspelled. In not every word is the ending a true suffix, but correct spelling is now your objective, not a study of word origins or of word-building.

FREQUENTLY MISSPELLED WORDS ENDING IN "-AR"

altar	familiar	pillar
beggar	grammar	popular
burglar	hangar	regular
calendar	insular	scholar
caterpillar	liar	similar
cellar	molar	sugar
circular	particular	vinegar
collar	peculiar	vulgar

FREQUENTLY MISSPELLED WORDS ENDING IN "-ER"

advertiser	diameter	messenger
adviser	employer	officer
announcer	examiner	partner
baker	jeweler	passenger
beginner	laborer	prisoner

believer	lawyer	teacher
boulder	manager	traveler
consumer	manufacturer	writer

FREQUENTLY MISSPELLED WORDS ENDING IN "-OR"

accelerator	author	bachelor
actor	aviator	behavior
commentator	escalator	neighbor
contributor	factor	pastor
councilor	governor	professor
counselor	humor	radiator
creditor	inferior	sculptor
debtor	legislator	senator
director	minor	supervisor
elevator	motor	traitor

-Ary, -ery

This suffix problem is simple. Hundreds and hundreds of English words end in *ary*. Only a half-dozen fairly common words end in *ery*. Learn the *-ery* words by whatever device presented in this book works best for you. Spell all others with *ary*. It's as elementary as that.

Here are the words you might use which end in *ery*:

cemetery	distillery	monastery
confectionery	millinery	stationery

End all other words with *ary*. You'll be right every time unless you happen to use such a rare word as *philandery*. You will have no spelling problems with the endings of *auxiliary, boundary, dictionary, elementary, honorary, imaginary, library, secretary,* and *voluntary*, and hundreds of other such everyday words.

-Cede, -ceed, -sede

These suffixes cause a large number of misspellings because they appear in several common words. But the problem they present is quite simple because so few words are involved. Only twelve words in the language end in this pronunciation, "seed," and not all of these are in common use.

First, only one word in English ends in *sede: supersede*. It has this ending because of its origin; it comes from the Latin verb *sedeo*, meaning "to sit." As with many other "borrowed" words in English it maintains some connection with its source.

Second, only three of the twelve words ending with the "seed" pronunciation are spelled with *ceed: exceed, proceed*, and *succeed*.

Finally, the eight remaining words end in *cede*, and of these only three of four are in general, everyday use:

accede	concede	recede
antecede	intercede	secede
cede	precede	

It won't help with spelling the *ceed* and *cede* words to know their origin, but it will help in avoiding a *sede* ending: the eleven *ceed, cede* words derive not from *sedeo* (as *supersede* does) but from Latin *cedo*, meaning "to go." Thus, *pre + cede* means "to go or come before"; *inter + cede* means "to go or come between," and so on.

-Efy, -ify

These two suffixes cause much spelling trouble, but here again the problem is simple when it is clearly looked at. Actually, only four words you are likely to use end in *efy* (and you probably won't use them every day, either). All the remainder, without exception, end in *ify*.

Therefore, learn these four words by whatever method seems best and spell all others with *ify*:

liquefy (to make liquid)
putrefy (to make or become rotten)
rarefy (to make or become rare)
stupefy (to make or become insensible)

Also, you should note that words built on these four tend to retain the *e* spelling:

liquefy, liquefies, liquefied, liquefying, liquefaction
putrefy, putrefies, putrefied, putrefying, putrefaction
rarefy, rarefies, rarefied, rarefying, rarefaction
stupefy, stupefies, stupefied, stupefying, stupefaction

-Ise, -ize, -yze

Some five hundred fairly common words in our language end in *ise, ize,* and *yze.* How can one master all these spellings, especially since correct pronunciation provides no help at all?

Consulting your dictionary will provide some help, and so will training your visual memory until a word you've spelled with *ize* just "doesn't look right" if it should end in *ise.* The best approach is to isolate the comparatively few words with *yze* and *ise* and to remember that *ize* is by far the most common suffix and that the chances of its being correct are mathematically excellent.

These are the only four fairly common words in English ending in *yze,* and of them you will normally use only two:

analyze
electrolyze
catalyze
paralyze

Study these four words carefully, especially the first and last. Master them by whatever method seems best: four words (or two) are a small matter.

The comparatively few words which end in *ise* can be grouped as follows:

1. Combinations with *-cise*:

exercise   exorcise   incise
excise   circumcise

These *cise* words are so spelled because they derive from a form, *incisus,* of a Latin word meaning "to cut."

2. Combination with *-guise*:

disguise

3. Combinations with -*mise*:

demise	premise
compromise	surmise

4. Combinations with -*prise*:

apprise	enterprise	reprise
comprise	emprise	surprise

5. Combinations with -*rise*:

arise	moonrise
sunrise	uprise

6. Combinations with -*vise*:

advise	improvise	supervise
devise	revise	

These *vise* words are derived from a form, *visus*, of a Latin word meaning "to see."

7. Combinations with -*wise*:

contrariwise	likewise	sidewise
lengthwise	otherwise	

8. Miscellaneous combinations with -*ise*:

advertise	despise	merchandise
chastise	franchise	

This makes a total of less than forty common words ending in *yze* and *ise*. All others with this suffixal pronunciation end in *ize*. Here are a few of the hundreds of words with this ending:

apologize	fertilize	pasteurize
authorize	generalize	patronize
baptize	humanize	philosophize
cauterize	jeopardize	realize
characterize	legalize	recognize
civilize	modernize	reorganize
colonize	monopolize	solemnize
criticize	moralize	subsidize

crystallize	nationalize	symbolize
economize	naturalize	tantalize
equalize	neutralize	utilize
familiarize	organize	vocalize

USE A DICTIONARY: PLURALS

You can consult your dictionary every time you are unsure about the spelling of a word but, as we have noted, if you do you'll be more a whirling dervish or page-flipper than a writer.

Many people find it fairly easy to spell the singular of a word (meaning "one") but have trouble forming and correctly spelling plurals (meaning "more than one"). This is quite understandable, since many English words form plurals in unusual ways. You can "look it up" in a dictionary when you are puzzled, but a few principles of plural-forming can easily be mastered.

1. The plural of most nouns is formed by adding *s* to the singular:

   book, books   hat, hats
   chair, chairs   pot, pots
   cracker, crackers   sheet, sheets

2. Nouns ending with a sibilant or *s* sound (*ch, sh, s, x, z*) form their plurals by adding *es*:

   arch, arches   fox, foxes
   box, boxes   loss, losses
   bush, bushes   tax, taxes
   buzz, buzzes   watch, watches

3. Nouns ending in *y* preceded by a consonant usually change *y* to *i* before adding *es*:

   activity, activities   forty, forties
   city, cities   library, libraries
   community, communities   sky, skies
   fly, flies   strawberry, strawberries

4. Nouns ending in *y* preceded by a vowel usually add *s* without changing the final *y*:

alley, alleys	money, moneys
attorney, attorneys	monkey, monkeys
chimney, chimneys	turkey, turkeys
key, keys	valley, valleys

5. Nouns ending in *o* preceded by a vowel add *s* to form their plurals:

cameo, cameos	radio, radios
folio, folios	rodeo, rodeos

6. Nouns ending in *o* preceded by a consonant often add *es* to form the plural:

buffalo, buffaloes	mosquito, mosquitoes
cargo, cargoes	potato, potatoes
echo, echoes	tomato, tomatoes
hero, heroes	volcano, volcanoes

7. Some nouns ending in *o* preceded by a consonant, including many musical terms, add *s* to form their plurals:

alto, altos	gigolo, gigolos
banjo, banjos	piano, pianos
canto, cantos	solo, solos
concerto, concertos	zero, zeros

8. Nouns ending in *f* form their plurals in such variable ways that you should *always* consult your dictionary when in doubt. Nouns ending in *ff* usually add *s*. Most nouns ending in *fe* change *fe* to *ve* and add *s*. The following examples will be sufficient to make you remember the formula: doubt + dictionary = correct spelling:

belief, beliefs	roof, roofs
chief, chiefs	self, selves
grief, griefs	sheriff, sheriffs
half, halfs (or halves)	staff, staves (or staffs)

handkerchief,
  handkerchiefs
life, lives
mischief, mischiefs

thief, thieves
wife, wives
wolf, wolves

9. Certain nouns of foreign origin retain the plural of the language from which they were borrowed. Some borrowed words have gradually assumed plurals with the usual English *s* or *es* endings. Finally, some words have more than one plural form. To reduce confusion, here is a list of fairly common nouns to fix in your mind by whatever device works best for you:

agendum, agenda
alumna, alumnae
alumnus, alumni
analysis, analyses
appendix, appendixes,
  appendices
axis, axes
bacterium, bacteria
basis, bases
crisis, crises
criterion, criteria,
  criterions
datum, data
erratum, errata
formula, formulas,
  formulae

genus, genera, genuses
hypothesis, hypotheses
index, indexes, indices
larva, larvae
memorandum,
  memorandums,
  memoranda
parenthesis,
  parentheses
phenomenon,
  phenomena
radius, radii, radiuses
stimulus, stimuli
thesis, theses
vertebra, vertebrae,
  vertebras

10. Compound nouns ordinarily form the plural by adding *s* or *es* to the important word in the compound. Sometimes the element considered most important comes first in the compound, sometimes at the end. The end element is usually the one pluralized if it and other elements are so closely related as to be considered a single word: *handfuls, housefuls, basketfuls.* Just to confound the pluralizing of compound words, occasionally more than one element is pluralized in the same word. Here again, the best advice is

consult your dictionary. The words listed below illustrate the erratic principles stated in this paragraph:

    attorney at law, attorneys at law
    attorney general, attorneys general
    brother-in-law, brothers-in-law
    commander in chief, commanders in chief
    consul general, consuls general
    father-in-law, fathers-in-law
    hanger-on, hangers-on
    master sergeant, master sergeants
    manservant, menservants

11. Some nouns have irregular plurals. Surely you expected to read this statement sooner or later. Here is a representative list of words with plurals that are irregular or plain nonsensical or that follow none of the principles stated above. Try to master them by whatever device you have found most useful:

    alkali, alkalies   mouse, mice
    brother, brothers,   photo, photos
       brethren   series, series
    child, children   sheep, sheep
    deer, deer   species, species
    foot, feet   swine, swine
    goose, geese   tooth, teeth
    louse, lice   woman, women
    man, men

12. Pronouns and verbs have plural forms just as nouns do. It is doubtful, however, that misspelling of pronouns is due to their number. If you misspell *their*, a plural pronoun, you are probably confusing *their* and *there*, rather than having trouble with a plural. *We, they, our, us, them,* all plural pronouns, are easy to spell.

    The plurals of verbs are quite simple. Main verbs have the same form for both singular and plural except in the third person singular, present tense: he *sees*, he *moves*, he *thinks*, he *does*, he *goes*. That is, most verbs add an *s (es)* in the third person to form a singular. It's easy to remember this: Most nouns and verbs form their plurals in directly opposite ways.

USE A DICTIONARY: APOSTROPHES

An apostrophe is a mark of punctuation, not a letter, and yet when one is improperly added or omitted it causes you to misspell. The apostrophe has several uses, all with some influence on spelling: to indicate the possessive case, to mark omission of letters, to indicate the plurals of letters and numbers. The use of an apostrophe influences both punctuation *and* spelling. Since this section deals only with spelling, we will concentrate on uses of the apostrophe that result in misspelling.

1. Use an apostrophe and *s* to form the possessive case of a noun (singular or plural) not ending in *s*:

    children, children's   horse, horse's
    doctor, doctor's   town, town's

2. Use only an apostrophe to form the possessive case of a plural noun ending in *s*:

    boys, boys'   students, students'
    ladies, ladies'   weeks, weeks'

3. Use an apostrophe alone or an apostrophe with *s* to form the possessive of singular nouns ending in *s*:

    Robert Burns, Robert   Charles, Charles'
      Burns' (or Burns's)
    She liked Robert Burns'   This is Charles' hat.
      (or Burns's) poetry.

4. In compound nouns, add the apostrophe and *s* to the last element of the expression, the one nearest the object possessed:

    my son-in-law's boat   King Henry IV's funeral
    somebody else's ticket   the city manager's salary

5. Use an apostrophe to show that letters or figures have been omitted.

aren't = are not   they're = they are
don't = do not   wasn't = was not
he's = he is   weren't = were not

The Civil War was fought 1861–65. (1861 to 1865)
He left home in '59. (1959)

This use of the apostrophe is reflected in the most misspelled short and simple word in the English language. *It's* means "it is" and can never be correctly used for *its* in the possessive sense: "When a dog wags *its* tail, that is a sign *it's* happy." Never write the letters *i-t-s* without thinking whether or not you mean "it is."

6. Use an apostrophe and *s* to indicate the plurals of figures, letters, and words considered as words.

Small children cannot always make legible 5's.
Uncrossed *t's* look like *l's*.
He uses too many *and's* and *but's* in speaking.

7. Never use an apostrophe in forming the plural of nouns and the possessive case of personal relative pronouns. The *Browns* (not *Brown's*) came to see us.

CORRECT	INCORRECT
ours	our's
ours	ours'
yours	your's
yours	yours'
his	his'
hers	her's
hers	hers'
its	it's
theirs	their's
theirs	theirs'
whose	who's

USE A DICTIONARY: COMPOUND WORDS

The general principle of word joining derives from actual usage. When two (or more) words first become associated with a single meaning, they are written separately. As they grow, through usage, to become more of a unit in thought and writing, they are usually hyphenated (spelled with a hyphen). Finally, they tend to be spelled as one word. This evolution may be seen in the following, the third word in each series now being the accepted form: *base ball, base-ball, baseball; rail road, rail-road, railroad.* This general principle, however, is not always in operation; many common expressions which one might think are in the third stage are still in the first: *mother tongue, boy friend, girl scout, in fact, high school.*

Here is another way to demonstrate how seemingly illogical is the spelling of many compound words: Look up in your dictionary some of the words which have *red* as the first part of the compound. Dictionaries differ among themselves, but the one the author consulted shows these distinctions: *red cedar, red cent, red clover, Red Cross, red deer, red light, red man, red oak, red pepper, red rose,* and *red tape; red-blooded, red-headed, red-hot,* and *red-letter; redbud, redcap, redcoat, redhead, redwing,* and *redwood.*

The hyphenated *red* words above offer a clue. The hyphen is a device to separate and also a mark to unify, to join. As a mark of spelling, it both joins and separates two or more words used *as an adjective.* And yet it may or may not be called for in forming compound adjectives because of position in a given sentence. For example, hyphens are generally used between the parts of an adjective preceding the substantive (noun) which it modifies, but may properly be omitted if the compound adjective follows. You may write "He saw the *red-hot* coil" and just as correctly write "The coil was *red hot.*" Since this is a section on spelling, not syntax, this illustration will have to serve as a warning and as a further plea for you to "look it up" whenever you are doubtful. But remember that dictionaries differ; they do not always indicate the distinction just made.

Finally, you should note that two or more words compounded may have a meaning quite different from that of the same two words not really joined:

Jim was a *battle-scarred* veteran.
The *battle scarred* the body and soul of Jim.
In this quarrel Sue served as a *go-between*.
The ball must *go between* the goal posts.

There is neither a short cut nor an all-inclusive rule for spelling compound words. But perhaps it will be of some help to remember that the present-day tendency is to avoid the use of hyphens whenever possible.

There are seven groups, or classes, of compound words with which the hyphen is used:

1. *Two or more words modifying a substantive and used as a single adjective:* The hyphen is especially needed in combinations placed *before* the word modified. Here are examples of these combinations:

    a. Adjective, noun, or adverb + participle (+ noun):

    Bob is a *sad-looking* boy.
    Bell-shaped hats are in fashion again.
    He jumped from a *fast-moving* train.

    b. Adjective + adjective (+ noun):

    Mary has *bluish-gray* eyes.

    c. Adjective + noun (+ noun):

    He is a *first-rate* musician.

    d. Noun + adjective (+ noun):

    There will be a *city-wide* search for the criminal.

    e. Prefix + capitalized adjective (+ noun):

    We took a *trans-Andean* clipper to Chile.

Here are other instances of these combinations:

above-mentioned	loose-tongued
absent-minded	ocean-blue
far-fetched	six-room
good-natured	soft-spoken
light-haired	ten-foot
long-needed	un-American

2. *Compound nouns*: Compound nouns consist of from two to as many as four parts. Practically every part of speech can become a component of a compound noun.

   a. Two-part compound noun:

   Coke is a *by-product* of coal. (preposition + noun)

   b. Three-part compound noun:

   My *brother-in-law* is a lawyer. (noun + preposition + noun)

   c. Four-part compound noun:

   Harry is a *jack-of-all-trades*. (noun + preposition + adjective + noun)

   Other examples of compound nouns:

court-martial	mother-in-law
ex-president	secretary-treasurer
fellow-citizen	son-in-law

3. *Compound words with "half," "quarter," or "self" as the first element*:

half-asleep	self-control
half-truth	self-interest
quarter-final	self-made
quarter-hour	self-respect

4. *Compound words made from a single capital letter and noun or participle*:

A-flat	S-curve
F-Sharp	T-shirt

5. *"Improvised" compounds*:

holier-than-thou   make-believe
know-it-all   never-say-die
long-to-be-remembered   never-to-be-forgotten

6. *Compound numerals from twenty-one through ninety-nine*:

thirty-three   sixty-seven
forty-six   eighty-five

7. *The numerator and denominator of fractions*:

four-fifths   three-quarters
one-half   two-thirds

If the hyphen already appears in either numerator or denominator, it is omitted in writing the fraction:

twenty-one thirds   three ten-thousandths

General Cautions in Using the Hyphen

1. All the examples cited above were checked in a good desk dictionary. If your dictionary differs, don't hesitate to take its word.

2. Do not use a hyphen when two adjectives preceding a noun are independent:

She wore a *faded yellow* hat.

3. Do not use a hyphen when an adverb modifies an adjective:

She was a highly trained secretary.

4. Do not use a hyphen between double terms that denote a single office or rank:

Major General Jones; *Executive Director* Adams.

5. Omit the hyphen in writing a fraction which is not an adjective:

He ate up *one half* of the pie.

6. Do not use a hyphen with reflexive pronouns:

herself, himself, yourselves

7. Many compounds formerly spelled separately or with a hyphen are now written as single words:

almighty, hateful, inasmuch, namesake

Once again, but finally, the only way to be sure about every compound word is to consult your dictionary.

USE A DICTIONARY: CAPITAL LETTERS

To misspell is to violate a convention; to use capital letters wrongly is to violate a convention. And breaking conventions, as all of us know, can cause us embarrassment, anguish, money, or all three. Many people firmly believe that mistakes in using capital and small letters are as serious as misspelling. Indeed, they feel that such mistakes *are* misspellings. Probably they are right.

The applications of capitalization are so numerous, and so loaded with exceptions, that firm rules and principles cannot apply to every possible example. A few underlying principles may be helpful and are given below. The only sound principle for you to follow is *use a dictionary.*

1. Capitalize the first word of every sentence and the first word of every direct quotation:

> The engine needs repair.
> He asked, "Does the engine need repair?"

When only a part of a direct quotation is included within a sentence, it is usually not begun with a capital letter:

> The reporter told me that the official said he felt "fine" but thought that he should "take it easy" for a few weeks.

2. Capitalize proper nouns. Proper nouns include:

    a. *Names of people and titles used for specific persons:* George Washington, Theodore Roosevelt, the President, the Senator, the Treasurer, the General, Mr. Chairman, Father, Mother.

    b. *Names of countries, states, regions, localities, other geographic areas, and the like:* United States,

England, Illinois, the Far East, the Dust Bowl, the Midwest, the Solid South, the Rocky Mountains, the Sahara Desert, the Connecticut River, Lake Michigan.

c. *Names of streets:* Michigan Boulevard, Fifth Avenue, Ross Street, Old Mill Road.

d. *Names of the Deity and personal pronouns referring to Him:* God, Heavenly Father, Son of God, Jesus Christ, Saviour, His, Him, Thy, Thine.

e. *Names for the Bible and other sacred writings:* Bible, the Scriptures, Book of Genesis, Revelations, Koran.

f. *Names of religions and religious groups:* Protestantism, Roman Catholicism, Presbyterian, Jesuit, Unitarian, Judaism, Shinto.

g. *Names of the days and the months (but not the seasons):* Monday, Tuesday, etc.; January, February, etc.; summer, winter, autumn, fall, spring.

h. *Names of schools, colleges, universities:* Woodberry Forest School, Kentucky Military Institute, Davidson College, Cornell University.

i. *Names of historic events, eras, and holidays:* Revolutionary War, Christian Era, Middle Ages, Renaissance, the Fourth of July, Labor Day, Thanksgiving.

j. *Names of races, organizations, and members of each:*

Indian, Malay, League of Women Voters, the Junior League, American Academy of Science, National League, San Francisco Giants, Big Ten Conference, an Elk, a Shriner, a Socialist.

k. *Vivid personifications:* Fate, Star of Fortune, Destiny, the power of Nature, the paths of Glory, the chronicles of Time, Duty's call.

l. Trade names: Bon Ami, Mr. Clean, Ry-Krisp, Wheaties, Anacin.

Note: If the reference is to any one of a class of persons or things rather than to a specific person or thing, do not capitalize the noun or adjective:

> He is not a captain.
> His name is Captain Draper.
> I am going to a theater.
> He is at the Bijou Theater.
> He attended high school.
> He attended Sumter High School.
> In college he took history and biology.
> In college he took History 12 and Biology 3.

3. Capitalize the first word of every line of poetry.

> I held it truth, with him who sings
> To one clear harp in divers tones,
> That men may rise on stepping-stones
> Of their dead selves to higher things.
> *Tennyson*

4. Capitalize all words except articles, conjunctions, and prepositions in the title of a book, play, magazine, musical composition.

> *The Decline and Fall of the Roman Empire*
> *You Can't Go Home Again*
> *Romeo and Juliet*
> *Atlantic Monthly*
> *Madame Butterfly*

5. Avoid unnecessary and careless use of capitals.

   a. Do not carelessly make small (lowercase) letters so large that they resemble capitals (uppercase letters).

   b. Do not capitalize names of points of the compass unless they refer to a specific section:

He lives in the West.
He walked west along the street.

c. Capitalize nouns such as *father* and *mother* if they are not preceded by a possessive:

Your father is a tall man.
I love Father very much.
My sister thinks I am noisy, but Grandpa says I am not.

LEARN A FEW SIMPLE RULES OF SPELLING

If you happen to study carefully a number of words that have similar characteristics you can make some generalizations about their spelling. In fact, observers have been doing just this for more than a century with the result that nearly fifty spelling rules have been formulated.

Generalizations about the groupings of letters that form classes of words will definitely help some people to spell more correctly. Those with good visual or motor memories will not need them. Other people apparently have a psychological block against rules. But experience has shown that rules—or at least a few of the more basic ones—do help some people to spell correctly certain classes of words. Applying spelling rules is only one approach to correct spelling; it may be more or less helpful to you than other methods of attack.

Before studying the rules that follow, you should understand a few basic principles about them.

First, it is doubtful that anyone ever improved his or her spelling merely by saying a rule over and over. Words come first, rules second; you should apply a rule, not merely memorize and mouth it.

Second, there are exceptions to every rule. And since there are so many exceptions you will need to use an additional approach: improve your visual or motor memory; use some remembering trick; consult your dictionary.

Third, the corollary and the reverse of every spelling rule are as important as the rule itself. For example, in the first rule given below, you are shown when not to use *i* before *e*, but the reverse of this pattern is fully as important and must be kept in mind and applied. Learning only part of a rule is about as silly and time-wasting as looking up a word in a dictionary and learning only one meaning of it, or only its spelling.

Words Containing *ei* or *ie*

One of the most frequent causes of misspelling is not knowing whether to write *ei* or *ie* in literally scores of everyday words. In fact, about one thousand fairly common words contain *ei* or *ie*. It helps to know that *ie* occurs in twice as many words as *ei*, but the problem is not thereby solved.

The basic rule may be stated in one of the best-known pieces of doggerel ever written:

> Write *i* before *e*
> Except after *c*
> Or when sounded like *a*
> As in *neighbor* and *weigh*.

This rule, or principle, applies only when the pronunciation of *ie* or *ei* is a long *e* (as in *he*) or the sound of the *a* in *fade*.

Here's another way to summarize the rule and its reverse:

When the sound is long *e* (as in *piece*), put *i* before *e* except after *c*.

When the sound is not long *e* (as it is not in *weigh*), put *e* before *i*.

Still another way to state this principle is this: When the *e* sound is long, *e* comes first after *c* but *i* comes first after all other consonants:

ceiling	conceive	perceive
conceit	deceitful	receipt
conceited	deceive	receive
achieve	belief	bier
aggrieve	believe	brief
apiece	besiege	cashier
chief	hygiene	retrieve
field	mischief	shield
fiend	piece	siege

frontier	pier	thief
grief	pierce	wiener
handkerchief	relieve	yield

This much of the rule is fairly simple: Usually you write *ie* except after the letter *c* when you write *ei*—provided the sound is long *e*. The last two lines of the doggerel refer to words in which *ei* or *ie* sounds like *a*. Fortunately, only a few everyday words fall in this group, among them:

beige	heir	skein
chow mein	neigh	sleigh
deign	neighbor	veil
freight	obeisance	vein
eight	reign	weigh
heinous	rein	weight

A few words are either exceptions to this basic *ei-ie* rule or are not fully covered by the four lines of doggerel. The best advice is to learn the following words by some method other than trying to apply the rule, which doesn't work here:

caffeine	height	seize
codeine	hierarchy	seizure
either	leisure	sheik
Fahrenheit	neither	sleight
fiery	protein	stein
financier	Reid (proper name)	weird

Summary:

1. Use *ie* generally when sounded as long *e* (*he*).
2. Use *ei* after *c* when sounded as *e* (*he*).
3. Use *ei* when sounded as *a* (*eight*).
4. Watch out for exceptions.

Final *y*

1. Words ending in *y* preceded by a consonant usually change *y* to *i* before any suffix except one beginning with *i:*

angry, angrily
carry, carries, carrying
easy, easier, easily
happy, happier, happiness
merry, merrier, merrily, merriment
pretty, prettier, prettiness
study, studied, studious
try, tried, trying

2. Words ending in *y* preceded by a vowel do not change *y* to *i* before suffixes or other endings:

annoy, annoyed, annoyance	employ, employer
betray, betrayal	stay, stayed, staying

To the two parts of this "final *y*" rule are so many exceptions that some experts feel the rule is not helpful. However, the exceptions among commonly used words are not numerous and can easily be mastered by some other approach suggested in this section. Here are some everyday words that follow neither part of the "final *y*" principle:

baby, babyhood	pay, paid
busy, busyness (state of being busy)	say, said
	shy, shyly, shyness
day, daily	slay, slain
lady, ladyship	wry, wryly, wryness
lay, laid	

Final *e*

Hundreds of everyday English words end in *e*, and hundreds and hundreds more consist of such words plus suffixes: *hope, hoping; come, coming; safe, safety,* and so on. In our pronunciation, nearly all *e*'s at the end of words are silent (not pronounced): *advice, give, live,* etc. Actually, the function of a final silent *e* is to make the vowel of the syllable long: *rate* but *rat; mete* but *met; bite* but *bit; note* but *not,* and so on.

With those facts in mind we can now proceed to a rule that covers more words than any other spelling rule, many of them common words frequently misspelled. Here it is:

Final silent *e* is usually dropped before a suffix beginning with a vowel but is retained before a suffix beginning with a consonant.

advice, advising	hate, hateful
argue, arguing	judge, judging
arrive, arrival	like, likable
bare, barely, bareness	live, livable
believe, believing,	love, lovable
believable	safe, safely, safety
care, careful, careless	sincere, sincerely
desire, desirable	sure, surely, surety
excite, exciting, excitement	

This basic rule is clear enough, but it does not cover all words ending in silent *e*. Here are some additions and exceptions to the general principle:

1. Silent *e* is retained when *ing* is added to certain words, largely to prevent them from being confused with other words:

   dye, dyeing to contrast with *die, dying*
   singe, singeing to contrast with *sing, singing*
   swinge, swingeing to contrast with *swing, swinging*
   tinge, tingeing to contrast with *ting, tinging*

2. Silent *e* is retained in still other words before a suffix beginning with a vowel. Sometimes this is done for the sake of pronunciation, sometimes for no logical reason at all:

acre, acreage	line, lineage
cage, cagey	mile, mileage
hoe, hoeing	there, therein

3. Silent *e* is dropped before a suffix beginning with a consonant in certain common words such as:

acknowledge,
  acknowledgment
argue, argument
awe, awful
due, duly
judge, judgment

nine, ninth
possible, possibly
probable, probably
true, truly
whole, wholly

4. Silent *e* is retained in words ending in *ce* or *ge* even when suffixes beginning with vowels (*-able* and *-ous*) are added. This is done for the sake of pronunciation: to prevent giving a hard sound (*k* or hard *g*) to the *c* or *g*:

marriage, marriageable
notice, noticeable
service, serviceable

advantage, advantageous
courage, courageous
outrage, outrageous

5. A few words ending in *ie* in which the *e* is silent change *ie* to *y* before adding *ing*. Presumably this change occurs to prevent two *i*'s from coming together:

die, dying
lie, lying

tie, tying (or tieing)
vie, vying

Inserted *k*

The letter *k* is usually added to words ending in *c* before a suffix beginning with *e*, *i*, or *y*. This is done in order to prevent mispronunciation. Note the different pronunciation, for example, of *picnicking* and *icing*. Only a few common words are involved in this rule, but they are frequently misspelled:

frolic, frolicked, frolicking
mimic, mimicked,
  mimicking
panic, panicky

picnic, picnicked, pic-
  nicker
shellac, shellacked,
  shellacking
traffic, trafficked, traffick-
  ing

This rule must be applied carefully. Note, for example, the words *frolicsome* and *mimicry*. Without adding a *k*, each *c* remains hard.

Doubling Final Consonant

The rule for doubling final consonants is complicated, but mastering it and its parts will prevent many common misspellings. Despite its complexity, it is one of the more useful rules for spelling.

1. Words of one syllable and those of more than one accented on the last syllable, when ending in a single consonant (except x) preceded by a single vowel, double the consonant before a suffix beginning with a vowel:

   acquit, acquitted, acquitting, acquittal
   admit, admitted, admitting, admittance
   begin, beginning, beginner
   control, controlled, controller
   equip, equipped, equipping
   forget, forgetting, forgettable, unforgettable
   occur, occurred, occurring, occurrence
   plan, planned, planning
   prefer, preferred, preferring
   refer, referred, referring
   run, running, runner
   swim, swimming, swimmer
   transfer, transferred, transferring

2. If the accent is shifted to an earlier syllable when the ending is added, do not double the final consonant:

   confer, conferring, *but* conference
   infer, inferring, *but* inference
   prefer, preferring, *but* preference

3. Cautions and exceptions:

   a. Derivatives from basic words that change pronunciation from a long to short vowel follow the doubling rule:

      write, writing, *but* written
      bite, biting, *but* bitten
      inflame, inflamed, *but* inflammable

b. Words ending in a final consonant preceded by *two* vowels do not double the final consonant:

> appear, appeared, appearing, appearance
> need, needed, needing, needy
> train, trained, training, trainee

c. Words ending in *two* consonants do not double the final consonant:

> bend, bending (*not* bendding)
> turn, turned (*not* turnned)
> insist, insisted (*not* insistted)

d. Words not accented on the final syllable do not ordinarily double the final consonant:

> happen, happened, happening
> murmur, murmured, murmuring
> benefit, benefited (*but* fit, fitted)

A helpful word in fixing this principle in your mind is *combat.* It may be pronounced with the accent on either syllable, but note the spelling:

> combat'   combatted   combatting
> com'bat   combated   combating

e. Like all spelling rules, this one for doubling has many exceptions or apparent exceptions. Rather than try to apply the rule slavishly you would gain by learning the following through some other approach:

> cancellation   gaseous   questionnaire
> chagrined   handicapped   tranquillity
> chancellor   humbugged   transferable
> excellence   metallurgy   transference
> excellent   outfitter   zigzagged

The "One-plus-One" Rule

When a prefix ends in the same letter with which the main part of the word begins, be sure that both letters are included.

When the main part of a word ends in the same letter with which a suffix begins, be sure that both letters are included.

When two words are combined, the first ending with the same letter with which the second begins, be sure that both letters are included.

Some spelling difficulties caused by prefixes and suffixes have been discussed earlier. The rule just stated in three parts is both supplementary and complementary to that discussion. It will take care of a larger number of often misspelled words such as:

accidentally	cleanness	dissatisfied
bathhouse	coolly	dissimilar
bookkeeping	occasionally	suddenness
drunkenness	overrated	underrate
illiterate	overrun	unnecessary
irresponsible	really	unneeded
meanness	roommate	unnoticed
misspelling	soulless	withholding

The only important exception to this rule is *eighteen*, which, of course, is not spelled *eightteen*. Also, keep in mind that the same three consonants are never written solidly together: *cross-stitch*, not *crossstitch; still-life*, not *stilllife*.

SPELL CAREFULLY

When writing, you concentrate on what you are trying to say and not on such matters as grammar, punctuation, and spelling. This concentration is both proper and understandable. But in your absorption, you are quite likely to make errors of various sorts, including some in spelling, which result from haste or carelessness, not ignorance. When you discover a mistake of this kind, or it is pointed out to you, you may reply: "Oh, I know better. I just wasn't watching"—or "thinking" or "being careful" or whatever excuse you choose to make.

Isn't it fair to suggest that since so many English words really are difficult to spell, we should be careful with those we actually know? And yet it is the simple, easy words that nearly everyone *can* spell which cause over half the errors commonly made. Listed below are words the author has repeatedly found misspelled in letters, reports, and student papers. They are so easy that you are likely to look at them scornfully and say "I would never misspell any one of them." The fact is that you probably do misspell some of these words, on occasion, or other words just as simple:

a lot, *not* alot	piano, *not* panio
all right, *not* alright	research, *not* reaserch
doesn't, *not* does'nt	religion, *not* regilion
forty, *not* fourty	surprise, *not* supprise
high school, *not* highschool	thoroughly, *not* throughly
in fact, *not* infact	whether, *not* wheather
ninety, *not* ninty	wouldn't, *not* would'nt

Errors of this sort are easy to make. Our pen or pencil slips; a finger hits the wrong key; our minds wander. Even excellent spellers often repeatedly make such silly mistakes. What's the remedy?

Well, merely glancing over or even rereading what you've written is not likely to uncover all such errors. When we read, we usually see only the outlines, or shells, of words. Only poor readers need to see individual letters as such; most of us comprehend words and even groups of words at a glance. As our eyes move along a line we neither see nor recognize individual letters. And this, of course, is as it should be.

But have you ever noticed how much easier it is for you to detect spelling errors in someone else's writing than in your own? This may be because we are looking for mistakes. Or it may be that we look more carefully at the writing of someone else than at our own because we are unfamiliar with it, are not previously aware of the context, and have to pay closer attention in order to comprehend.

Whatever the reason for closer scrutiny, we narrow the range of our vision and thereby pick up mistakes hitherto unnoticed. In short, we detect careless errors in spelling not by reading but by *proofreading*.

It is indeed naive for any of us to think that we can write rapidly without misspelling some words, even though we are good spellers. Only careful proofreading will uncover spelling errors in our own writing or, indeed, in anyone else's.

This kind of reading requires that we see words and phrases not as such but that we actually see every letter they contain. When each letter stands out distinctly, it is simple to detect errors in spelling.

Here is a list of forty frequently misspelled words. Some are spelled correctly here; some are not. In which of them can you identify each letter at a single glance? Which require you to move your eyes, even if only slightly?

1.	acquaint	21.	mere
2.	against	22.	noblity
3.	all right	23.	noticeable
4.	amount	24.	occupying
5.	apear	25.	opportunity
6.	arise	26.	optomistic
7.	around	27.	pamplet
8.	basas	28.	perseverance
9.	begining	29.	preferable
10.	before	30.	primative
11.	careless	31.	process
12.	clothes	32.	pursue
13.	comming	33.	recomendation
14.	considerable	34.	representative
15.	decided	35.	restaurant
16.	extremely	36.	sandwitch
17.	field	37.	siege
18.	finishing	38.	twelfth
19.	likelyhood	39.	unmanageable
20.	lonely	40.	yield

Eleven of these words are misspelled. Did your proofreading catch them all? Check your findings: the following contain errors—5, 8, 9, 13, 19, 22, 26, 27, 30, 33, 36.

Keep in mind that at least 50 percent of all errors come from omitting letters or transposing or adding them, writing two words as one or vice versa, and other similar acts of carelessness. Check

and recheck, read, and reread your writing until you have eliminated at least all the careless mistakes everyone makes. There will
still be errors enough of other kinds to keep us humble or angry.

USE MEMORY DEVICES

Suppose that someone suddenly asks you, "How many days in
March?" You may be able to answer instantly, but if you are like
most of us you will come up with the answer, "31," only after you
have run through your head the familiar lines beginning, "Thirty
days hath September." If so, what you have done is to use a device
to aid memory.

One special kind of memory device has the rather imposing
name of *mnemonics*. The word is pronounced *nee-MON-iks* and
comes from a Greek word meaning "to remember." (Mnemosyne
was the goddess of memory in Greek mythology.) A mnemonic is a
special aid to memory, a memory trick based on what psychologists refer to as "association of ideas," remembering something by
associating it with something else. You may have been using
mnemonics most of your life. The term applies to a very basic
characteristic of the human mind.

Mnemonics *can* be used to improve spelling. The system will
help some more than others and may not help some people at all.
The entire system of association of ideas has been criticized because, of course, you can place a greater burden on your mind with
elaborate mnemonics than is involved in the original item to be
remembered. In addition, a memory aid that works for you may be
useless to me, and vice versa. But a set of mental associations has
proved useful to some people for spelling certain words, and a
system of mnemonics is one legitimate approach to better spelling.

Any mnemonic is a sort of crutch, something we use until we
can automatically spell a given word without even thinking. But
so is a rule a crutch, and, in a different sense, a dictionary is, too.
In time, we can throw away our spelling crutches except on rare
occasions; until then we can use them to avoid staggering and
falling.

A mnemonic will be most helpful when you contrive it from
some happening, or base it upon some person, meaningful in your

life. That is, you must invent, or use, only mnemonics that have a *personal* association of ideas. Some of the mnemonics suggested below will help you; others will seem meaningless or downright silly. Some words that trouble you will not even be covered. You can then try devising mnemonics of your own for your particular spelling demons.

A clue about the origin of a word will sometimes provide a mnemonic. Sometimes exaggerated pronunciation will form the association, the bond of relationship between word and spelling. Occasionally, breaking the word into parts will help. Sometimes a play on words will give a useful memory device. As you read the mnemonics below, you will note these and various other methods used in manufacturing them. On occasion you will see that more than one method is used to phrase a mnemonic for the same word. Adapt for your use the most helpful one.

If none of these mnemonics proves helpful, you will at least have suggestions for "rolling your own." If another approach to correct spelling better suits your learning abilities, then skip what follows. At any rate, these memory clues have helped some people to spell correctly the words listed:

all right. Two words. Associate with *all correct* or *all wrong.*

anoint. Use *an oil* to *anoint* him (each *n* appears alone).

argument. I lost an *e* in that *argument.*

balloon. Remember the *ball* in *balloon.*

battalion. This comes from *battle*; it has the same double *t* and single *l*.

believe. You can't *believe* a *lie.*

business. Business is no *sin.*

calendar. The *D.A.R* will meet soon.

capitol. A capit*o*l has a dome (associate *o*).

cemetery. (1) There is *ease* (*e's*) in the cemetery.

(2) A place we get to with *ease* (*e's*).

compliment. A compliment is what *I* like to get.

conscience. con + science.

corps. Don't kill a live body of men with an *e* (corpse).

definite. Def*inite* comes from *finite.*

dependable. An *able* worker is depend*able.*

descendant. A descend*ant* has an *ancestor*.

desert. The Sahara (one *s*).

dessert. Strawberry sundae (two *s*'s).

dilemma. In a dil*emma* was *Emma*.

disappoint. dis + appoint.

dormitory. The French word for sleep is *dormir*.

ecstasy. There is no *x* in ecstasy.

embarrassed. (1) Double *r*, double *s*, double trouble.

     (2) *R*obert and *R*ose were *sh*op *s*tewards.

February. Feb*r*uary makes one say *"Br!"*

genealogy. Al is interested in gen*ea*logy.

grammar. (1) Accent the trouble spot: grammA*r*.

    (2) Don't *mar* your writing with bad gram*mar*.

    (3) Write *g—r—a—m*: then start back: *m—a—r.*

hear. I h*ear* with my *ear*.

indispensable. (1) *Able* people are indispens*able*.

     (2) This word refers to a thing one is not *able* to *dispense* with.

infinite. In*finite* comes from *finite*.

*inoculate. I*noculate means to *in*ject.

irresistible. (1) *I* am ir*r*esis*t*ible to the opposite sex.

    (2) *L*ipstick is irre*sist*ible.

laboratory. People *labor* in a *labor*atory.

literature. It was an *era* of good lite*r*ature.

medicine. Associated with *medicinal*.

occasion. (1) An *occasion occurs*.

    (2) Don't be an *ass* on this occasion (one *s*).

occurrence. An occurrence may be a *current* event.

outrageous. The out*rageous* idea put me in a *rage*.

parallel. All lines are pa*rallel*.

piece. Have a *piece* of *pie*.

potatoes. Pota*toes* have eyes and *toes*.

preparation. (1) From the base word *prepAre*.

     (2) This comes from *prae* + *parare* (to make ready).

principal. A princip*al* rule is a m*a*in rule.

principle. A princip*le* is just a ru*le*.

privilege. Some special priv*i*leges are *vile.*

professor. The abbreviation is *prof* (one *f*).

pronunciation. The *nun* knew pro*nun*ciation.

pursuit. A pickpocket took my *purse.*

recommend. re + commend.

*relative. Relati*ve comes from *relate.*

repetition. Associate with "repeat."

resistance. Increase resis*tan*ce with *tan.*

ridiculous. Associate with *ridicule.*

seize. Seize him by the *ear* (*e* before *i*).

separate. (1) Sep*ar*ate means "*apart.*"

         (2) Accent the trouble spot: sep*A*rate.

         (3) There is a *rat* in sepa*rat*e.

sergeant. Think of serge + ant.

siege. An army *si*ts before a city (*i* before *e*).

significant. "Sign if I cant" (can't).

stationary. This word means "standing."

stationery. This is used for writing *le*tters.

superintendent. A superintend*ent* collects *rent.*

supersede. (1) Both first and last syllables begin with *s.*

         (2) The word comes from Latin *sedeo,* "to sit."

surprise. That was *sur*ely a *sur*prise.

temperature. She lost her *temper at* the heat.

together. to + get + her.

tragedy. (1) Every *age* has its tr*age*dy.

         (2) Old *age* may be a tr*age*dy.

tranquillity. Associate with *quill* (pens used in olden days).

vaccine. Va*cc*ine is measured in *c*ubic *c*entimeters (*cc*'s).

villain. The villain likes his *villa in* the country.

Wednesday. This word means "Woden's day."

LISTING MISSPELLED WORDS

Learning to spell is an individual, highly personal matter. As we have discovered, a single approach to correct spelling will work for one person and not for another. Also, the words whose spelling gives you trouble may not be the words that bother me or any of your friends and acquaintances. Perhaps it would be more precise to say that, although certain words cause trouble for a majority of people, any list of commonly misspelled words will contain some that give you no difficulty and omit others that do. The very best list of words for you to study is the one you prepare yourself to meet your own needs and shortcomings.

There's a lot of waste in any spelling list. It is simple to prepare a list of "spelling demons" and assert that these are the "most frequently misspelled" words in the language. In a sense, this statement would be correct, but it fails to recognize that, although these words are likely to be misspelled when used, they aren't used very often. Learning to spell a long list of difficult words is about as silly as trying to swallow a dictionary or an encyclopedia. You use a dictionary when you need to tap its resources, just as you turn on a faucet to get water from a reservoir. You consult a list of misspelled words only when you have a definite need.

This section should serve primarily to start you on a list of your personal spelling demons. These words will be ones you need to learn to spell because you use them. And they may be simple or difficult; short or long; everyday words or ones which, although rare to others, are a part of your working vocabulary. The only basis for any list of misspelled words is its *use* value.

Regardless of whether we are homemakers, businesspeople, clerks, truckdrivers, or physicians, we all use certain basic words many scores of times more often than any others in the language. Any spelling list should start with them. But fortunately, they are never (or hardly ever) misspelled by anyone who can write at all. The most frequently used words in the English language are *and*, *the*, *to*, *you*, *your*, *in*, *for*, *of*, *we*, *is*, *I*, and *its*. These give no trouble except for some occasional confusion between *your* and *you're* and *its* and *it's*.

Once past this basic list, however, selecting frequently used words becomes more difficult. *Table* is an everyday word, but a baker might use *bread* and a physician might use *temperature* more often. It is reassuring to know, however, that it is neither the most simple and common words nor the ones primarily used in a trade, profession, or industry that provide major spelling difficulty. The words in between are the troublemakers. And here we do have some authoritative studies of frequency of word use and frequency of misspelling. The short list that follows is based upon one of these major studies.

Of the 500 words occurring most frequently in our speech and writing only 20 ever cause anyone except very poor spellers any trouble whatever. Probably few, if any, of them bother you. Here is the list:

across	dollar	possible	suppose
almost	don't	quite	their
believe	friend	receive	through
brought	government	should	whether
business	laugh	supply	your

Keep in mind that these 20 words, along with 480 even more easily spelled ones, are certain to appear in your speech and writing many times as often as all other words in the language. The best approach of all to correct spelling is to *master* the simple, everyday words that you use over and over. Doing so will solve the greater part of your spelling problem.

Note: No exercises are provided for spelling problems. In lieu of doing exercises, you are urged to form the habit of consulting your dictionary again and again in accordance with the spelling principles discussed in preceding pages.

A final word about spelling. If you are using a word processor, much of this chapter can be disregarded. Why? Because a separate program or function within a word processor tests for correctly spelled words. It can test the spellings within an entire paper or just a marked block of that paper. A spelling checker simply compares words to a dictionary of words so that the wrong use of a correctly spelled word cannot be detected. But although a spelling checker cannot test for exact diction it can surely detect misspellings.

Yet this chapter will not be useless because on many occasions you need to know the correct spelling of a word without having to write it. And also many writers do not use word processors.

INDEX

ABOUT THE AUTHOR

HARRY SHAW is well known as an editor, writer, lecturer, and teacher. For a number of years he was director of the Workshops in Composition at New York University and teacher of classes in advanced writing at Columbia, at both of which institutions he has done graduate work. He has worked with large groups of writers in the Washington Square Writing Center at NYU and has been a lecturer in writers' conferences at Indiana University and the University of Utah and lecturer in, and director of, the Writers' Conference in the Rocky Mountains sponsored by the University of Colorado. In 1969, Mr. Shaw was awarded the honorary degree of Doctor of Letters by Davidson College, his alma mater.

He has been managing editor and editorial director of *Look*, editor at Harper and Brothers, senior editor and vice-president of E. P. Dutton and Co., editor-in-chief of Henry Holt & Co., director of publications for Barnes & Noble, Inc., and also an editor at W. W. Norton & Co., Inc. He has contributed widely to many popular and scholarly national magazines and is the author or co-author of a number of books in the fields of English composition and literature, among them *Spell It Right!* and *Punctuate It Right!*